REDISCOVERING GANDHI

VOLUME 2 : Ahimsa: The Way to Peace

Series Editor: ***Prof. R.P. Misra***

Vol. 1. Hind Swaraj: *Gandhi's Challenge to Modern Civilization*
—R.P. Misra

2. Ahimsa: *The Way to Peace*
—Jonathan K. Crane & Jordi Agusti-Panareda

Forthcoming Volumes

- Satyagraha: *Gandhian Approach to Conflict Resolution*
—Jai Narain Sharma

- Consensual Democracy: *Gandhi on State, Power, and Politics*
—Ashu Pasricha

- Humanizing Science and Technology: *Some Case Studies*
—Vinnie Jauhari and ***Parul Goyal***

- Truth is God: *Gandhi's Search for Religion of Religions*
—R.P. Misra

- Swadeshi: *Gandhi on Self-Reliant Development*
—M.L. Sharma

About the Authors

Jonathan K. Crane is a graduate of Wheaton College (Norton, MA), the University of Notre Dame, Gujarat Vidyapith (Ahemdabad, India), and received rabbinic ordination from Hebrew Union College-Jewish Institute of Religion. He has taught in the fields of politics, peace studies, religion in general and Judaism in particular. He has published articles and chapters on conflict resolution organizations, nonviolence, lethal personal and international conflict, gender issues, Jewish law and ethics, and interfaith relations. He is currently a PhD candidate in modern Jewish ethics at the University of Toronto. He and his wife, Lindy Miller, live in Chennai, India.

Jordi Agusti-Panareda is a lawyer and researcher on conflict management. He holds a master's degree in law from London School of Economics and Politics, and doctoral degree in judicial sciences from Stanford University, USA. He has worked and researched in the field of conflict management, mediation, law and society, nonviolence, intercultural relations, international organizations, development, and human rights. He has written articles on dispute resolution, mediation, and the role of law in cross-cultural relations.

REDISCOVERING GANDHI

Series Editor
Prof. R.P. Misra

Volume 2

AHIMSA

The Way to Peace

By
Jonathan K. Crane: Jordi Agusti-Panareda

In Collaboration with
GANDHI SMRITI & DARSHAN SAMITI, NEW DELHI

Published by
CONCEPT PUBLISHING COMPANY, NEW DELHI

Cataloging in Publication Data—DK
Courtesy: D.K. Agencies (P) Ltd. <docinfo@dkagencies.com>

Crane, Jonathan K.
Ahimsa : the way to peace/ by Jonathan K. Crane, Jordi Agusti-Panareda.
p. cm. — (Rediscovering Gandhi ; v. 2)
Includes bibliographical references ( )
Includes index.
ISBN 13: 9788180694684
ISBN 10: 8180694682

1. Ahiṃsā. 2. Nonviolence. 3. Passive resistance. 4. Gandhi, Mahatma, 1869-1948. I. Agusti-Panareda, Jordi, joint author. II. Title. III. Series: Rediscovering Gandhi ; v. 2.

DDC 322.409 54 22

ISBN -13: 978-81-8069-374-8 (Series) ISBN -10: 81-8069-374-0 (Series)
ISBN- 13: 978-81-8069-468-4 (Vol. 2) ISBN- 10: 81-8069-468-2 (Vol. 2)

First Published 2007

Published and Printed by
Ashok Kumar Mittal
Concept Publishing Company
A/15-16, Commercial Block, Mohan Garden
New Delhi-110059 (INDIA)
Phones : 25351460, 25351794 *Fax* : 091-11-25357103
Email : publishing@conceptpub.com

Preface

This is the second volume of *Rediscovering Gandhi,* a multi-volume series of books published by Gandhi Smriti and Darshan Samiti, Rajghat, New Delhi, India. It focuses on Ahimsa or non-violence as the means and end of continuing development of human race and survival of planet earth. The volume contains contributions by two young researchers from the USA. Jonathan Kadane Crane, and Jordi Agusti-Panareda. Jonathan did his M. Phil at the International Centre of Gandhian Studies, Gujarat Vidyapeeth, Ahmedabad; and Jordi his LL.M. at the London School of Economics, London. Both the dissertation centre on non-violence, one from the points of view of its meaning and relevance in the violence-ridden world we live; and the other from its contribution to the theory and practice of conflict resolution.

There are two important reasons why these contributions are being published under the title *Ahimsa: The Way to Peace*. First, they deal with a theme, that forms the core of Gandhian thought and second, they have been written by two young researchers from the west. If the future is going to be shaped by the youth, then the future of Gandhian thought too depends on how deeply are the youth imbued with it. Both reasons are germane to the purpose for which this series is being published. The volume points to the growing interest in Gandhian philosophy and the theory and practice of non-violence in the world, west included.

The concept of Ahimsa and its application to remove all barriers that come in the way of man to become human and get enlightenment even while living in the world as it is today, is a distinct contribution of India to the world. It was through Ahimsa that Buddha and Mahavira transformed the war hungry worlds of their times; it is through Ahimsa that Gandhi liberated India from the clutches of British colonialism in 1947. It was through Ahimsa that the coloured peoples of the USA got equal civil rights; it was through Ahimsa that

South Africa gained independence; and it was through Ahimsa that Poland could get rid of a government imposed by the USSR. There are over 50 countries in the world where non-violent movements in one form or the other are underway to solve national and local problems: in Latin America, North America, Asia, Africa, and Europe. Ahimsa is now widely recognized as the sure means to resolve conflicts within individuals, and among individuals, groups, communities, regions and nations.

Practice of Ahimsa is not easy. It needs training, forbearance and attitudinal preparedness. But then, if the society can invest so much in preparedness for violence (army, police, arms and ammunitions etc.), there is no reason why it cannot invest in peace making through non-violence.

I would like to thank the two researchers for putting their research outputs at the disposal of Gandhi Smriti & Darshan Samiti for publication and thereby helping us to carry their ideas and thoughts to a wider circle of readers interested in Gandhi and his philosophy.

R.P. Misra

Contents

Editorial

Ahimsa constitutes the foundation of Gandhian philosophy. It is through Ahimsa that man can reach Truth, that is God and attain self-realization. 'I do not envisage God other than truth and non-violence…. My religion is based on truth and non-violence.' Gandhi considered ahimsa to be the greatest force available to humankind. 'It is mightier than the mightiest weapon of destruction devised by the ingenuity of man.'

Gandhi demonstrated that Ahimsa was more powerful than even atom bomb, were it used truthfully and strategically even by a single man army. And he and his brand of Ahimsa are now increasingly recognized as the sole means to bring peace in the individual oppressed by tension and the world oppressed by violence and thus to help man to scale higher reaches of consciousness and the world to ensure continuance of life on planet earth. True, there is more violence today than ever before but it is more likely to be a storm before the lull than lull before the storm. There is growing realization that there is something fundamentally wrong with the way we are managing ourselves. Even in the west, which was responsible for inflicting violence on other parts of the world during the last three centuries, Ahimsa has been progressively recognized as the only instrument for peaceful resolution of conflicts. It has been used not in one but many countries during the last few decades to resolve long standing political, social and economic problems; South African struggle for independence; the Civil Rights Movement led by Martin Luther Kings in USA; and the Solidarity Movement in Poland are only too well known to be mentioned here.

He firmly believed that violence could never produce peace; it would always produce more violence even if it were employed in the name of justice and peace. It "was not simply a political tactic which was supremely useful and efficacious in liberating his people from foreign rule. … On the contrary, the spirit of non-violence sprang from an inner realization of spiritual unity in himself," (Thomas

Merton, p. 6). A normal human being would not employ violence against those who are near and dear to him. Who does not love his own children? As the consciousness of individuals expands to include 'others' too among the near and dear, violence becomes rare. For Gandhi, all that is live constitutes a single family—animals and plants included.

Mark Shepard elaborated further his views on Ahimsa in following words: "Ahimsa was the expression of the deepest love for all humans, including one's opponents; this non-violence, therefore, included not only a lack of physical harm to others, but also the absence of hatred or ill-will towards them. Gandhi rejected the traditional dichotomy between me, and they; he believed in winning over the opponents by changing their hearts; not by punishing them, and in this way one could win their friendship and one's own freedom. If need be, one might need to suffer or die in order that they may be converted to love". And to add punch to his views, Ganathi says:

"If the function of himsa (violence) is to devour all it comes across, the function of ahimsa (non-violence) is to rush into tested only in the face of himsa." (Harijan, 13-5-1939, p. 121) "The hardest metal yields to sufficient heat. Even so the hardest heart must melt before sufficiency of the heat of non-violence. And there is no limit to the capacity of non-violence to generate heat."

AHIMSA AS CONCEIVED AND PRACTICED BY GANDHI

True meaning, role, and practice of Ahimsa in real life have often been misconceived and distorted. Many see it in the narrow sense of non-killing, or to desist from inflicting any physical harm to other human beings or living species. Some relate it to vegetarianism, while others to passivity. Many deride it as the weapon of those who are physically weak; and as an easy escape route for cowards. And those who treat it as impractical and an ideal not worth pursuing are not few. '*Mazboori ka nam Gandhi hai' i.e.* the other name for helplessness is Gandhi, is often heard in common parlance. Atenborough's film *Gandhi* did help people understand Ahimsa better; and the recently released film *Lage Raho Munna Bhai* has also popularized the potential use of Ahimsa in the current contexts but the misconceptions are so deep rooted that lot more needs to be done in practical terms to tilt the balance in favour of Ahimsa.

In the so-called developed countries of the world, the situation is far worse. Ahimsa has yet to take fancy of the people as an alternative way to create a peaceful world. War has been the principal means to bring peace ever since man descended on the earth. Disputes have generally been resolved by fighting physically with or without the aid of weapons (all the way from stones and bamboo sticks to atom bombs) for too long a time to be forgotten and abjured. Man has not forsaken his brute ancestry. But there is a silver lining on the dark horizon. Man's war against nature and his fellow human beings has taken him too close to *Pralaya* - planetary destruction. The search for a new paradigm and new style of life has already begun, and many statesmen of the world have recognized the potentials of Ahimsa in saving the world from total chaos.

Unfortunately, fresh thinking on the issue of war and peace has not been as widely publicized as the old ways of solving problems by resorting to wars. Conflicts, murders, and physical or psychological assaults catch the attention of the people (media especially) more than peace, births and happiness. We rarely realize that human beings have protected more life than destroyed. How else are there more than six billion people in the world today? As Gandhi said, eye for eye would leave everyone blind. Even animals protect more of their species than they kill other animals to satisfy their hunger. If many of the species of plants, insects, animals and even human races/ communities are disappearing, it is not because they kill each other but because we the humans destroy them and their habitats to satisfy our avarice and greed.

The problem is not that there is so much violence today; the problem is that the evolutionary journey that man started millenniums back has taken a wrong turn and hence non-violence, the antidot for violence, has failed to counter violence. Instead of taking man to higher levels of consciousness, it is taking him backwards to his animal ancestry. What makes man different from animal is not just his physical structure standing on two legs; it is his capacity to reason and his proclivity to transform himself into a super-conscious being, that separates him from the animal. Reasoning refines and perfects knowledge; and ahimsa takes him to higher reaches of consciousness and finally converts knowledge into wisdom. One can get knowledge from books and teachers; higher consciousness, however, comes from adherence to Dharma and the pillar on which Dharma stands is Ahimsa or Non-violence.

No two human beings are exactly the same. Even twins who have same parents and are born within a time distance of minutes are different in many physical as well as psychological traits. It happens partly because the genes despite having common origin differ in many respects, and post birth circumstances in which they are brought up are different. The parents are different, as are the social, economic, and technological contexts in which children grow to become adults. But human beings are human beings and as a species they have certain common traits and proclivities for imaging, reasoning, and action. Their upbringing and training can make or mar their life; turn them into saints or criminals; and make them self-centred or other centred.

The hand, an organ of the body, can be used for creative as well destructive purposes; thinking and feeling too can be creative or destructive. Much depends on the environment in which one is brought up and training he gets in the family, community, society and schools of various levels. Man, ever since he was born as Homo sapiens has been brought up in a situation, which is full of conflicts. He is trained to be aggressive and to defend his rights and privileges by any means at his disposal. And the means most readily available and about which he has full knowledge and training is physical force i.e. violence. So the world is violent.

In any conflict situation, there are two parties to the dispute. To settle the dispute, one party resorts to himsa and harms the other physically, verbally, legally, or otherwise. If the attacked party is defeated, it waits for the chance to retaliate more forcefully. And thus the process goes on generations after generations. To revenge one murder, several murders take place before one of the parties in the dispute has no power left, or loses interest because there are other fronts to fight on or realizes the futility of revenge. The situation is reversed when the party being attacked decides to counter non-violently not because it is weak, meak or coward but because it knows the futility of violence and decides to change the heart of the attacker. He does not meekly submit to the dictates of the attacker; he rather pits his soul against his ill will and brute force. He suffers him and his violence as long as the opponent is not a changed person and comes on a negotiating table to settle the dispute.

It is something like some one in the family unhappy with some other member resorting to fasting until he is convinced that no wrong is done or the so-called wrong done to him is corrected. The family unable to bear the suffering of a dear one talks to him and brings him back to the dining table. This is a very crude example of use of non-violence at the family level. Gandhi carried this idea beyond the confines of the family and used it as a social force to change the society as a whole. In the words of Gandhi: "Working under this law of our being, it is possible for a single individual to defy the whole might of an unjust empire to save his honour, his religion, his soul and lay the foundation for that empire's fall or its regeneration." (Young India, 1-8-1920, p. 3)

If the world is violent today, it does not mean that tomorrow it cannot be non-violent. It is violent today, because most of the people use violence to settle their differences. It would become non-violent, when most of the people start using non-violence as the means to settle their differences.

It is unfortunate that some people equate non-violence with vegetarianism. "Ahimsa is not a mere matter of dietetics, it transcends it. What a man eats or drinks matters little; it is the self-denial, the self-restraint behind it that matters. By all means practice as much restraint in the choice of the articles of your diet as you like. The restraint is commendable, even necessary, but it touches only the fringe of ahimsa. A man may allow himself a wide latitude in the matter of diet and yet may be a personification of ahimsa and compel our homage, if his heart overflows with love and melts at another's woe, and has been purged of all passions. On the other hand a man always over-scrupulous in diet is an utter stranger to ahimsa and pitiful wretch, if he is a slave to selfishness and passions and is hard of heart." (Young India, 6-9-1928, pp. 300-301)

Ahimsa is outside the purview of those who are cowards. Non-violence and cowardice are contradictory terms. Non-violence is the greatest virtue, cowardice the greatest vice. Non-violent conduct is never demoralising, cowardice always is. Non-violence springs from love, cowardice from hate. Non-violence suffers; cowardice inflicts suffering. Perfect non-violence is the highest bravery.

Most of the fully armed persons are cowards at heart. The very possession of arms implies an element of fear. Nowadays people are prepared to bribe to get a gun licence. A large number of them keep arms without lincence. Such persons cannot be non-violent nor can they be brave. Non-violence without complete fearlessness is impossible. Those who are gripped by pride and egoism, cannot be nonviolent either, for "Non-violence is impossible without humility." (Harijan, 28-1-1939, p. 442).

Thus ahimsa or non-violence of Gandhi has a far deeper meaning, a meaning, which goes a step beyond what Lord Buddha, Mahavira and Jesus had enunciated. This is not to compare Gandhi with these great personages; it does, however, mean that Gandhi carried their message of Ahimsa a step forward and made it an instrument of mass movement for social change. Moreover, he gave it a scientific touch thereby brought science and spirituality on a common platform. The power of ahimsa never fails. "Ahimsa is a science. The word 'failure' has no place in the vocabulary of science. Failure to obtain the expected result is often the precursor to further discoveries." (Harijan, 6-5-1939, p. 113)

The Gandhian, theory and practice of Ahimsa, have been elaborated further under the following ten reads:

To remain athentic to Gandhi's views, I have tried to present the discussion using his own words, as far as possible.

1. Ahimsa is the law of our species;
2. Ahimsa and truth go togather;
3. Ahimsa is an active force;
4. Ahimsa alone can counter brute force;
5. Ahimsa has no winners and losers;
6. Ahimsa is a social virtue;
7. Ahimsa is the bed-rock of all religions;
8. Ahimsa leads to true democracy;
9. Ahimsa is the sure way to peace and harmony;
10. India is most suited to practice ahimsa.

Ahimsa Is the Law of Our Species

'Non-violence is the law of the human race and is infinitely greater than and superior to brute force.' In these words of Gandhi is hidden his theory of evolution of species. Gandhi goes with Darwin in so far as the physical evolution of life forms is concerned, but unlike Darwin he postulates an evolutionary process that did not stop with the emergence of the Homo sapiens with larger brain than any other species. In his scheme of things, the evolutionary journey of the Homo sapiens has continued beyond the purview of mind to super-consciousness. There is an inborn tendency in man to rise above the sub-conscious brute to ultimately become the master of his own destiny. Further, he believed that the emergence of the Homo sapiens was not just a chance; it was designed by nature to perfect man into super-conscious spiritual being something far above what he is today i.e., intellegent being.

In Gandhian conception of God, there was just one ultimate Power that turned the wheel of the universe as it keeps each living cell functioning. And that Power is not any physical entity; it is Truth or *Ric* as the first richa of the Rig Veda says. The way to reach the truth is Non-violence, "an active force of the highest order. It is soul force or the power of Godhead within us. Imperfect man cannot grasp the whole of that Essence — he would not be able to bear its full blaze, but even an infinitesimal fraction of it, when it becomes active within us, can work wonders." Gandhi was well aware of the fact that man could never become perfect because God alone was perfect. "The sun in the heavens fills the whole universe with its life-giving warmth. But if one went too near it, it would consume him to ashes. Even so it is with Godhead. We become Godlike to the extent we realize non-violence; but we can never become wholly God." (Harijan, 12-11-1938, p. 326)

Pointing to the scientific basis of Ahimsa, the Mahatma says: "Every action is a resultant of a multitude of forces even of a contrary nature. There is no waste of energy. So we learn in the books on mechanics. This is equally true of human actions. The difference is that in the one case we generally know the forces at work, and when we do, we can mathematically foretell the resultant. In the case of human actions, they result from a concurrence of forces of most of which we have no knowledge. But our ignorance must not be made to serve the cause of disbelief in the power of these forces. Rather is our ignorance a cause for greater faith. And non-violence being the mightiest force in the world and also the most elusive in its working, it demands the greatest exercise of faith. Even as we believe in God in faith, so have we to believe in non-violence in faith". (Harijan, 7-1-1939, p. 417)

Ahimsa, to Gandhi, was the Law of Love that helped man become Godlike or reach the stage of self-realization. "The rishis who discovered the law of non-violence in the midst of violence were greater geniuses than Newton. They had themselves known the use of arms, they realized their uselessness, and taught a weary world that its salvation lay not through violence but through non-violence." (Young India, 11-8-1920, p. 3)

"The fact is that non-violence does not work in the same way as violence. It works in the opposite way. An armed man naturally relies upon his arms. A man who is intentionally unarmed relies upon the Unseen Force called God by poets, but called the Unknown by scientists. But that which is unknown is not necessarily non-existent. God is the Force among all forces known and unknown. Non-violence without reliance upon that Force is poor stuff to be thrown in the dust." (Harijan, 28-6-1942, p. 201)

"Consciousness of the living presence of God within one is undoubtedly the first requisite." (H, 29-6-1947, p. 209). This means that we must "cultivate in our daily life, as between ourselves, truthfulness, humility, tolerance, loving kindness. Honesty, they say in English, is the best policy. But, in terms of non-violence, it is not mere policy" for policies change through time but non-violence does not. It has to be pursued even if one's life is in danger and there is violence all around as it is today. "A non-violent person looks so ordinary unless and until he is pitted against violence, then and then alone one realizes the difference between the two provided that we are 'ever wakeful, ever vigilant, ever striving.'" (Harijan, 2-4-1938, p. 64).

Non-violence is not a cloistered virtue to be practiced by the individuals for their 'peace and final salvation', it is a "a rule of conduct for society if it is to live consistently with human dignity and make progress towards the attainment of peace for which it has been yearning for ages past." (GCG, pp. 42-44, pp. 170-1). Once it is used in mundane matters, we come to know of its true value as a means to 'bring heaven upon earth'. "There is no such thing as the other world. ...There is no 'here' and no 'there'. As Jeans has demonstrated, the whole universe including the most distant stars, invisible even through the most powerful telescope in the world, is compressed in an atom. ... I hold it, therefore, to be wrong to limit the use of non-violence to cave dwellers and for acquiring merit for a favoured position in the other world. All virtue ceases to have use if it serves no purpose in every walk of life." (Harijan. 26-7-1942, p. 248)

Since nonviolence has generally been used only by some very exceptional individuals, people doubt the possibility of its 'exercise by groups, much less by masses of people'. (H. 8-9-1946, p. 296). "I have been practicing with scientific precision non-violence and its possibilities for an unbroken period of over fifty years. I have applied it in every walk of life, domestic, institutional, economic and political. I know of no single case in which it has failed. Where it has seemed sometimes to have failed I have ascribed it to my imperfections. I claim no perfection for myself. But I do claim to be a passionate seeker after Truth, which is but another name for God. In the course of that search, the discovery of non-violence came to me. Its spread is my life mission. I have no interest in living except for the prosecution of that mission." (Harijan, 6-7-1940, pp. 185-6)

And he finally asserts that, "The only thing lawful is non-violence. Violence can never be lawful in the sense meant here, i.e., not according to man-made law but according to the law made by Nature for man." (Harijan, 27-10-1946, p. 369)

Ahimsa and Truth Go Togather

Given the present stage of spiritual evolution each individual is different from others and has different ways of looking at realities of life and living. Conflict is built in human psyche and society. What is wrong for one appears right for many and *vice versa* is also true. Very few really see the Truth dispassionately. The perspective is blurred by self-interest, past experiences, and images of the future. Thus each person converts Truth into his own truth. And hence conflict is built in the interpersonal and social relations. Non-violence does not and cannot do away with conflicts among individuals, groups and nations. It does, however, convert conflicts into opportunities to bridge the gaps between opponents and bring both sides on a negotiating table to find the Truth, which in Gandhian praxis is the same as God.

In the words of the Mahatma, "This ahimsa is the basis of the search for truth. I am realizing every day that the search is vain, unless it is founded on ahimsa as the basis. It is quite proper to resist and attack a system, but to resist and attack its author is tantamount to resisting and attacking oneself. For we are all tarred with the same brush, and are children of one and the same creator, and as such, the divine powers within us are infinite. To slight a single human being is to slight those divine powers, and thus to harm not only that Being but with Him the whole world." (Auto biography, p. 203)

"My experience teaches me that truth can never be propagated by doing violence. Those who believe in the justice of their cause have need to possess boundless patience and those alone are fit to offer civil disobedience who are above committing criminal disobedience or doing violence." (Young India, 28-4-1920, p. 8). "My love for non-violence is superior to every other thing mundane or supra-mundane. It is equaled only by my love for Truth, which is to me synonymous with non-violence through which and which alone I can see and reach Truth." (Young India, 20-2-1930, p. 61)

Gandhi separates man from his deeds. A good deed should be appreciated, and a wicked one should invite disapprobation. But "the doer of the deed, whether good or wicked, always deserves respect or pity as the case may be. Those who seek to destroy men rather than manners ...become worse than those whom they destroy under the mistaken belief that the manners will die with the men. They do not know the root of the evil." (Young India, 17-3-1927, p. 85)

"By reason of life-long practice of ahimsa, I claim to be an expert in it, though very imperfect. Speaking in absolute terms, the more I practice it the clearer I see how far I am from the full expression of ahimsa in my life. It is his ignorance of this, the greatest duty of man in the world, which makes him say that in this age non-violence has little scope in the face of violence, whereas I make bold to say that in this age of the Atom Bomb unadulterated non-violence is the only force that can confound all the tricks put together of violence." (Harijan, 16-11-1947, p. 412)

If a person does not practice non-violence in his personal relations with others, and hopes to use it in bigger affairs, he is vastly mistaken. Non-violence like charity must begin at home.

Ahimsa Is an Active Force

"In my opinion, non-violence is not passivity in any shape or form. Non-violence, as I understand it, is the most active force in the world...Non-violence is the supreme law. During my half a century of experience, I have not yet come across a situation when I had to say that I was helpless, that I had no remedy in terms of non-violence." (Harijan, 24-12-1938, p. 393)

"The non-violence of my conception is a more active and more real fighting against wickedness than retaliation whose very nature is to increase wickedness. I contemplate a mental and, therefore, a moral opposition to immoralities. I seek entirely to blunt the edge of the tyrant's sword, not by putting up against it a sharper-edged weapon, but by disappointing his expectation that I would be offering physical resistance. The resistance of the sword that I should offer instead would elude him. It would at first dazzle him, and at last compel recognition from him, which recognition would not humiliate him but would uplift him. It may be urged that this again is an ideal state.

And so it is. The propositions from which I have drawn my arguments are as true as Euclid's definitions, which are nonetheless true because in practice we are unable to even draw Euclid's line on a blackboard. But even a geometrician finds it impossible to get on without bearing in mind Euclid's definitions. Nor may we...dispense with the fundamental propositions on which the doctrine of Satyagraha is based." (Young India, 8-10-1925, p. 346)

"I admit that the strong will rob the weak and that it is sin to be weak. But this is said of the soul in man, not of the body. If it be said of the body, we could never be free from the sin of weakness. But the strength of soul can defy a whole world in arms against it. This strength is open to the weakest in body." (Young India, 6-5-1926, p. 164)

"Non-violence is the greatest force at the disposal of mankind. It is mightier than the mightiest weapon of destruction devised by the ingenuity of man. Destruction is not the law of the humans. Man lives freely by his readiness to die, if need be, at the hands of his brother, never by killing him. Every murder or other injury, no matter for what cause, committed or inflicted on another is a crime against humanity." (Harijan, 20-7-1935, pp. 180-81)

"Non-violence is like radium in its action. An infinitesimal quantity of it embedded in a malignant growth acts continuously, silently and ceaselessly till it has transformed the whole mass of the diseased tissue into a healthy one. Similarly, even a little of true non-violence acts in a silent, subtle, unseen way and leavens the whole society." (Harijan, 12-11-1938, p. 327) "I do believe that, where there is only a choice between cowardice and violence, I would advise violence....I would rather have India resort to arms in order to defend her honour than that she should, in a cowardly manner, become or remain a helpless witness to her own dishonour."

"But I believe that non-violence is infinitely superior to violence, forgiveness is more manly than punishment. Forgiveness adorns a soldier...But abstinence is forgiveness only when there is the power to punish; it is meaningless when it pretends to proceed from a helpless creature....But I do not believe India to be helpless....I do not believe myself to be a helpless creature....Strength does not come from physical capacity. It comes from an indomitable will." (Young India, 11-8-1920, p. 3)

"We do want to drive out the beast in the man, but we do not want on that account to emasculate him. And in the process of finding his own status, the beast in him is bound now and again to put up his ugly appearance." (Young India, 15-12-1921, p. 419)

"The world is not entirely governed by logic. Life itself involves some kind of violence and we have to choose the path of least violence." (Harijan, 28-9-1934, p. 259)

"An armed soldier relies on his weapons for his strength. Take away from him his weapons-his gun or his sword, and he generally becomes helpless. But a person who has truly realized the principle of non-violence has the God-given strength for his weapon and the world has not known anything that can match it." (Harijan, 19-11-1938, pp. 341-2)

"My non-violence does not admit of running away from danger and leaving dear ones unprotected. Between violence and cowardly flight, I can only prefer violence to cowardice. I can no more preach non-violence to a coward than I can tempt a blind man to enjoy healthy scenes. Non-violence is the summit of bravery. And in my own experience, I have had no difficulty in demonstrating to men trained in the school of violence the superiority of non-violence. As a coward, which I was for years, I harboured violence. I began to prize non-violence only when I began to shed cowardice. Those Hindus who ran away from the post of duty when it was attended with danger did so not because they were non-violent, or because they were afraid to strike, but because they were unwilling to die or even suffer an injury. A rabbit that runs away from the bull terrier is not particularly non-violent. The poor thing trembles at the sight of the terrier and runs for very life." (Young India, 28-5-1924, p. 178)

"Non-violence is not a cover for cowardice, but it is the supreme virtue of the brave. Exercise of non-violence requires far greater bravery than that of swordsmanship. Cowardice is wholly inconsistent with non-violence."

Change over from violence to non-violence is possible and, at times, even easy. "Non-violence, therefore, presupposes ability to strike. It is a conscious deliberate restraint put upon one's desire for vengeance. But vengeance is any day superior to passive, effeminate and helpless submission. Forgiveness is higher still. Vengeance too is weakness. The desire for vengeance comes out of fear of harm, imaginary or real. A dog barks and bites when he fears. A man who fears no one on earth would consider it too troublesome even to summon up anger against one who is vainly trying to injure him. The sun does not wreak vengeance upon little children who throw dust at him. They only harm themselves in the act." (Young India, 12-8-1926, p. 285)

"The path of true non-violence requires much more courage than violence." (Harijan. 4-8-1946, pp. 248-9) "The minimum that is required of a person wishing to cultivate the ahimsa of the brave is first to clear one's thought of cowardice and, in the light of the clearance, regulate his conduct in every activity, great or small. Thus the votary must refuse to be cowed down by his superior, without being angry. He must, however, be ready to sacrifice his post, however remunerative it may be. Whilst sacrificing his all, if the votary has no sense of irritation against his employer, he has ahimsa of the brave in him.

Assume that a fellow-passenger threatens my son with assault and I reason with the would-be-assailant who then turns upon me. If then I take his blow with grace and dignity, without harbouring any ill-will against him, I exhibit the ahimsa of the brave. Such instances are of every day occurrence and can be easily multiplied. If I succeed in curbing my temper every time and, though able to give blow for blow, I refrain, I shall develop the ahimsa of the brave which will never fail me and which will compel recognition from the most confirmed adversaries." (Harijan, 17-11-1946, p. 404)

"While I admit my impotency regarding the spread of the ahimsa of the brave and the strong, as distinguished from that of the weak, the admission is not meant to imply that I do not know how the inestimable virtue is to be cultivated....It is truer (if it is a fact) to say that India is not ready for the lesson of the ahimsa of the strong than that no programme has been devised for the teaching. It will be perfectly just to say that the programme....for the ahimsa of the strong is not as attractive as that devised for the nonviolence of the weak has proved to be." (Harijan, 29-6-1947, pp. 209-10)

"Inculcation of cowardice is against my nature. Ever since my return from South Africa, where a few thousand had stood up not unsuccessfully against heavy odds, I have made it my mission to preach true bravery which ahimsa means." (Harijan, 1-6-1947, p. 175)

"No matter how weak a person is in body, if it is a shame to flee, he will stand his ground and die at his post. This would be non-violence and bravery. No matter how weak he is, he will use what strength he has in inflicting injury on his opponent, and die in the attempt. This is bravery, but not non-violence. If, when his duty is to face danger, he flees, it is cowardice. In the first case, the man will have love or charity in him. In the second and third cases, there would be a dislike or distrust and fear." (Harijan, 17-8-1935, p. 211)

"My creed of non-violence is an extremely active force. It has no room for cowardice or even weakness. There is hope for a violent man to be some day non-violent, but there is none for a coward. I have, therefore, said more than once....that, if we do not know how to defend ourselves, our women and our places of worship by the force of suffering, i.e., non-violence, we must, if we are men, be at least able to defend all these by fighting." (Young India, 16-6-1927, p. 196)

"Let me repeat for the thousandth time that non-violence is of the strongest, not of the weak." (Young India, 8-5-1941). It is better to use arms than to run away from danger. It amounts to "deny one's faith in man and God, even one's own self. It were better for one to drown oneself than live to declare such bankruptcy of faith." (Harijan, 24-11-1946, p. 410). "My non-violence does admit of people, who cannot or will not be non-violent, holding and making effective use of arms."

Ahimsa Alone Can Counter Misuse of Power

Can a modern nation state become non-violent yet protect itself against external aggression, and internal revolt? Gandhi says no, it cannot, so long as it is based on force of arms. "A man cannot serve God and Mammon, nor be 'temperate and furious' at the same time. There have been cases of states based on non-violence, which offered "non-violent resistance against a world combination based on armed force. Such a State was Ashoka's. The example can be repeated. But the case does not become weak even if it be shown that Ashoka's State was not based on nonviolence. It has to be examined on its merits....." (Harijan, 15.9.1946, p. 309)

"The Government cannot succeed in becoming entirely non-violent, because it represents all the people. I do not today conceive of such a golden age. But I do believe in the possibility of a predominantly nonviolent society. And I am working for it." (H, 9-3-1940, p. 31). "There remains the question as to whether in an ideal society there should be any or no government. I do not think we need worry ourselves about this at the moment. If we continue to work for such a society, it will slowly come into being to an extent, such that the people can benefit by it. Euclid's line is one without breadth, but no one has so far been able to draw it and never will. All the same, it is only by keeping the ideal line in mind that we have made progress in geometry. What is true here is true of every ideal.

"Those who are militarily strong would not use non-violence." Says Gandhi. "In order to be a nonviolent state, it must "discard all her power of doing violence. … if those, who were at one time strong in armed might, change their mind, they will be better able to demonstrate their non-violence to the world and, therefore, also to their opponents." (Young India, 12-5-1946, p. 128)

"If the government does not depend on organized violence, it will have "less to do with the unorganized violence of the people. I would prefer to be crushed between the two." (Young India, 24-11-1921, p. 382) "For me popular violence is as much an obstruction in our path as the Government violence. Indeed, I can combat the Government violence more successfully than the popular. For one thing, in combating the latter, I should not have the same support as in the former." (Young India, 24-4-1930, p. 140)

Gandhi was therefore totally against the way the revolutionaries toppled governments in countries like France, USSR, China, and many others using violence. In India too there were revolutionaries who wanted to throw the British out by force of arms. He appreciated the their heroism and sacrifice. "But heroism and sacrifice in a bad cause are so much waste of splendid energy and hurt the good cause by drawing away attention from it by the glamour of the misused heroism and sacrifice in a bad cause.

"I am not ashamed to stand erect before the heroic and self-sacrificing revolutionary because I am able to pit an equal measure of non-violent men's heroism and sacrifice untarnished by the blood of the innocent. Self-sacrifice of one innocent man is a million times more potent than the sacrifice of a million men who die in the act of killing others. The willing sacrifice of the innocent is the most powerful retort to insolent tyranny that has yet been conceived by God or man."

Gandhi invited the attention of the Indian revolutionaries to the three great hindrances to Swaraj: one, unemployment (he referred to the need to spread spinning wheel among the masses), two, disharmony among various religious groups (discord between Hindus and Muslims), and three, inhuman treatment to suppressed classes among the Hindus. They must remove these obstacles by patient social construction. "It may not be spectacular enough. But on that very account it requires all the heroic patience, silent and sustained effort and self-effacement of which the tallest among the revolutionaries is capable. Impatience will blur the revolutionary's vision and lead him astray." (Young India, 12-2-1925, p. 60)

"To compare their (revolutionaries') activities with those of Guru Govind Singh or Washington or Garibaldi or Lenin would be most misleading and dangerous. But, by test of the theory of non-violence, I do not hesitate to say that it is highly likely that, had I lived as their contemporary and in the respective countries, I would have called every one of them a misguided patriot, even though a successful and brave warrior.... Kemal Pasha and De Valera, too, I cannot judge. But, for me as a believer in non-violence out and out, they cannot be my guides in life in so far as their faith in war is concerned. I believe in Krishna. But my Krishna is the Lord of the Universe, the creator, preserver and destroyer of us all. He may destroy because He creates....

"By its very nature, non-violence cannot 'seize' power, nor can that be its goal. But non-violence can do more; it can effectively control and guide power without capturing the machinery of government. That is its beauty. ...There is an exception, of course. If the non-violent non-cooperation of the people is so complete that the administration ceases to function or if the administration crumbles under the impact of a foreign invasion and a vacuum results, the people's representatives will then step in and fill it. Theoretically that is possible.

"To me political power is not an end but one of the means of enabling people to better their condition in every department of life. Political power means capacity to regulate national life through national representatives. If national life becomes so perfect as to become self-regulated, no representation become necessary. There is then a state of enlightened anarchy. In such a state everyone is his own ruler. He rules himself in such a manner that he is never a hindrance to his neighbour.

"In the ideal State, therefore, there is no political power because there is no State. But the ideal is never fully realized in life. Hence the classical statement of Thoreau that Government is best which governs the least." (Young India, 2-7-1931, p. 162)

"It is my firm conviction that if the State suppressed capitalism by violence, it will be caught in the coils of violence itself, and fail to develop non-violence at any time. The State represents violence in a concentrated and organized form. The individual has a soul, but as the State is a soulless machine, it can never be weaned from violence to which it owes its very existence. Hence I prefer the doctrine of trusteeship.

"The fear is always there that the State may use too much violence against those who differ from it. I would be very happy, indeed, if the people concerned behaved as trustees; but if they fail, I believe we shall have to deprive them of their possessions through the State with the minimum exercise of violence.

"What I would personally prefer would be not centralization of power in the hands of the State, but an extension of the sense of trusteeship, as, in my opinion, the violence of private ownership is less injurious than the violence of the State. However, if it is unavoidable, I would support a minimum of State-ownership.

I look upon an increase in the power of the State with the greatest fear because, although while apparently doing good by minimizing exploitation, it does the greatest harm to mankind by destroying individuality, which lies at the root of the progress. We know of so many cases where men have adopted trusteeship, but none where the State has really lived for the poor." (Modern Review, October, 1935, p. 412)

Ahimsa Has No Winners and Losers

"It is the acid test of non-violence that, in a non-violent conflict, there is no rancour left behind, and in the end the enemies are converted into friends. That was my experience in South Africa, with General Smuts. He started with being my bitterest opponent and critic. Today he is my warmest friend." (Harijan, 12-11-1938, p. 327). More recently, Smuts son related the story of a pair of sandals especially made by Gandhi and presented to General Smuts. The General never used these chappals and kept them safe in his cupboard. When he was asked the reason behind not using the sandals and keeping them safe, he responded something like this: 'they are too big for my small feet.' Smuts cherished his association with Gandhi all through his life.

Ahimsa in us "ought to soften and not to stiffen our opponents' attitude to us; it ought to melt him; it ought to strike a responsive chord in his heart. An ahimsa-ite to be a genuine practicener of Ahimsa should be ready to receive the arrows of the opponent on his bare breasts without returning them? He should not be angry nor should he be perturbed by his criticism?" (Harijan, 13-5-1939, p. 121). 'Individuals or nations who would practice non-violence must be prepared to sacrifice (nations to last man) their all except honour.'

"Non-violence affords the fullest protection to one's self-respect and sense of honour, but not always to possession of land or movable property, though its habitual practice does prove a better bulwark than the possession of armed men to defend them. Non-violence, in the very nature of things, is of no assistance in the defence of ill-gotten gains and immoral acts.

"For the way of non-violence and truth is sharp as the razor's edge. Its practice is more than our daily food. Rightly taken, food sustains the body; rightly practiced non-violence sustains the soul. The body food we can only take in measured quantities and at stated intervals; non-violence, which is the spiritual food, we have to take in continually. There is no such thing as satiation. I have to be conscious every moment that I am pursuing the goal and have to examine myself in terms of that goal.

"Non-violence is a power which can be wielded equally by all children, young men and women or grown-up people, provided they have a living faith in the God of Love and have, therefore, equal love for all mankind. When non-violence is accepted as the law of life, it must pervade the whole being and not be applied to isolated acts. In the last resort it does not avail to those who do not possess a living faith in the God of Love." (Harijan, 13.5.39)

Ahimsa Is a Social Virtue

Ahimsa has never been new to India. India without the concept of Ahimsa would not be real India. The idea of Vasudhaiva Kutumbakam is as old as the Harappan Civilization and its contemporary Ganga civilization further east. Each generation of Indians added newer dimensions that enriched it both in theory and practice. Ashok used it as a state instrument to spread the message of peace. Gandhi, the latest of the great Ahimsa-ites, uplifted it from the cloistered preserve of individuals to the wide-open social field. He made it a means of social change to remove the tyranny of exploitation that man and state heaped on human beings and nature. "I hold that non-violence is not merely a personal virtue. It is also a social virtue to be cultivated like the other virtues. Surely society is largely regulated by the expression of non-violence in its mutual dealings. What I ask for is an extension of it on a larger, national and international scale." (Harijan, 7-1-1939, p. 417). "It is a profound error to suppose that, whilst the law is good enough for individuals, it is not for masses of mankind." (Harijan, 5-9-1936, p. 236)

"All society is held together by non-violence, even as the earth is held in her position by gravitation. But when the law of gravitation was discovered, the discovery yielded results of which our ancestors had no knowledge. Even so, when society is deliberately constructed in accordance with the law of non-violence, its structure will be different in material particulars from what it is today. But I cannot say in advance what the government based on non-violence will be like. What is happening today is disregard of the law of non-violence and enthronement of violence as if it were an eternal law." (Harijan, 11-12-1939, p. 8)

Many have shaken their heads and said, "But you can't teach non-violence to the masses. It is only possible for individuals and that too in rare cases. ...That is, in my opinion, a gross self-deception. If mankind was not habitually non-violent, it would have been self-destroyed ages ago. But in the duel between forces of violence and non-violence, the latter have always come out victorious in the end.

"It is a blasphemy to say that non-violence can only be practiced by individuals and never by nations, which are composed of individuals." (Harijan, 12-11-1938, p. 328) "The truth is that we have not had patience enough to wait and apply ourselves whole-heartedly to the spread of non-violence among the people as a means for political ends." (Young India, 2-1-1930, p. 4)

Ahimsa Is the Bed-rock of All Religions

"Non-violence is common to all religions, but it has found its highest expression and application in Hinduism, Jainism and Buddhism. Hinduism believes in the oneness not of merely all human life, but in the oneness of all that lives. Its worship of the cow is, in my opinion, its unique contribution to the evolution of humanitarianism. It is a practical application of the belief in the oneness and, therefore, sacredness of all life. The great belief in transmigration is a direct consequence of that belief." (Young India, 20-10-1927, p. 352)

Gandhi considered himself to be a Sanatani Hindu, a Hindu who considered truth and nonviolence as the fundamentals of this religion from ancient most times. Some Hindus, however, did not consider him a true Hindu for a number reasons. He did not go to temples although he did not object to others doing so. He also has great respect for other religions specially Christianity and Islam. Some of his ardent followers were Christians and Muslims. Many Hindus felt that it was because of the Ahimsa preached by Buddhism that invaders from the west Asia could come to India, destroy Hindu temples and forcibly convert Indians to their religion. According to them Hinduism never preached the type of non-violence Gandhi was preaching and practicing. Hinduism should be militant in order to save itself from oblivion.

"My claim to Hinduism has been rejected by some because I believe and advocate non-violence in its extreme form. They say that I am a Christian in disguise. I have been even seriously told that I am distorting the meaning of Gita, when I ascribe to that great poem the teaching of unadulterated non-violence. Some of my Hindu friends tell me that killing is a duty enjoined by the Gita under certain circumstances. A very learned shastri only the other day scornfully rejected my interpretation of the Gita and said that there was no warrant for the opinion held by some commentators that the Gita represented the eternal duel between forces of evil and good, and inculcated the duty of eradicating evil within us without hesitation, without tenderness.

"I have also been asked wherefrom in Hinduism I have unearthed ahimsa. Ahimsa is in Hinduism, it is in Christianity as well as in Islam. Whether you agree with me or not, it is my bounden duty to preach what I believe to be the truth as I see it. I am also sure that ahimsa has never made anyone a coward." (H, 27-4-1947, p. 126). "I state these opinions against non-violence in detail, because it is necessary to understand them, if we would understand the solution I have to offer....My religion is a matter solely between my Maker and myself. If I am a Hindu, I cannot cease to be one even though I may be disowned by the whole of the Hindu population. I do, however, suggest that non-violence is the end of all religions." (Young India, 29-5-1924, p. 175)

Gandhi saw some merit in what others felt and said about ahimsa. But he did not agree with them. He was of the view that the invaders could come not because Indians had become non-violent but because they had deviated from the non-violent path. Many of the kings sided with the invaders; and those who were cowards and did not face the challenge posed by the invaders, were not scarce. Gandhi also averred that non-violence has been the bedrock of great religions of the world. The prophets and avatars willed so but their followers often did just the opposite.

"(Barisaheb) assured me that there was warrant enough for Satyagraha in the Holy Koran. He agreed with the interpretation of the Koran to the effect that, whilst violence under certain well-defined circumstances is permissible, self-restraint is dearer to God than violence, and that is the law of love. That is Satyagraha. Violence is concession to human weakness, Satyagraha is an obligation. Even from the practical standpoint it is easy enough to see that violence can do no good and only do infinite harm." (Young India, 14-5-1919, quoted in Communal Unity, p. 985)

Some Muslim friends tell me that Muslims will never subscribe to unadulterated non-violence. With them, they say, violence is as lawful and necessary as non-violence. The use of either depends upon circumstances. It does not need Koranic authority to justify the lawfulness of both. That is the well-known path the world has traversed through the ages. There is no such thing as unadulterated violence in the world. But I have heard it from many Muslim friends that the Koran teaches the use of non-violence. It regards forbearance as superior to vengeance. The very word Islam means peace, which is non-violence. Badshahkhan, a staunch Muslim who never misses his namaz and Ramzan, has accepted out and out non-violence as his creed. It would be no answer to say that he does not live up to his creed, even as I know to my shame that I do not one of kind, it is of degree. But, argument about non-violence in the Holy Koran is an interpolation, not necessary for my thesis." (Harijan, 7-10-1939, p. 296)

"Gandhi's intense study of Christ and Christianity, especially in South Africa, had a major impact on his *satyagraha* campaigns in both South Africa and India. Although *satyagrahis* often considered only in its political aspect, and although several studies of his religious beliefs have been done without reference to their political implications, Gandhi himself emphasized throughout his life that he sought to spiritualize the political, to establish a spiritual basis for all his social and political work. Gandhi was especially moved by the similar themes he found in the Sermon on the Mount and the *Bhagavad Gita*. Christ's ethic of Love, expressed especially in the admonitions to "resist not evil" and to "make this world the Kingdom of God," deepened Gandhi's inclusive Hindu faith and contributed to his theory of nonviolent direct action." (*Richard L. Johnson & Eric Ledbetter, 1997*)

"Prophets and supermen are born only once in an age. But if even a single individual realizes the ideal of ahimsa in its fullness, he covers and redeems the whole society. Once Jesus had blazed the trail, his twelve disciples could carry on his mission without his presence.

It needed the perseverance and genius of so many generations of scientists to discover the laws of electricity, but today everybody, even children, use electric power in their daily life. Similarly, it will not always need a perfect being to administer an ideal State once it has come into being. What is needed is a thorough social awakening to begin with. The rest will follow.

To take an instance nearer home, I have presented to the working class the truth that true capital is not silver or gold, but the labour of their hands and feet and their intelligence. Once labour develops that awareness, it would not need my presence to enable it to make use of the power that it will release." (Towards New Harizons, pp. 91-93)

The scriptures of Christians, Mussalmans and Hindus are all replete with the teaching of *ahimsa*. I make bold to say that violence is the creed of no religion and that, whereas non-violence in most cases is obligatory in all, violence is merely permissible in some cases. But I have not put before India the final form of nonviolence." (Young India, 2-3-1922, p. 130)

"I object to violence because, when it appears to do good, the good is only temporary; the evil it does is permanent." (YI, 21-5-1925, p. 178). "I do not believe in armed risings. They are a remedy worse than the diseases sought to be cured. They are a token of the spirit of revenge and impatience and anger. The method of violence cannot do good in the long run." (Young India, 9-6-1920, p. 3)

Ahimsa Leads to True Democracy

"Science of war leads one to dictatorship pure and simple. Science of non-violence can alone lead one to pure democracy." (Harijan, 15-10-1938, p. 290) "Democracy and violence can ill go together. The States that are today nominally democratic have either to become frankly totalitarian, or if they are to become truly democratic, they must become courageously non-violent." (Harijan, 12-11-1938, p. 328)

The above statement of Gandhi is backed not only by the happening of the distant past but also recent present. Let us look at the freedom struggles of the twentieth century. Russia became USSR to once again become Russia. The USSR founded on violence could not survive. Even the places named after Lenin have reverted to old names: Petersburg became Leningrad to once again become Petersburg. Look at Mao's China. The Chinese, both leaders and commoners, do not want to recall those old days of 1940s and 50s. The commune system is gone and the capitalism has returned in the guise of communism. Let us look at what happened in Vietnam, Cambodia, Laos, Mongolia and the countries of Eastern Europe. And then look at the social and political scenario in Latin America. Some of the worst dictators of Africa are gone after ruining their respective countries. The forced aparthied has disappeared. And if the South

Africans did not retaliate violently against the Whites, it was because the struggle for freedom had the Gandhian touch.

Why is it that practically no West Asian country has democracy? To say that Islam and democracy do not go together is to display ignorance about Islam. It is largely because non-violence, the essence of Islam, has yet to be recognized by the leaders and laity of these countries as the means to social, economic and political reform. Islamic societies would continue to have dictators and despotic kings as long as they continue to ignore the Islamic edicts on truth, non-violence and self-purification. Even the prophet had to leave Mecca and settle down in Medina to avoid bloodshed. He was able to convince the people of Medina and then came back to Mecca to convince the unconvinced by logic, persuasion and demonstration.

Gandhi was convinced that no constitutional or democratic government could exist without the recognition of non-violence as the means to settle disputes not only at the personal and group levels but also at the national and global levels. He therefore devoted his energy to the propagation of non-violence as the law of human life. " ...The conclusion is irresistible that for one like me, wedded to non-violence, constitutional or democratic government is a distant dream so long as non-violence is not recognized as a living force, an inviolable creed, not a mere policy. While I prate about universal non-violence, my experiment is confined to India. If it succeeds, the world will accept it without effort. There is however a bit BUT. The pause does not worry me. My faith is brightest in the midst of impenetrable darkness." (Harijan, 11-12-1939, p. 8)

The goal of human life is complete independence in personal as well corporate life. And this was just not possible without adherence to non-violence as a means to reach the truth. "I have often said that if one takes care of the means, the end will take care of itself. ...It is an unshakable faith with me that a cause suffers exactly to the extent that it is supported by violence. I say this in spite of appearances to the contrary. If I kill a man who obstructs me, I may experience a sense of false security. But the security will be short-lived for I shall not have dealt with the root cause. In due course, other men will surely rise to obstruct me. My business, therefore, is not to kill the man or men who obstruct me, but to discover the cause that impels them to obstruct me and deal with it." (Young India, 26-2-1931, p. 1)

"He was of the view that there could be no international League (a sort of overarching world government), so long as all nations, big or small, composing it are fully independent. The nature of that independence will correspond to the extent of non-violence assimilated by the nations concerned. One thing is certain. In a society based on non-violence, the smallest nation will feel as tall as the tallest. The idea of superiority and inferiority will be wholly obliterated." (Harijan, 12-10-1935, p. 376)

Ahimsa Is the Sure Way to Peace and Harmony

Man has waged wars against others for millennia in the hope that the conflict would end in peace. But it has not happened so far nor is it likely to happen in future for himsa breeds himsa. Ahimsa is the antedote of himsa. How does ahimsa bring peace? It extinguishes the fire of himsa by the water of self-sacrifice. By facing the adversary bravely without retaliating the himsa perpetrated by ahimsa, and by willingly suffering the pain inflicted despite the fact that the attacked has the physical power to retaliate physically, the sufferer becomes bolder and more tolerant and the attacker feels the remorse of being a tormenter. That is why Gandhi says, "I have been a 'gambler' all my life. In my passion for finding truth and in relentlessly following out my faith in non-violence, I have counted no stake too great. In doing so I have erred, if at all, in the company of the most distinguished scientist of any age and any clime." (Young India, 20-2-1930, p. 61). And he adds, "I know only one way—the way of ahimsa. The way of himsa goes against my grain. I do not want to cultivate the power to inculcate himsa...The faith sustains me that He is the help of the helpless, that He comes to one's succor only when one throws himself on His mercy. It is because of that faith that I cherish the hope that God will one day show me a path, which I may confidently commend to the people." (Young India, 10-10-1928, p. 342)

"Hate the sin and not the sinner' is a precept which, though easy enough to understand, is rarely practiced, and that is why the poison of hatred spreads in the world. Non-violence to be a creed has to be all-pervasive. I cannot be non-violent about one activity of mine and violent about others." (Harijan, 12-10-1935, p. 376)

"But if it is necessary for the individual to be trained in non-violence, it is even more necessary for the nation to be trained likewise. One cannot be non-violent in one's own circle and violent outside it. Or else, one is not truly non-violent even in one's own circle; often the non-violence is only in appearance. It is only when you meet with resistance, as for instance, when a thief or a murderer appears, that your non-violence is put on its trail. You either try or should try to oppose the thief with his own weapons, or you try to disarm him by love. Living among decent people, your conduct may not be described as a non-violent.

Mutual forbearance is non-violence. Immediately, therefore, you get the conviction that non-violence is the law of life, you have to practice it towards those who act violently towards you, and the law must apply to nations as individuals. Training no doubt is necessary. And beginnings are always small. But if the conviction is there, the rest will follow." (Harijan, 28-1-1939, pp. 441-42)

"I am an irrepressible optimist. My optimism rests on my belief in the infinite possibilities of the individual to develop non-violence. The more you develop it in your own being, the more infectious it becomes till it over-whelms your surroundings and by and by might over sweep the world." (H, 28-1-1939, p. 443). "There is no hope for the aching world except through the narrow and straight path of non-violence. Millions like me may fail to prove the truth in their own lives that would be their failure, never of the eternal law." (Harijan, 29-6-1947, p. 209)

India Is Most Suited to Practice Ahimsa

Gandhi considered India to be a fertile ground for the practice of Ahimsa. Hindu religion, as also Buddhism and Jainism extol and value ahimsa more than anything else. Minus Ahimsa, these religions especially Buddhism and Jainism would become boxes without any contents. Independent India of Gandhi's dream was to be non-violent India.

"It must be remembered that nowhere in the world does a State without government exist. If at all it could ever come into being, it would be in India; for, ours is the only country where the attempt has, at any rate, been made. We have not yet been able to show that bravery to the degree, which is necessary and for the attainment of which there is only one way. Those who have faith in the latter have to demonstrate it. In order to do so, the fear of death has to be completely shed, just as we have shed the fear of prisons." (Harijan, 15-9-1946, p. 309)

Giving his outline of non-violent free India, Gandhi says: "In Swaraj based on ahimsa, people need not know their rights, but it is necessary for them to know their duties. There is no duty but creates a corresponding right, and those only are true rights, which flow from a due performance of one's duties. Hence rights of true citizenship accrue only to those who serve the State to which they belong. And they alone can do justice to the rights that accrue to them." Following this dictum, Gandhi never tried to be unfaithful to even the British Empire and was ever willing to undergo punishment for violating unjust laws.

"Swaraj of a people means the sum total of the Swaraj (self-rule) of individuals. And such Swaraj comes only from performance by individuals of their duty as citizens. In it no one thinks of his rights. They come, when they are needed, for better performance of duty." (Young India, 25-3-1939, p. 64). Under Swaraj based on non-violence there would be no enemies, all would serve the society, all will be literate and educated and their knowledge would continue to grow as new experiences are gained. People will lead a life of simplicity, eat healthy food and hence sickness and disease will be reduced to the minimum. No one would be poor nor would there be people using their wealth to browbeat others. There is no place under such a government for gambling, drinking and immorality or for class hatred.

"The rich will use their riches wisely and usefully, and not squander them in increasing their pomp and worldly pleasures. It should not happen that a handful of rich people should live in jewelled palaces and the millions in miserable hovels devoid of sunlight or ventilation..... "In non-violent Swaraj there can be no encroachment upon just rights; contrariwise no one can possess unjust rights. In a well-organized State, usurpation should be an impossibility, and it should be unnecessary to resort to force for dispossessing a usurper. (Young India 25-3-1939, p. 65)

"I suggest that, if India is to evolve along non-violent lines, it will have to decentralize many things. Centralization cannot be sustained and defended without adequate force. Simple homes from which there is nothing to take away require no policing; the palaces of the rich must have strong guards to protect them against decoity. So must huge factories. Rurally organized India will run less risk of foreign invasion than urbanized India well equipped with military, naval and air forces. Centralization as a system is inconsistent with non-violent structure of society." (Young India, 18-1-1942, p. 5)

Regarding the maintenance of law and order, Gandhi considered the police force as a necessary evil even in non-violent India.

"Throughout my life it has been part of my creed not to avoid the police but to assist them in prying into all my work; for I have always abhorred of secrecy and it has made my life and work easy because of my indifference to this kind of surveillance. This indifference, and invariable courtesy shown to the police, result in the silent conversion of several amongst them.

My indifference, however, is one thing and personal to me. As a system the police surveillance cannot but be described as a despicable thing, unworthy of a good government. It is a useless burden upon an already over-burdened tax-payer. For, the whole of this extraordinary expenditure, it must be remembered, comes from the pockets of the toiling millions." (Young India, 16-5-1929, p. 159)

"Even in a non-violent State a police force may be necessary. This, I admit, is a sign of my imperfect ahimsa. I have not the courage to declare that we can carry on without a police force, as I have in respect of an army. Of course, I can and do envisage a State where the police will not be necessary; but whether we shall succeed in realizing it the future alone will show.

The police of my conception will, however, be of a wholly different pattern from the present-day force. Its ranks will compose of believers in non-violence. They will be servants, not masters, of the people. The people will instinctively render them every help and through mutual co-operation they will easily deal with the ever-decreasing disturbances.

The police force will have some kind of arms, but they will be rarely used, if at all. In fact the policemen will be reformers. Their police work will be confined primarily to robbers and dacoits.

Quarrels between labour and capital and strikes will be few and far between in a non-violent State, because the influence of the non-violent majority will be so great as to command the respect of the principal elements in society. Similarly there will be no room for communal disturbances." (Harijan, 1-9-1940, p. 265)

Gandhi had a very unique conception of crime and punishment. He relies on Jesus Christ when he says: "In Independent India of the non-violent type, there will be crime but no criminals. They (criminals) will not be punished. Crime is a disease like any other malady and is a product of the prevalent social system. Therefore, all crime including murder will be treated as a disease. Whether such an India will ever come into being is another question." (Harijan, 5-5-1946, p. 124)

The jails of independent India would not be very palatial as they were in his days and today for they would not be meant to keep criminals; they would be something like hospitals for the mentally sick who needed treatment and cure. The causes of the disease should be investigated and removed. The "outlook of the jail staff should be that of physicians and nurses in a hospital. The prisoners should feel that the officials are their friends. They are there to help them to regain their mental health and not to harass them in any way. The popular governments have to issue necessary orders, but meanwhile the jail staff can do not a little to humanize their administration.

And the prisoners should behave as ideal prisoners; avoid breach of jail discipline; put "their heart and soul into whatever work is entrusted to them. ...They should so behave in their little community as to become better men when they leave the jail than when they entered it." (Harijan, 2-11-1947, p. 395)

ABOUT THE PRESENT VOLUME

'Ahimsa: The Way to Peace' is the second volume of the series Rediscovering Gandhi. It focuses on Non-violence for which Mahatma Gandhi is so well known. In general parlance, non-violence means non-killing, but Gandhi gave a social meaning to the term through its practical demonstration as much as verbal exposition. Even than people find it difficult to understand it, let alone follow it in real life situations. This volume is yet another addition to innumerable others written on the subject since the Mahatma passed away on January 30, 1948.

The volume consists of two parts. The first six chapters of Part I constitute M. Phil. dissertation by Jonathan Kadane Crane, an American student of Jewish background at Gujarat Vidyapeeth, Ahmedabad during 1997-98.

The other three chapters constitute articles on related themes the authors wrote subsequently.

Chapter 1 tells how Gandhi inspires him; it tells about the objectives, and structure of the dissertation and concludes by saying:

Religion, gender and nonviolence are urgent issues. There is a sense of immediacy with them: they are intensely personal, historical, communal, and implicate the quality of our futures. All involve three basic dimensions. First, they attempt to understand the status quo, *what I call the Establishment. Second, they envision a ways of constructing Identity. Finally, mediating between establishment and identity, are techniques used to analyze, resist, subvert and transform violence into non violence. As such, gender, religion and non-violence, as fields of philosophical and practical engagement, are normative projects - since they all have visions of how relationships ought to be, and offer ways to get there.*

Chapter 2 is devoted to a discussion on theories of non-violence. After noting Gandhi's multi-faceted approach to non-violence, the author finds a common thread in them all. Enemy is not a person, group or institution, it is the violence that underlies the relationship. 'Thus the target is not the individual per se but the acceptance of violence as a viable means of relating.' There must be differences of opinion, ways of perceiving and doing things; even the imaging of God must differ. All these must be resolved without recourse to violence; violence in thought, words and action. We should agree to disagree without hating each other, abusing each other and killing each other in the hope that through time as love pervades the adversaries would see the truth differently. The here will be concord. 'Living according to harmlessness and compassion also addresses needs/wants. Harmlessness urges the reduction/elimination of (violent) wants; compassion is the pursuit of maximizing needs being met (for *all* sentient beings).'

Once this happens, people start seeing themselves differently; the self-expands and interdependence in the pursuit of truth increases. And thus the differences take the form of strengths rather than weaknesses. The needs of all must be met and all must endeavour singly and jointly to create a world order wherein the needs of all are met. Here all includes the present and future generations; it also includes the non-human sentinels too.

The next chapter (chapter three) focuses on feminism. The issue of gender inequality and exploitation arises from the proneness of the human mind to violence. The author brings out a parallel between gender inequality and inequalities perpetuated in the society on other grounds and violence related thereto. Once diversity is recognized as a strength, the attitude of males towards females would undergo change and patriarchal oppression will weaken and finally disappear. The relationships between men and women would undergo change from one based on antagonism of interests to one based on mutual respect and interdependence on terms of equality.

Theories of religion are discussed in chapter four. There is a similarity between Hinduism and Judaism in terms of history and evolution. It is the relationship between the individuals and the divine power that makes the differences among the religions. Each religion tends to consider itself as superior and its God the real God. Gandhi changed the whole context and content and redefined the concept of God as Truth. Worshiping Truth requires serving others; it is immaterial how one imagines the God so long as one serves others. God does not bestow anything to anyone; it is service of others that ennobles people and gives them bliss. In Gandhian praxis then the divinity emanates from the relationships we develop with the creation; human and non-humans and the service we render to others.

The next chapter takes the reader to the crucial issue of Facing Violence. The author alludes to various types of violence: direct, structural, cultural, natural, and time. Direct violence refers to physical or verbal attack; structural violence is more enduring but untended often borne out of unequal power relations in a community or society; cultural violence is a collection of mechanisms to legitimize the above two types of violence; natural violence is biological in nature and is most visible among carnivorous animals; and time violence is one that impact future generations.

'Violence engenders refugees, weakens immune systems, impoverishes environments with which to cope with deadly, debilitating microbes, and broader structure of disease transmission, gives rise to widespread disturbances: prostitution, rape, prison camps exchange of diplomats, interaction with entertainers and reporters, and economic modes of production and transportation.' It divides people between 'us' the righteous and 'they' the villains.

The author concludes that non-cooperation (breaking of laws and suffering willingly the penalty for it), and with which Gandhi started his movement in 1907 in South Africa, is not enough for it leaves the violent power structure intact. That is why Gandhi had to improve upon it and convert it into Satyagraha, which is non-cooperation plus a vision of a new future.

Implications of the study are discussed in chapter 6. 'Non-violence suggests transferring the locus of traditional notions of power over the others to power over the self.' But that does not guarantee that the others would not do violence to me. Real power lies in the relationship; the way we relate to our environment around us. We can persuade only if there is relatedness. Thus non-cooperation does not deny relationship; rather it reaffirms it. This applies to individuals as well as nation states. If all countries decide to non-cooperate with a rogue country, that country would have to rethink about its proneness to exert power over others.

Withdrawing from the scene and let things settle down does not help either. We can influence the emerging future by being there and relating ourselves to the rest of the world in ways that are conducive to peace.

The remaining three chapters, 'Beyond Gandhi's Ahimsa: A Necessity'; 'Marin Buber and Mohandas Gandhi'; and 'Towards a Culture of Peace' do not form part of the dissertation of the author. In the first paper the author has traced the Gandhi's concept of Ahimsa to Gita; he dwells on the concept of Truth and non-violence and comes to the conclusion that by the time he came closer to his death, he did say more than once that violence was better than cowardice. "People must everywhere learn to defend themselves against misbehaving individuals, no matter who they are. The question of non-violence and violence does not arise. No doubt, the non-violent way is always the best, but where that does not come naturally, the violent way is both necessary and honourable. Inaction here is rank cowardice and unmanly. It must be shunned at all cost."

While non-violence is the real way to resolve conflicts, in certain situations defensive violence may become necessary not as a rule but as an exception. Defensive violence can be of two types: one, to kill oneself rather than see some one being tormented, physically eliminated or sexually abused; and two, to kill the tormenter if there is no other way out. Offensive violence to stop something gruesome happening is prohibited but it is better than cowardice, running away from the scene fearing being injured or killed or showing unconcern for others. And thus in Gandhi's scheme of things non-violence must be norm but there are situations when one can use defensive as well offensive violence but in no case the fourth choice i.e. cowardice. A society that consists of cowards is doomed to remain in chains; and the one that is violent will torment others and will be tormented by others and the one that is non-violent would make this world a better place to live.

Chapter 8 compares Martin Buber (1878-1965), a Jewish non-violent activist and Gandhi (1869-1948). Buber won freedom for Israel in 1948 and Gandhi for India in 1947. They were contemporaries similar in many ways; they exchanged their thoughts until 1939. They were great leaders to whom their countrymen looked for guidance. The chapter explores what these men said on the topic of rights of the Jews to have their own homeland. While they were on a common wavelength in so far as religion is concerned they differed with each other on many issues especially the issue of Israel. The chapter offers explanations for the disagreements and concludes that 'may be, both did not fully integrate their thoughts into their own religio-mystical or philosophical groundings.'

The last chapter takes the reader 'Towards a Culture of Peace'. It is related to author's own interaction with a group of students. He developed a dynamic model of experiential and reflexive dialogue to enable the students to learn by experiencing what they already knew.

Part II of the volume contributed by Jordi Agusti-Panareda constitutes his LLM dissertation submitted to London School of Economics, London in 2001-02. Jordi has looked at the potentials of broadening the sphere of ADR by bringing Gandhian philosophy especially the theory and practice of Satyagraha as a tool to resolve conflicts that plague humanity. After examining the present approaches of ADR, the author comes to the conclusion that the ADR would become a more powerful process of dispute resolution if it is impregnated with Satyagraha and all that it connotes. Then dispute resolution would take the form of conflict resolution with the broader aim of bringing about systemic changes in the power structure of the society and thus, to produce more enduring peace.

The dissertation is presented in six chapters. The first chapter asserts that both ADR and Satyagraha are the products of nineteenth century and have similar aims and objectives, but have not benefited from each other to make resolution of conflicts that plague humanity easier and more enduring. 'The aim is to draw a subjectively Gandhian perspective to conflict and to interrelate it creatively with an existing and varied Alternative Dispute Resolution Moverments.'

Chapter 2 looks at Satyagraha in a nutshell defines the Gandhian approach to conflict resolution. Satyagraha of it is built around Truth; means truth force. Since truth is relative, satyagraha accepts and respects differences of opinion. To come to a common understanding on any issue, people must recognize the difference and have dialogue with love and affection for each other. While dealing with each other both the ends and means must be pure, uncontaminated by violence in thought, words and action. The idea behind the whole exercise is to convert the opponent into friends. Satyagraha often involves self-suffering and appeals to the conscience of the opponent. Satyagraha thus has much larger and broader goals and objectives; not merely dispute resolution that ADR aims at.

Convergence of ADR and Satyagraha constitutes the third chapter. The author feels that the exploration of possible links between satyagraha and ADR has not been done although many strands of satyagraha do find echo in ADR. Both look at conflict as a positive opportunity to make the society more peaceful; second, both lay emphasis on relationships; thirdly, both approach the problem in an integrated way; fourthly, both emphasize consensual and non-violent process of settling disputes; both lay emphasis on human transformation through conflict resolution. And then the superiority of Satyagraha is brought out particularly with respect to the comprehensiveness of its goals.

The last chapter tries to enrich and impregnate ADR with satyagraha, and discusses various tenets of satyagraha to convince the reader that ADR would benefit immensely, both in theory and practice, if it comes closure to the Gandian approach.

What do we learn from this book? We learn that Ahimsa, even if it is limited to the western concept of non-killing, alone can ensure the survival and development of hurnanictry; that Satyagraha is the most inclusive and potent approach to conflict resolution; and that ADR would benefit a lot if it comes closer to or under the umbrella of Satyagraha. This is what the two authors of this volume advise all those who are involved directly or indirectly in dispute resolution, conflict resolution, and peace process through negotiations, mediations, etc.

Both the authors are from outside India and Indian cultural realm. Janathan has focused on what it means to be non-violent when faced with annihilation, partial or total, and Jordi sees the concept of ADR highly enriched if it takes Gandhi's concept of Ahimsa as a part of its toolbox.

REFERENCES CITED

Apart from various issues of *Harijan* and *Young India* already cited in the text, the editorial has referred to the following books:

1. Thomas Merton, *The Nonviolent Alternative,* University of California Press, 1980, p. 6.
2. Mark Shepard, *Mahatma Gandhi and His Myths: Civil Disobedience, Nonviolence, and Satyagraha,* Los Angeles; Shepard Publications, 2002.

3. *Gandhi's Correspondence with the Government: 1942-44,* Ahmedabad: Navajivan Press, April 1945.
4. M.M. Gandhi, *An Autobiography or The Story of My Experiments with Truth,* Ahmedabad: Navajivan Press, 1959.
5. *Modern Review,* Oct. 1935, p. 412.
6. Richard L. Johnson & Eric Ledbetter, 'Spiritualizing the Political: Christ and Christianity in Gandhi's Satyagraha', in *Peace and Change,* Vol. 22, No. 1, Jan. 1997, pp. 32-48.
7. Towards New Horizons: (reprinted from Mahatma Gandhi: The Last Phase by Pyarelal), Ahmedabad: Navajivan Press, 1959.

PART I

BE(COM)ING NON-VIOLENT

by

Jonathan Kadane Crane

1

Introduction

To speak about non-violence, gender or religion is futile. Yet, to be silent on these immediately personal and urgent subjects is absurd. The balance is found through dialogue and reaction. Inspired by Gandhi's relentless pursuit of truth, this project engages these three topics in search of more meaningful, wholesome and peaceful ways of relating. Of special concern is how to transgress conventional modes of believing/thinking/doing, which perpetuate the violences we manifest, impose and suffer. The parallel discussions of non-violence, gender and religion, critique conventional modes of understanding the establishment, identities, and the techniques used to shape these very entities. There is no attempt to answer hypotheses; there are only observations of human relations. These have certain implications, which spontaneously lead to imperatives. Like other academic and non-academic projects, this is normative. I seek to challenge the way we traditionally perceive ourselves, each of us, our surroundings, and our (violent) relationships. This challenge begins at the conclusion with an invitation for each of us to respond to the question: how can we relate differently?

To what extent I have succeeded in so difficult a task, only the reader can judge. But I feel mighty pleased that I got an opportunity to work on a theme that is so dear to me. I consider Mohandas Gandhi the greatest man of the twentieth century. If he were not given the Nobel Peace Prize, I can only say that the prize did not deserve him. From what I have read, thought and contemplated about the Mahatma and his philosophy, I have come to the conclusion that he offers a ray of hope for the tormented humanity.

To do justice to Gandhi and his philosophy, one has to go beyond him to where he might have gone had he lived longer. He was a dynamic personality ever experimenting and modifying his strategies to suit the time, place and problem while sticking steadfastly to truth and non-violence.

Given my Jewish background, I had a whole series of questions in my mind about the relevance of Gandhi's Ahimsa. I found answers to some but each answer has produced new questions. I am inquisitive to find answers to the new questions too. But I doubt I would ever be without questions to ask myself, and you all, my teachers, friends and colleagues; the world around me. Success of an academic journey lies in reaching a milestone, not in reaching the destination, for there is no end to knowledge. I have travelled on the road; not even reached a milestone in the hope that many others would start where I ended and move forward.

Major portion of my contribution to this volume is drawn from the M. Phil dissertation I submitted in 1998 at the Gujarat Vidyapeeth, Ahmedabad. Then there are three papers, which I wrote subsequently. I have included them under different chapters for they further elaborate what I wrote in my thesis and also broaden the picture I had drawn therein.

Gandhi, in all his complexity, has inspired my work and he continues to inspire me, and my work with Jewish people in different parts of the world. Gandhi to me belongs to all religions. He was born Hindu but he lived and died as a true follower of all religions of the world. He was right indeed when he said that all religions are great; it is their followers who maligned them and used them in their own image.

Mohandas Gandhi (1869-1948) was a dynamic personality; he gave voice to millions of oppressed people, first in Africa, then in India. After his death in 1948, he is reaching the oppressed and tormented people the world over. He gently toppled old empires and constructed new ones. Owning virtually nil, his poverty concerned the wealthiest in the world. He was but a single man yet so powerful to influence the globe economically, politically, religiously, socially, even militarily. His days were full, his mind ever active. He wrote often and his words now fill hundreds of volumes—too much for a scholar of my ilk. But the spirit of his life and words is what is most exciting, because it is so familiar to common sense and so novel because it is so different from the absurdities of contemporary society. I (try to) listen to his spirit.

Gandhi often said that he did not want Gandhism or even a social following. Yet despite his wishes, many people explore Gandhi's life and words in attempts to understand him. Some who consider themselves Gandhians know very little about Gandhi, his philosophies, or his visions. Their ignorance belies their title. Some other self-proclaimed Gandhians live according to dictates, vows, rules and regulations Gandhi endorsed. They do not question the relevance of these disciplinarian mechanisms to contemporary society; they follow them because they were Gandhi's. They live in the past. Others adhere to some parts of Gandhi's philosophies while simultaneously and blatantly ignore or oppose other parts. Some consider themselves armchair Gandhians—moral supporters of Gandhian ideals in only words, not actions. Others memorize Gandhi's words and life and regurgitate them on demand. Still others take inspiration from Gandhi, listen to his words of wisdom, and apply a Gandhian-like approach to modern life and contemporary struggles.

I would dare myself not call a Gandhian, but Gandhi does inspire me and when I feel dismayed, I turn to him for answer. He rarely fails me but the fast changing world we live in today does fail me. But not always, follow his footsteps, not because I should not but because I am so overwhelmed by the violence around me that I do not know where to begin, when to begin and how to begin. And thus time goes ahead leaving me behind. Thus I am among those people who are highly inspired by Gandhi, listen to what he said and try to apply his thoughts to the complex world of the twenty first century.

The chapters that follow should, therefore, not be treated as purely academic. Gandhi urges us to dissolve the barriers between academia and daily life, between intellectualism and pragmatism. The subject matter is broad indeed i.e. our relationships and identities. Focal themes are non-violence, gender in general and feminism in particular, and religion, and central influence (Gandhi) are not academic issues only. They are living entities. They are at once concrete and abstract, individual and collective, pragmatic and visionary. We must explore them on these levels simultaneously.

The book is not so much about mapping the dimensions of non-violence, the feminist social movement(s), or Gandhian philosophy. Many other scholars have developed, and continue to expand, these discourses. Rather, this project explores behind the maps (what is hidden underneath) and attempts to see where these maps lead us (what is required of us). Nor do I quote many people, especially Gandhi. Nor should I; Gandhi wants people to listen to the spirit of his life rather than his particular words. Also, Gandhi often changes his position on topics and it would be fairly easy to find quotes to counter quotes I put forth here. I am pre-empting that process by drawing more from Gandhi's philosophical spirit than his letters. (Ironically, to quote is to use second-hand thinking, as Krishnamurti says. I'd rather be guilty of first-hand thinking.)

What is of most interest is how to transgress conventional modes of believing/thinking/doing, which perpetuate the violence we manifest, impose and suffer. In what ways do non-violence, feminism(s), and religion transgress these violences? Or, more importantly, how relevant ought non-violence, feminisms and religion be for you and me today? Concisely, *how can we relate differently?*

The reader may think that my goal is to answer these questions. It is not. Here I attempt to begin to think about them. There are no answers. There are only beginnings. If I *do* answer these questions, then I am guilty of defining them—and no definition is the thing itself. Nor can I do justice to the complexity, density, and diversity of issues embedded within these topics. Thus, I limit myself to discussing certain aspects of them in hopes of contributing to broader discourses—and to our daily lives. These are some of my thoughts thus far. I invite you to think and engage with me about these issues—and hopefully we can find some indications of where to go next.

The Approach

My approach in these chapters is non-linear. Non-violence is multidimensional; so are gender issues and religion. Through parallel discussions we explore how similar, and in which ways different, non-violence, gender issues (specifically feminisms), and religion seem to be. This is done because the three overlap, interface, complement, ansd reinforce each other. While they have parallel structres, the presentation is sequential to ease reading; however, please consider them simultaneous discussions. This dialogue precedes a discussion of contemporary society with its (not so) glorious condition of violence. We also highlight how conflict resolution theories address these problems. How to counter such violence (a question I hope you the reader are avidly concerned about) is explored in the last section: Implications and Imperatives.

The reader may find it easier to skip about. While sections are relatively free standing arguments, there is much cross-referencing, which encourages reading the whole document. I am sorry for that burden, and hope the reading is not too painful. For this, I kept the techno-jargon to a minimum. I believe as Gandhi does—that any writing, especially about topics so central to our lives (like non-violence, gender and religion), ought to be targeted to the largest audience possible. Also, the non-linearity of this project is an attempt to challenge traditional modes of thinking about causality, time, and argumentation. These issues exist and interrelate simultaneously within each of us; they ought to be discussed simultaneously. Gandhi, I think, would have wanted it this way.

Structure of the Book

Because we are exploring non-violence, feminism(s), and religion, a brief introduction to them will facilitate a more nuanced dialogue. Even before this—one may ask why these topics are important in the first place, so important to receive such explication here. My response to this is: please look around. What do you experience? What do you see? Oddly, most of us experience what we want, and we see what we want, too. We think this is the whole of our existence. Most of us do not see the poverty right outside our doors. Most of us do not see the suffering we cause other sentient beings, human and non-human, in our daily lives. Most of us do not recognize the violence in our relationships. Nor do we understand why such violence and suffering exists in the first place. Nor do many of us care to think about it.

Once we look around and reflect upon what you experience and see, you may find that your experiences and views of the world differ from others'. This is good. You may also see general patterns of human behaviour and attitudes. Notice, too, that *how* we think about our experiences, and *how* we think we experience something: all these shape how we respond, who we are, and how we relate (Peterson 1997a). Our actions with others are shaped by, and influence, how we think and perceive our self and our life events. Our actions (really, our relations), and I dare say *all* of them, reveal more than just how we think. They disclose what and how we believe. Our behaviours are extensions of our thinking pattern—which could also be called our soul.

All of us are conditioned to think in certain patterns, depending on our contexts. Such conditioning is imposed upon us by our cultural heritage, education, economic background, political system, religious doctrine, geographical terrain, personal physiobiology, and historical exigencies, among others. A little while ago, someone decided that a particular thinking pattern is better than another and convinced others to think so, too. They in turn convinced us of this. But we did not know we were being convinced; we figured it was the way things should be. We are taught these things. We are taught what to think, what to experience, what to say—in short, how to live. Our behaviours (the ways we relate) are, in part, exogenous. They reflect the preferences of someone *else*. It begs the question: why should we live according to someone else's preferences, mode of thinking and behaving—especially when we witness the suffering it causes me and those around me? Then Who are we, ourselves individually or other people's preferences?

If I want to be me, and not who (and what) someone else wants me to be, then I must engage with myself. I must understand who I am. At the most fundamental level each of us is biologically different. A piece of our biological difference is our sex. There appear to be many "men" and many "women" in the world. But these diametric categories can be deceiving. There are also people who exhibit blends of male and female sex organs. And there are people who exhibit blends of male and female hormonal proportions. There are no "pure" males, and no "pure" females. We are more or less male and female.

But, society tells us differently. Society tells us that there are (only) two categories of humans: men and women. What society (comprising the majority of acculturation mechanisms listed above) teaches us is both "the effect of historically specific configurations of power" and a lie (Peterson 1997a:190). But on top of this lie, society dictates that men and women ought to think, look, feel, believe, behave, grow, make love, work, and die in different and particular ways. Society builds on this basic lie structures of preferences. These hierarchical structures are commonly called patriarchal systems, since most (if not all) benefit men. Patriarchal systems not only prefer (male) men, they also dictate who and what not-(male) men are.

Such ascription of characteristics and identity profoundly affects each person, regardless of sex. It even affects how you read this paper and respond to it. Sadly, women (and "less-than-male" men) have been historically oppressed by such patriarchal systems. If we can assume that oppression is unjust, then this sex-ascription is also unjust. To consider it not unjust is to decide arbitrarily between issues, rendering the concept of justice meaningless. And if we can assume that the pursuit of justice, or at least the reduction of oppression, is a worthy cause of modern civilization, then this topic is worthy of our attention here. And not just here on paper, but here in my life, and in yours—for we are victims (and perpetrators) of the patriarchal systems in which we are embedded. This issue is not an academic question (Peterson 1997b). This is a personal issue. This is also a political issue.

So while individually we cope with the sex(uality) society ascribes to us, we may also see and experience around us other kinds of oppression. Linked with oppression are exploitation and coercion. These are different words for the concept of violence, which we will explore in greater detail later. Violence pervades our lives. We exploit others even without intending to. We ourselves are coerced and oppressed by individuals and systems. We are taught to respond to such violence in a variety of ways, many if not most of which are retaliatory violent mechanisms. This occurs on all levels: (inter- and intra-) personal, societal, regional/national, and international/global. If you doubt this, read any newspaper instead of this paper. We surround ourselves with violence. We embellish our lives with it. We tell ourselves it is good, necessary, inevitable. But is this Truthful?

If we assume violence is unjust (leaving for later the debate about whether *all* violence is unjust) then it ought to concern us now to at least minimize its presence in our personal, communal, regional, and global lives—if not eliminate it altogether. If we assume that violence *is* just, then we could assume that violence is fundamental to human society. However, this is a false conclusion. False, because you are reading this paper (evidence of my existence) and you are responding to it (evidence of your existence). If humans are fundamentally violent, then we would not exist today: I would not exist (no paper), you would not exist (no reader). There would be no modern civilization. Eons ago our predecessors would have eliminated each other in a futile competition for dominance. And, if we were fundamentally violent, today it would not take such a long time or many resources to train soldiers (most of them men) how to kill, or create in them the spirit to execute their training (Pettman 1996; see Hitler's *Mein Kempf* regarding how difficult it is to provoke people to instigate violence, as quoted in Radhakrishnan 1947 : 200). If we are fundamentally violent, then I ought to kill you because you threaten, or pose a potential threat, to my future resource security. Even my mother would have killed me at birth (if not before) because my presence would threaten her own survival. Thankfully, she did not think so. Since I am not killing or trying to oppress you, nor you me, then such an assumption seems absurd.

If humans are *not* fundamentally violent, so what? It means that what society teaches us, to relate with violence, contradicts our fundamental human nature. We are *not* fundamentally violent creatures, but we are taught to believe (and do live) so. But this begs the question: if we are not fundamentally violent, are we non-violent? I do not know if there could ever be a final or complete answer to this. Some say yes, others say yes to a degree, others say it does not matter. However, I do know that we must engage this question. Not to engage with it is to perpetuate the violence, which we suffer. This is not an academic question. This is a personal issue. And it is political.

Yet another conditioning influence in our lives are our religions. These complex webs of belief systems, laws, histories, lores, practices, communities and prejudices inform, in part, how we perceive the world and ourselves. A quick glance at religions around the world shows they all speak about one fundamental aspect of existence: relationships. They recognize that humans must relate to exist. They seek to shape how those relationships form and evolve. They focus on how each of us needs/ought to relate. Religions give us (sometimes in coercive mechanisms, like forced excommunication if you do not adhere to particular teachings) prescriptions of *how* to relate, how to think about our relationships, and how to change them. These relationships are inter/intrapersonal, communal, this/that religion, this/that society, with time, the environment, history/heritage, and of course, with divinity.

Religions are normative projects, seeking particular matrices of relations. To the degree you (do not) adhere to a religion's prescriptive and proscriptive doctrines and practices you are eligible for a series of rewards and punishments. Through these inducements each of us is normalized into conforming to particular religious worldviews and ways of relating. Which religion I conform to becomes an identifying marker of my self. By declaring myself a "Jew" or a "Hindu" or a "Zoroastrian" I name myself—I demarcate where and how my relationships begin, evolve and end. By naming myself (or am named by others) I subject myself to the idea(l)s of a particular religion. That is, I agree to pursue what that religion tells me: how I *ought* to relate (with myself, the world, god, you, everything). My religion, more or less, forces me to relate in certain ways, ways different from how you are taught in your religion.

Religions even erect more insidious barriers: they induce us to *believe* we ought to relate in these (different) manners. What we believe shapes how we think, and how we think informs our behaviours, and *vice-versa*. In essence, religions isolate us from each other (and ourselves!); they violently impose marginalization of non-conformers and alienation of mal-adherents. The differences between religions are not merely academic or theological issues; they are very human and concrete issues. In fact, my religious identity is not just a personal issue; it is also political.

Religion, gender and non-violence are urgent issues. There is a sense of immediacy with them: they are intensely personal, historical, communal, and implicate the quality of our futures. All involve three basic dimensions. First, they attempt to understand the status quo, what I call the *Establishment*. Second, they envision a ways of constructing *Identity*. Finally, mediating between establishment and identity, are *Techniques* used to analyze, resist, subvert and transform violence into non-violence. As such, gender, religion and non-violence, as fields of philosophical and practical engagement, are normative projects—since they all have visions of how relationships ought to be, and offer ways to get there.

Let me take this opportunity to express my gratitude to all those teachers, colleagues and friends who made my task easier. I had the privilege to live with a host family, which proved to be my real family too. Each of them has played a pivotal role in my life, from the minutiae of playing with me in the evenings to "the big picture" discussions at lunchtime. While I talked with most of them about my project, all of them inspired and influenced this project in various ways. They are (in no particular order): Pushpa, Raunak, Saumil, Karan, Mitali, Puran, S.B. (Dada), Savatree (Mammiji), Chetan, Mohnish, Vandana (Bhabi). Pal, Pratap, Ramu, Raju, Ramshankar and Pandit offered comic relief and constant care. They laughed with me, peed on me, cried with me, ate with me. Each is my friend; together they are my family. They gave me the greatest gift I could ever receive: familial love. Thank you.

Many thanks to my professor, guru, and humor tutor, the wise and "crazy old man" Devavrat Pathak. His wit, wisdom and wonderful encouragement spurred me to "experiment with truth."

To my classmates and close friends at Gujarat Vidyapith, Nityanand Satapathy and Neema Vaishnava I owe gratitude. Our adventures were crazy indeed. Elsewhere, Sunalini Kumar's tender insights, questions and intensity pushed me in directions I didn't think possible. Conversations with Aaron Gross slipped between the absurd and profound, yet constantly enlightened me. Adam Loving's quiet observations and Marcy Michaud's curiosity encouraged me to listen more intensely to the world.

Thanks are due to the faculty and staff at the Peace Studies Center at Gujarat Vidyapith: Sadhana Vora for helping me swim through administrivial details; Pushpa Motyani for becoming my big sister; and the morning spinning squad for allowing me to sit on the cushion.

My presence in India was sponsored by the Rotary Foundation of Rotary International on a Paul Harris Ambassadorial Scholarship. Rotary's generosity is heartily appreciated. The Rotary Club of Kankaria in general, and my host counsellor Narendra Patel in particular, deserve thanks for being such wonderful hosts, inviting me to various events, and making sure I stayed out of trouble.

I also want to thank Hilary (short for Hilarious), the cow with the curiously bad hairdo, who lives near Jawahar Chowk. Her presence reminded me to turn onto this street so I did not get lost too often when returning from crazy adventures. She is my ruminating, and roaming, compass.

As usual, my family: Kay and Garry, Paul and Heidi, and Daniel and Audrey, never doubted my capacity to do something strange. I extend to them gratitude beyond words, and love for enabling and encouraging me to venture in a field that is so germane and greatly needed today than ever before.

And finally, I express my thanks to Professor R. P. Misra who found my work satisfactory enough to include it in volume two of his prestigious multi-volume series 'Rediscovering Gandhi' published by the Concept Publishing Company for the International Centre for Gandhian Studies and Peace Research, Gandhi Smriti & Darshan Samiti, New Delhi.

Jonathan Kadane Crane

2

Theories of Non-violence

There is ample scholarly discussion on the various kinds of non-violence and how non-violence is used in historical and modern situations. This project does not explore this discourse *per se*. Rather, this is an attempt to understand in what ways non-violence is relevant to our relationships. It may be helpful here to briefly highlight some conceptualizations of non-violence, especially those inspired by Gandhi.

Gandhi conceived non-violence in many ways, one as the *Renunciation of Violence*. Renunciation implies making a conscious choice between violence and non-violence. A meaningful choice emerges only *vis-a-vis* one's knowledge of and capacity to enact one's decision. Here, one must know how and have the capacity to be violent (e.g., exploit, coerce, physically damage). If you do not know how to kill me then you cannot choose *not* to kill me. Thus, according to this conceptualization, most of us are not non-violent; only those soldiers trained in the art of war and killing *and* who renounce such training can be considered non-violent (see Gandhi's letter 30th June, 1918 in Erikson 1969:374; also Brock 1994).

A different Gandhian conceptualization of non-violence is *Obedience to Truth*. Gandhi embedded mechanisms into ashramic and freedom struggle life that ensured compliance with the vows[1], rules and regulations he set forth for their non-violent pursuits. These surveillance mechanisms served as disciplinary measures and normalized people into obedient subjects. Through micro-surveillance, even over such details as the *desire* to propagate, Gandhi became an engineer of conduct and an orthopedist of individuality.

The norm to which he urges others to adhere is what Gandhi calls Truth. A Truth is some piece of knowledge which can be understood and communicated between people. However, such transactions are always filtered through experiences (which are biased), and often through language (which is locked into a power system of symbols and meaning). Here, Truth (to which we ought to adhere) is another name for existing violent power structures and relations—themselves targets of non-violent struggles. A different interpretation of Truth is God. If God implies absolute perfection, then the norm to which we ought to adhere is something which we can never attain. If God implies striving toward perfection, then the presence of surveillance mechanisms betrays the concept that the means are the ends, since such mechanisms would be redundant once perfection obtains.

A third version of non-violence is the *Abandonment of Coercion.* This requires surrendering to (that is, accepting) the way things are, and not trying to impose one's will (thus, being coercive). Individual abandonment of coercion also implies not allowing oneself to be coerced. However, this self-oriented conceptualization does not prevent or pre-empt others using coercive measures (Gross 1997a, b; 1996).

A fourth vision of non-violence is the *Deconstruction of Coercion.* Gandhi encourages consistency in the moment between one's thoughts, emotions, words and actions. Society, though, encourages (and often demands) us to be inconsistent in the moment and through time. Individual consistency ought to be conceived of not through the majority of one's attitudes and behaviours, but through *all* of them (Unnithan 1987). If one is allowed to pick and choose which facets are consistent with the exigencies obtaining in a certain moment, then the concept of consistency is meaningless. Being wholesomely consistent requires deviating from what society dictates (inconsistency). Through deviation we become true to ourselves, and our circumstances.

Deconstruction means revealing the Truth. As discussed above, the concept of Truth is problematic. If, however, we conceive of the Truth as the nature of relationships then we can recognize that each thing, including ourselves, exists because of and through these relations. Though the quality of these relations varies, the relationships themselves cannot be erased, denied or ignored. Revealing these relationships and their power asymmetries requires recognizing, appreciating, and preserving differences. (This does not mean preserving power asymmetries—see below.) Affording equal consideration to different perspectives does *not* mean considering all things equal; they are not. Intrinsic values are relatively equal regardless of circumstances; utility, though, varies greatly depending on the situation. Equal consideration does mean: (a) nothing and no body is so unimportant enough to be ignored; (b) nothing and no body is so important as to demand one to ignore others; and (c) all things and all bodies concern each of us in varying degrees (Hesse 1943; Pandeya †).

Since it is our pursuit to minimize suffering, considering all perspectives leads us to harmlessness and compassion (Gross 1997a). Living according to the former is to minimize the suffering imposed on others (a passive aspect); the latter maximizes the reduction of existing suffering (an active aspect). By refusing to participate in coercive power relations, we simultaneously dismantle the violence in relations, and promote harmlessness and compassion—two elements of sharing, which is the root of all civilization. More importantly, by deconstructing violent relations, we empower others to be more internally (and externally) consistent. Through my compassion, I enable you to be more truthful (just, non-violent) to yourself and thus also to me. It is in *my* interest to be compassionate. It is in *my* interest *not* to be self-interested (only).

Establishment

These theories of non-violence enable us to understand extant circumstances through several lenses. First, the concept of the *Enemy* is understood as not the person(s) with whom one is engaged in conflict. Rather the "enemy" is the fundamental violent nature of the conflict. It could be the violent nature of the other's policy, structure or behaviour (among other things). Thus, the target is not an individual *per se* but the acceptance of violence as a viable means of relating. Here, all people involved are held responsible for their actions; they are not absolved from the consequences but they themselves are not the targeted enemy.

This shift from a personified enemy to focusing on the quality of relationships emphasizes the role of *power* and *knowledge* in conflicts. Gandhi's approach to power was through "power-over-oneself", or self-control (Galtung 1992 : 64), which echoes traditional Indian power concepts (Nandy 1980). "Power over", however, suggests that something (here, the "self") needs to be suppressed, manipulated or controlled. Alternatively, power can be expressed as the potential to exercise such control. Having the resources (mental, emotional, material or whatever) necessary to exercise control, though, does not make anyone powerful (Unnithan 1987). Rather, non-violent power emerges from non-coercive, voluntary active adherence to morality.

This differs radically from traditional conceptualizations of power as "power-over-others." By changing the locus of the concept, Gandhi undermines the fundamental nature of relationships: each relation is no longer confined to a zero-sum game *vis-a-vis* power. Now in every relationship each party can be as powerful as it wants. Power is relative—to the self. This is profound: it affects how each party perceives itself, the other(s), and the relationship itself.

Related to the shift in understanding power is a change in what is considered *knowledge*. Non-violence recognizes that each situation is different and requires particular actions. It also says that each party understands a certain situation differently, and each perspective is equally valid. This does *not* mean each perspective is equally just. It demands us to consider how other party(s) perceive a conflict, and appreciate why they see it so. No one has the monopoly on knowledge.

This decentralization of knowledge is another profound contribution to the way violent relationships can be addressed. It changes the assumption that only one side (mine) works with valid knowledge and the other(s) (yours) does not. Now all parties are understood to be working with valid information about the relationship. By appreciating others' knowledge, you can work with them from within their informational base, rather than against them from outside their known-world. This encourages cooperation rather than blind competition.

Through cooperating with adversaries you can influence how they perceive the *Truth* of a particular situation. Influence, and not coerce. Because you understand how and why your adversaries know what they do, you can work with them to expand their knowledge and reveal silences and gaps which prohibit or prevent them from understanding your position. You deconstruct their informational boundaries and thus shift their knowledge center (Truth) closer to one which is compatible with yours. Of course, all the while, you yourself are open to such endeavors by them. This is a reciprocal engagement. If you remain closed to their influence, then your Truth is self-centered, and doomed to perpetuate the relationship's violent nature.

A shift in the concept of *justice* emerges from such mutual influencing through sharing of information. What is just in one particular historical moment may not be just in another. Informational, power, and adversarial matrices fluctuate. Nevertheless, an underlying question guides all non-violent action: "for whom will you live?" (Pandeya †). If only for yourself, then the concept "justice" is meaningless; if only for others, the concept is equally absurd. Relations are more or less just, depending on how one balances the needs of the self with others' needs. As needs and resources change over time, relations must reflect these changes. Thus, what is just is extremely personal and fluctuates with contexts.

This is a radical departure from traditional conceptualizations of justice which conceive it as (mostly) static and universal. Many conventional legal systems enforce such justice through revenge (to destroy the other), retaliation (to harm the other), or punitive (to hinder the other) mechanisms. Within the philosophy of non-violence, justice is not enforced *per se* but engendered through (voluntary) mutual, non-coercive engagement in pursuit of Truth. Again, this profoundly impacts how people perceive themselves: each individual is no longer a passive victim of an externally determined criterion of what is not/ just. Each is an active creator, and sustainer, of contextually just relationships. Each of us is empowered to manifest justice through all our actions and relations. Each becomes an evolving agent of justice.

Similar to how contexts change, so do personal requirements. A body's needs change over time. A child, for example, has particular nutritional needs an adult does not. Hormonal changes also influence an individual's needs—say, for sexual relations—and these differ for each person. Traditional "needs" tend to be static and universal. Non-violence sees "needs" as highly individualized and contextual. What are considered "wants" through non-violent theories are often seen as "needs" by society. For example, society tells us we "need" life insurance. But, I have yet to find any life insurance, which will guarantee me that I will live forever. I will die; so will you. When and how is not up to me, really. Somebody wants me to buy life insurance. But do I *need* it to enjoy life just because someone tells me I "need" it? Non-violence encourages us to distinguish between needs and perceived needs (wants). Non-violence seeks to empower each of us to secure our needs and minimize our wants (which are often times exploitative).

To ensure our needs are met requires performing our duties. Gandhi often said that duties are primary, rights secondary. What good are individual rights when no one performs her/his duty? Only by executing one's duties secures one's rights. Again, this profoundly impacts how an individual perceives herself: she is no longer only a recipient of rights (by birth or national affiliation). She is an active executor of duties, which in turn secure for herself (and others) rights and privileges. Living according to harmlessness and compassion also addresses needs/wants. Harmlessness urges the reduction/elimination of (violent) wants; compassion is the pursuit of maximizing needs being met (for *all* sentient beings).

Identity

As seen above, theories of non-violence reconceptualize the establishment which also changes how people see themselves. Non-violence also deconstructs traditional ways of seeing and understanding the individual self and offers alternative ways of appreciating the individual. The *self* is no longer seen as a separate ego, which is simultaneously vulnerable to attacks from without and must be defended at all costs from within. The ego self-defines itself over and against what it perceives as not itself. Through negating what it perceives as "other"—not-self—the ego comes to define what it is. This absolute boundary between the self and other is challenged by non-violence by showing how no individual can exist within a vacuum (real or otherwise). All selves are interdependent, or as the Buddha says, interpenetrating. It is this truth, which prompts Gandhi to speak about reducing the ego to the point of eliminating it. Once the ego, the "I" is gone, then altruistic behaviour (a basic essence of non-violence) manifests more readily.

This is not the same as eliminating one's individual identity. Rather, it is reducing the barriers to identify *with* other sentient beings, especially with those who are your adversaries. There is no reduction of one's self-identity; there is only expansion. Or, put differently, non-violence dismantles the identity prisons society dictates for each of us. In short, this process could be considered one of sympathy (literally: with-thinking/feeling). By reducing the barriers to sympathy, our individual self-identities transcend our (partially) socially constructed egos of competition. Through sympathy we are able to cooperate with others and reduce potentials for violent conflicts.

Theories of non-violence also deconstruct how we think about and interact with *others*. In tangent with reconceiving the "enemy", nonviolence perceives the "other" as not an inherently evil or irrational entity *per se*. The other is assumed to be a relatively rational (according to that other's perspective) actor responding to the Truths apparent to her/him. More importantly, the other is seen as a locus of sentience, a potential sufferer. Since it is our pursuit to minimize suffering imposed on others, then we must do whatever we can to protect other(s), even our adversary, from suffering. The rational other deserves sympathy and protection from suffering. Sympathy reduces psychological distance between people. Through sympathy we (can) obliterate the "otherness" of the other. Sympathy leads to altruism.

The construction of identity through non-violent philosophical assumptions expands notions of the self, brings the other closer, and thus reshapes how people think about and identify with *community*. The community is no longer seen as a static collection of nameless egos with which the individual must compete to secure resources. A non-violent conceptualization of community reveals the intricate, evolving and expanding web of interdependencies between sentient beings and ideas. Gandhi speaks of oceanic circles of humanity, each centering around the individual and expanding to be more inclusive. Gandhi encourages people to consider the community as their own family. This shift, or rather expansion of one's own kin network, is non-threatening, especially for women (Gokani †). In fact, it empowers women: it gives them justification to leave their homes and work for communal causes—because every "other" is a family member. Again, this does not eliminate traditional concepts of family or kinship, but expands them to bring closer seemingly disparate groups.

Nor does this reconceptualization of community obliterate *diversity*. Differences are needed, especially when pursuing the ever elusive Truth. We must rely upon others to assist in our pursuits of Truth since each of us "has to regard oneself as less than perfect" (Galtung 1992:102). In brief, each person is incomplete by her/himself; *and* each person offers unique insights into the Truth. Thus, each individual is needed, especially when countering violence, because each different perspective helps locate the Truth. Diversity is both needed and reinforced through collective effort, catalyzed by sympathy and altruism.

Techniques

Construction of self-identities through theories of non-violence encourages diversity. In other words, nonviolence encourages each individual to be, think, feel, and express differently from others. (Blind) Conformity to arbitrary norms runs against non-violent philosophy. Anarchy (no rule or order), however, is not sought; self-rule (swaraj) is. On the other hand, forcing differentiation is equally coercive. What one chooses to make known as one's identity is a political process. Here, the *personal is political.*

Gandhi personalizes politics and politicizes personality. This is one of the central techniques Gandhi and non-violence theorists use to address violent situations. Depending on one's perspective, it either burdens each individual or empowers each individual with the responsibility of developing the quality of her/his relationships. "The onus is placed on each individual to ensure that rather than the conflict becoming a competitive encounter in which as one gains, the other loses, the encounter remains cooperative and thus maximizing the chances of a productive conflict resolution" (Weber 1991: 24). No matter if you look at this responsibility negatively or positively, the important notion is that you are no longer a passive victim of your relationships, even with the structures in which you live. You, and I, are political/personal agents; and we must be (and are) held responsible for our relations.

Coupled with this notion of personal agency is a changing of the rules of relationships themselves. Traditional relating separates means from ends. Gandhian philosophy, from economics to religion, from non-violence to dietary reform, boils to the simple tautology: *the means are the ends, the ends are the means*. The two cannot, ought not, be distinguished or separated. However, such a simple guiding principle can lead potentially to disastrous results. For example, there is a debate whether non-violent resistance did, or could have, countered Nazi Germany during World War II. Regardless of one's perspective on this topic, it may be more useful to think about future conflicts with an adaptation of Gandhi's question of "does the end justify the means?" as suggested by Alinsky: does this particular end justify this particular means. (see Weber 1991: 54). Or, are these the right means for the right ends (Gokani †).

Another aspect of means/ends is openness, or *open-endedness*. Non-violence theories encourage engaging in conflicts without a preconception of some specific end or goal. Actions of the adversary require spontaneous responses attuned to the subtleties of the (new) situation. This dialectic maximizes a nonviolent activist's chances of influencing an adversary by working with the adversary in the moment rather than against the adversary toward some preconceived goal. This is the process of satyagraha. In contrast, engaging in conflicts with a set of prejudgments (about adversaries or desired ends) is called duragraha (Bondurant 1968).

Related to openness is the willingness to see all parties in a conflict as simultaneously victim and perpetrator. Viewing certain parties as one or the other limits how you interact with them, and also limits how you think about yourself. Each party is both victim and perpetrator of the violent relationship. For example, Gandhi recognized that the masses of Indians were oppressed by British rule. At the same time he saw that the masses allowed themselves to be oppressed: they were simultaneously victim and perpetrator. The British, on the other hand, were oppressors of the Indian masses. Yet at the same time their fears of insecurity stemmed from oppressing (increasing the grievances of) the masses, giving the masses reasons to violently rebel. The British, too, were simultaneously victim and perpetrator. Knowing this, Gandhi was able to work with all parties involved by showing them how much they actually had in common, and that their desires for security could be met by changing how they saw themselves, each other, and their relationships. Without this philosophical openness, such a dialogue could not obtain.

This leads to a final couple of techniques of non-violence. Gandhi levels the playing field of relationships: no longer were there powerful/weak distinctions, victim or perpetrator. Everyone involved in a (violent) conflict is a sentient being (most times human) and requires equal consideration. In hierarchical relations, diplomatic relations often become debates where the dominant dictates conditions to the subservient. In horizontal relations, diplomatic discussions become *dialogues* between (relative) equals. No one side has the monopoly on truth, power, resources, or the future. Through dialectical interaction parties mutually influence each other and creative alternatives (to violence) emerge as viable ways of relating.

The magic of dialogue both reinforces a horizontal playing field, and it shreds the illusion of center/periphery dichotomy. Each person is a locus of sentience, a contributor to collective Truth, a center of meaning. No person is so far removed from a(ny) relation as to be excluded from dialogue, or worse—from even being considered by others in dialogue. If all peoples are to be considered, regardless of their "closeness" to a particular (violent) relationship, then this requires a huge shift in the way we are taught to think. Society teaches us to pursue results, to think about the final product, to achieve, to succeed. For example, schools want us to "pass" classes: schools are more worried about the final product (graduates), than whether those products are worthy of existing (that is, moral and kind human beings). Because I jump through administrative hoops, regurgitate particular pieces of information on exams, and conform to institutional rules and norms, I am awarded a degree. But does this mean I'm a nice person? Society is teaching me how to achieve and accrue accreditations, but is this product worth it? I wonder. Someone who uses this result-oriented thinking in dialogues reduces the discussion to debates toward some preconceived and desired goal. The means separate from the ends; the process melts from satyagraha to duragraha.

However, if all peoples are worthy of consideration in horizontal relations, then a different kind of thinking is required. This is what I call *consequential thinking*. Here, ends and means are intimately linked. *How* one moves from A to B matters. This requires considering the impact of (*all* of) one's actions on *all* those who would be effected. "All" means those existing today and, more importantly, those who will exist tomorrow. "All" also means the more-than-human world: the environment, animals, atmosphere. This, too, is a radical shift from traditional thinking. We humans may be special, but our specialness does not give us permission or justification not to consider (and respond to) the needs of all those we affect. Rather, we are just as necessary to the community of life as the community of life is necessary for and to us. Consequential thinking expands our horizons of accountability to the whole community of life (extant and yet to be).

Reference

1. The vows Gandhi followed and encouraged others too as well were: truth, non-violence, continence, non-possession, control of the palate, non-stealing, fearlessness, removal of untouchability, bread labour, equality of religions, and use of Swadeshi.

3

Theories of Feminism

The growing discourse on feminisms is well documented and analyzed. This project will not burden you with yet another extensive summary of the various strains of feminism. What is of interest here are the common threads among the strains, and how these (inter)weave into a philosophical fabric with which to face violence. However, a brief discussion of the strains may be useful here.

Liberal feminisms tend to assert the (once radical) idea that women can (potentially) do whatever men do. (This begs the question, why would women want to do everything men do, including coercing each other to kill?) This commitment to equality is "manifested in demands for equal access to and representations in the public sphere" (Sargisson 1996:70). To challenge the patriarchal systems defining who/what is (not) male, liberal feminisms offer the concept of sexual neutrality, or androgyny (Kumar 1998). However, the pursuit of (legal) equality and elimination of (sexual) difference does not lead to equal participation, representation, access or influence (Pettman 1996).

Radical feminisms challenge the liberal pursuit of material equality and suppression of differences. Instead, radical feminisms emphasize the basic fact that women and men are physiologically and psychologically different entities. By examining how sex influences all relations, radical feminist theories and practices subvert the traditional political/private dichotomy, but they also constantly face the trap of biological determinism (Kumar 1998; Sargisson 1996).

Among other strains of feminism are *socialists* which argue that productive and procreative activities are defined, controlled and manipulated for majority (i.e., patriarchal) purposes. *Black* feminisms critique other feminisms for their purported universalistic claims (Sargisson 1996).

What is important here is that the equality/difference debate within the various strains of feminism leads to an observation relevant for our discussion. That is, it is dangerous to dissect issues into "either/or" (for example: *either* for pursuing equality *or* maintaining differences). It may be more helpful to think "and/and." This will be touched on below.

Establishment

These theories collectively offer insights into understanding the *status quo*. First, the concept of the *Enemy* is not men *per se* but the structures, policies, attitudes, institutions, and language designed to dominate women (and "not-male" men). These patriarchal systems are the target of feminisms' projects. Through active analysis and critique, theoretical and practical feminisms challenge, subvert and dismantle such exploitative systems. Some feminisms even challenge the concept of sex itself, saying sexual distinctions are also subject to political (power) struggles to determine who/what is fe/male (Kumar 1998). One of the most fundamental contributions of the feminist theories is the engagement in discourse about gender issues in the first place. That is, they criticize how gender affects the nature of relationships. One's sex is not the target, but rather how one's sex/ed/ualized identity affects relationships.

One's sex, according to feminist theories, impacts and is influenced by the concepts of *power* and *knowledge*. By problemitizing sexual politics, feminisms challenge traditional patriarchal modes of conceptualizing and expressing power. Modes of power (ideology, force, discipline and resources) operate through historically specific technologies, located in particular sites, and produce certain effects (Cooper 1995). Feminisms also point out that any concept of power implicates the presence of resistance (Grimshaw 1993). Understanding how power, and access to power, reinforces itself encourages a reconceptualization of power to one which is less vulnerable to implosion: from power-over to power-to. The former is acquisitive and "grounded in appropriation (of autonomy, for instance), while the latter is to do with internal empowerment (individually or by a society)" (Sargisson 1996 : 206).

Locating the center of power away from external coercive potential to internal capacity profoundly impacts how people relate. There is no dichotomy between those "in" power, and those who resist. The blurring of such distinctions reduces epistemological barriers to identifying with others. It also undermines the perpetuation of differences and also of hierarchies based on sex/ed/ualized identities. Each individual, regardless of sex, is (or can be) an empowered agent. This differs from the traditional patriarchal power concept whereby (only) one agent in a relationship "has" power.

The decentralization of power also affects how *knowledge* is understood. Feminisms problematize traditional patriarchal knowledge (re)production. Through various critiques they argue that knowledge is an extension of power structures: it is usually men who determine what is "knowledge" and this knowledge usually reinforces extant (patriarchal) systems. What women know, in fact, differs from what men know; what women know "is outside the masculine sphere of control/knowledge" (Sargisson 1996:188). Recognizing the sexualized nature of knowledge leads us to consider how others in a particular relationship are victims (and perpetrators) of their own knowledge. It also reveals how complex knowledge is, and that no one individual can claim perfect, unbiased knowledge of a certain object, situation or relationship.

Knowledge, because it is sex/ed/ualized through socialization oriented to perpetuate patriarchal domination, is partially mythological. Recognizing the imaginary nature of one's own, or someone else's, knowledge may transform violent relationships, as the violence may be more socially (re)constructed than objectively real. The elimination (or reduction) of such social constructions decreases the complex webs of myths which cloud our vision of more peaceful relationships.

Through active engagement, or dialogue, feminists do not so much discuss the *Truth* of a particular situation but rather reveal Truth(s) by shedding socially determined knowledge perpetuating systems of domination. This does not mean feminists impose their own political agendas onto the knowledge with which they engagse in a particular relationship. The alternative(s) to patriarchal knowledge is not matriarchal knowledge; it is the elimination of all forms of oppressive knowledge (Peterson 1997a). It may seem that such deconstruction reduces what is considered legitimate knowledge. Rather, deconstructing patriarchal knowledge de-silences the hitherto ignored information and envoices those who previously were denied (en)knowledgeable status (Crane 1997b). Thus, the sphere of legitimate knowledge expands.

If all forms of non-oppressive knowledge are legitimate, then feminisms' contribution to the debate on *justice* is that normalization is unjust. In other words, differences ought to be preserved and protected. Forcing normalization to particular socially determined idea(l)s (for example, gender roles) is essentially the suppression, even denial, of differences; this is unjust. Hence justice is no longer conceived of as merely an either/or issue. Justice is more complex, fluctuating according to subtle differences and deviances from norms.

By encouraging individuals to adhere less tos socially constructed and static norms and more to individual deviances from those norms, feminisms undermine the monolithic nature of traditional justice. This transforms the individual from a passive observer/victim of justice to an active creator of a dynamic system of give and take. Feminisms also propose a justice of caring (as different from more traditional conceptualizations of justice as liberty, equality, or welfare). Caring, or sharing, is founded on performance of duties and, at the same time, honors differences of needs. An example may clarify this. Similar to how mothers instinctively care for the needs of children, children also instinctively care for the needs of pets and replicas of humans. These are just relationships based on caring: voluntary performance of duties and recognition of differences.

Identity

One of feminisms' projects is to deconstruct patriarchal identities and construct more suitable and sustainable identities. Patriarchal systems institutionalized masculinist identities of the self, and this made the identities "naturalized; and that which is natural has no history and no politics—and no visibility..." (Peterson 1997a:192). The concept of identity itself is challenged by the observation that identities draw boundaries demarcating exclusive territories (conceptual, textual, physical—among others) and distinguishing between inside/outside (Young, in Sargisson 1996:177). Feminisms criticize this process and by doing so make visible women as viable and meaningful loci and shapers of identity.

The construction of *self* identity through feminist theories shakes patriarchal domination. While patriarchal systems rule through dividing reality into hierarchical binarisms, feminisms show that what is (arbitrarily) privileged is privileged only in relation to what is not. That is, what is negated undergirds what is privileged; or, what is subservient props up the entire hierarchical system. Take away the negated, and patriarchal thinking/systems are powerless: there is no one to dominate or control. Gandhi understands this and encourages the oppressed "masses" not to cooperate with the dominating few; this topples empires.

The concept and identity of the self, then, is political. Feminisms understand the self, particularly the woman-self, as subject to multiple layers of pressures. It is each individual's task (developing one's identity) to decipher which pressures are worthy of listening to and to disregard if not outright dismantle others. Recognizing the interference of external pressures indicates that individuals are embedded in political networks to which they must respond and contribute.

It is this interpenetration (a term some radical feminists would balk at because it suggests sexual intercourse, and intercourse in their eyes is rape) between selves which also influences how feminists reconceptualize the *other*. Traditional masculinist thinking systems perceive the other as different, and anything different is inferior, dangerous and must be controlled. "The other is the stranger, the strange, and thereby becomes the estranged" (Sargisson 1996:179). Feminisms tend to think of others as (potentially) creative sites of political identification and social solidarity—and this can be based on the politics of sex/uality, (re)production, and materiality. To hinder, coerce, or destroy the other's efforts to shape her/his self identity is to fall into the trap which patriarchal systems are known for: interfering unwarrantedly and imposing identity characteristics. The other is viewed not so much as a completely separate entity, nor the relationship between the self and other as irrelevant. Being sensitive to how one's own identity influences others, one empowers others to more freely shape their own (politic/al/icized) identity.

By acknowledging that others are different from one's own self also dismantles the conceptual paradigm of binarisms. There is no *one* opposite from the self. The concept of difference shifts from binary opposites to multiplicity. *Diversity* becomes more important than sameness. *Community* is then seen not much as a collection of like individuals, or people who ascribe to similar identities. Feminist conceptualization of community is seen more as diversity co-existing: "community as 'being-in-common' as opposed to (the opposite) 'being-common' or being the same" (Neufeld 1997:17). Personal identity and community mutually constitute each other. This honors and supports notions of personal growth and responsibility for collective diversity, just as Gandhi sought (Thakkar †). It also changes thinking about such issues like development by bringing women into the (inter/intra-national) picture as knowledgeable subjects and (re)sources (of creativity) (Pettman 1996).

Techniques

One of the central tenets of feminisms is the concept that the *personal is political.* While some feminists seek to minimize public intrusion into personal space (like, sex/uality, and reproduction), many feminists encourage the personalization of the political. That is, walk your talk. Or as Gandhi says, be consistent between your thoughts, emotions, words and deeds. So it goes multiple ways: the "sprivate" self you've constructed is a political statement; your "public" self (politics) is an extension (or reflection) of your internal conceptualization of your self; and the two are mutually constituting. You become an active participant in your private (sex/ed/ual) political construction and the public (sex/ed/ual) political structures surrounding you. You are no longer a passive victim of environmental pressures; and you are held accountable for this.

Women, as centers of politicized identities, are no longer silenced by patriarchal mechanisms of ascription. Women can and ought to voice their identities on their own terms; not only women, but all subaltern groups previously denied voices by oppressive systems founded on binarisms. This challenges conventional identities of individuals, communities, and even national groups. Nationalism is revealed as a technique of dichotomizing us/them, inside/outside, inclusion/exclusion, sameness/difference, and rendering these binarisms into hierarchical values which must be (and are) defended through violence (Pettman 1996; Nordstrom 1994). Following feminisms' philosophical assumption that all oppressive structures are unjust, then what traditionally was considered a just way of identifying with a nation must be dismantled.

The same can be said about individual identities. We each are subject to sex/ed/ualized socialization according to how others perceive us, and how we are taught to see ourselves. We are taught that some ways of believing/thinking/doing are better than others; some good, some bad. This arbitrary (masculinist) valuing of characteristics suppresses each individual's capacity to shape her/his own identity. By revealing this insidious process, feminisms empower women, other subaltern groups, and even men themselves, to become active deconstructors of their patriarchal identities and generators of more truthful identities.

To say this process threatens male dominance is an understatement. It leads to a dramatic shift in the way people relate: with themselves and each other. Let me explain with a short diversion. Feminist scholars challenge traditional analytical/explanatory theories, which more often than not reinforce extant worldviews and policies. Instead, feminisms offer critical theory as a way of approaching subjects. Criticism de-silences silences, renders visible the invisible (the oppressed), and shatters previously held universal assumptions (especially in the realms of international relations, development theory, sociology, literature, and sex/uality). Only by approaching extant systems with a critical eye can one begin to understand why things are they way they are now. This requires going beyond simple binaristic thinking (e.g., either/or, sameness/ difference). It means eliminating the concepts of finality, linearity, and boundary (among others). In short, critical theories lead us to transgressing patriarchal thinking (and doing/being). There are no conclusions, no blueprints, no predetermined identities toward which we as individuals or as societies must strive or for which we must kill. Critical theories lead us to open potentialities, fluidity, and influence. As there are no set ends *per se*, then the *means are the ends, the ends are the means*. Transgressing traditional thinking, identification and acting transforms extant violent relations into evolving mutually constituting relation-ships.

A mutually constituting relationship requires active interaction. It also presupposes a degree of interdependence—for why would there be any relationship between non-interdependent beings? In the human sphere, and inspired by feminist teachings, such interaction occurs through *dialogue*. Traditional ways of relating, however, encourage defending particular stances, identities, territories (e.g., geographical, emotional, intellectual, spiritual, sexual). What I protect is considered static, concrete, exclusive(ly mine), and symbolic of my worth. I defend it from your intrusion. In fact, I declare anyone and anything not mine eligible for destruction because you all threaten my identity (that is, everything I'm protecting). You are also doing the same: you perceive me as a threat to your matrix of possessions (we "own" our identities in this line of thinking) and condemn me to forever being an outsider (even if we are co-nationals I still threaten your personal security) (Fromm 1976). We should probably call this interaction "mutually assured destruction" or mutually assured defense, rather than relating. Yes, this is also the name for national nuclear policies to stockpile enough armaments to ensure destruction of (all) adversaries who also prepare the same. We do this individually too. Why else would I (and you) have a stockpile of emotional defense mechanisms, insults, stereotypes, prejudices, and fears of otherness/difference? To defend (and destroy) ourselves.

Feminisms emphasize the ridiculousness of this way of relating. There are no legitimate dialogues when adversaries seek only to defend themselves from external (and internal) threats. Defensive adversaries perceive themselves as superior to/different/separate from others. These "relations" include debates, impositions, sanctions, even abandonment. Feminisms, however, dismantle the otherness of the other, level the playing field, and empower each individual to engage in dialogue.

Gandhi also ridicules traditional ways of relating based on such defensive fears and masculinist binaristic identification. He negates traditional Indian masculine/feminine dichotomy, renames colonialism as exploitation, and asserts an egalitarian ethic: "He rejected the British as well as the Brahmanic-Kshatryia equation between manhood and dominance, between masculinity and legitimate violence, and between femininity and passive submissiveness" (Nandy 1980:74). By obliterating the otherness of the other, Gandhi levels relational playing fields, empowering each individual to actively engage in dialogue.

Now that relations are more or less level and all adversaries are legitimate centers and envoicers of real experience, what does this mean? Following feminisms concept of *open-endedness*, such dialogues then are events of mutual influence. No one person is a set identity. In fact, no one *is*. For declaring what one *is* is to define oneself, demarcate (set) boundaries, admit staticness. If one *is* then one is stagnant; you are (spiritually, emotionally, intellectually, possibly even physically) dead. Feminisms thus encourage conceptualizing the self as an entity becoming.

What and how you become is political (Asopa †). Who you are, and will be, affects (all) those around you. As one of feminisms' projects is to eliminate, by reducing, oppression, then it is up to each of us to eliminate, through reducing, our own oppressiveness. Choosing *not* to reduce the extent to which I exploit others is a political statement. It says that while others are worthy of being exploited, so am I. (To say that others should be exploited but I am exempt, is to disassociate myself from the community of life. It says I am so unlike other (human) beings and am so superior that only I can decide who exploits whom how. This kind of thinking, sadly, has led us to the brink of environmental destruction.)

However, choosing to reduce the oppression I cause others presupposes that I recognize that I impact others in the first place. This relates to the feminist concept of the self as an open system, multidimensional, and embedded within broad networks of relations. The quality of those relations is of concern here. Feminisms reveal that we are indeed related to everything around us (see ecofeminist theories on this), and they also encourage us to think about how we relate to everything. This *consequential thinking* expands the concept of the self, empowers each to reduce the oppression one imposes on others, and plants the seeds for evolving relations with the broader community of life.

4

Theories of Religion

Just as the bunyan tree stretches back down into the soil for added nourishment, so, too do religions stretch back into history to bind again (*re-legere*) humans to our heritages. Through parallel connections with its environment, the bunyan tree can then generate new branches from below and from above. It is a living organism, interweaving its historical base with its contemporary moment, be it in the shade or light, wind or rain. So, too, are religions: they reach through generations to find moral nourishment and guidance for new ways of living intensely in the moment. Religions, like trees, are living entities: they must spread themselves into their environments to gather strength, must hold fast to their roots for centering, must forever shift, expand and contract according to exigencies, and yes even religions must eventually die. But their seeds live on....

Gandhi recognizes that religions are living, breathing entities. They *must* be, or otherwise they are blind dogmas, mere propaganda, sets of stagnating rituals. Religions are mechanisms to help us understand our experiences, locate us within history and the environment, and guide our actions. They mediate and balance our knowledge, desires and behaviours. They assist us in making wrongs right. This transformation toward "right" living is not so much about there being *one* way of living, but more about a move toward making things whole, or be(com)ing wholesome ourselves (Krishnamurti 1980). Each religion teaches us different ways of be(com)ing wholesome. Through time and experience, these ways change.

It is not the task of this paper to outline how each religion puts forward ways to live wholesomely. However, two religions in particular are of interest here: Judaism and Hinduism. The latter because it, along with many others, influenced Gandhi; the former because it, along with many others, influences me. A brief discussion of elements of each may be useful as we then explore how religions in general teach us to view what's around us and inside us, and what techniques they provide to engage with reality. Gandhi's reconceptualization of religion is woven throughout this section.

Some notes to consider on Hinduism and Judaism: these religious traditions are relatively old, each claiming origination over three thousand years ago. The geographical locations of germination are also relatively close, both taking place in or near the Fertile Crescent of Mesopotamia. Both employ a similar symbol of fertility—the six-pointed star, which also suggests some cross-fertilization of other elements during their genesis. While one religion is adhered to by nearly 1/6th of the world's population, the other claims but a fraction of one per cent of the total population. Both enjoyed periods of political and religious sovereignty; both suffered lengthy periods of subjugation and intolerance. A different note to consider: these religious traditions are *not* all the religions of the world, nor can they represent other religious traditions or experiences. For example, indigenous religions of African tribes may find little in these religions with which they can identify. Thus, the universal claims made in this section should be taken in light of this fundamental shortcoming of this paper...

Hinduism is a vast and evolving religion. Its complexity cannot be understated. Nor can its influence on Gandhi be precisely measured, though many scholars attempt this. Contrary to popular belief, Hinduism is monotheistic: the massive pantheon of deities are the multiple faces of the single God (Gandhi 1955). The concept of *karma* produces not so much a sense of fatalism but of acceptance of the moral law of consequences. Yet within this attitude of acceptance is room for the exercise of will power. People act according to four techniques: (a) knowledge (*jnana yoga*); (b) devotion or faith (*bhakti yoga*); (c) work, function or action (*karma yoga*); and (d) psychophysical exercises (*raja yoga*). One of the central texts, the *Bhagavad Gita*, explores the dynamics of listening to morality and engaging as informed agents in the illusory, multiplicitous, moral, middling, and teaching world (Smith 1991). A central tenet of Hinduism is that there is no one particular teaching, deity, or even God, (in) which one must believe—to be a Hindu.

Similar to Hinduism, there is no one doctrine within *Judaism* (in) which all Jews must believe. In fact, Judaism encourages active critique and engagement with its teachings. The central text, the *Torah*, is simultaneously a historical document, a meta-historical collection of moral stories, a guide to mysticism, and a prophetic vision of a messianic era (among other things). Rooted deep within the tradition is the philosophy that justice (*tzeddek*) is both historically contextual and needs constant pursuit and maintenance. Relatedly, charity (*tzeddakah*) is viewed as righteousness.

Curiously, while both religious communities have been accused of being misogynist, both religions elevate the woman, womanliness, and even femininity into positions worthy of worship. For example, in Hinduism, Mira, Draupadi and Sita are strong woman figures who are revered for their resistance to male oppression, their expression of self-reliance, and conferring with their individual consciences in the face of moral dilemmas (Thakkar †). In Judaism, the holiest of all holy days, the Sabbath, is viewed as a woman—the queen of Judaism. One of the most revered prophets in the *Torah* is Ruth, who displays great courage in balancing respect for elders' wishes with her needs of self-identity. The discrepancies between religious beliefs and modern communal practices show the dire need for contemporary Jews and Hindus, men and women, to listen more closely to their belief systems and relate accordingly (Bumiller 1990).

Establishment

Religions are complex systems of beliefs, rituals, norms, lores, languages, histories, geographical terrains, and visions (among other things). They are, for the most part, dynamic, communal and personal, historical and contemporary, this-worldly and other-worldly. How they perceive reality is often influenced by where they are located: historically, geographically, and (according to Marx) also economically (political and technological means of production). All religions, though, attempt to explain origins. What obtains differs widely.

Whose origins? Determining this requires distinguishing between who are the "chosen" and who are not. Who are *not* eligible for inclusion are the "other" and are often demonized, condemned, or sometimes sought after for conversion. Also related to origins of religions is the concept of God, or some divinity. While some religions conceptualize the divine outside this world, others locate the divine within it. Those with other-worldly gods, like Judaism, Christianity and Islam, are often accused of allowing the development of a negligent attitude toward the earth because divinity is not here but "elsewhere" (Abram 1996: 94). Likewise, those with this-worldly gods are often met with disdain because they do not transcend reality into abstractions where many humans find greater meaning.

Nevertheless, while the location of a religious divinity is important, how people relate to it/them is of special interest here. The relationship between the individual and the divine is, for lack of a better term, the *Enemy*. Or, more precisely, how religions teach us to relate with the divine(s) is the enemy. That is, some religions teach us that the divine is beyond human comprehension, its qualities (perfection, completeness, infiniteness—among others) beyond human capacity of be(com)ing, its emotions and intellect beyond human ability. They teach us to worship that which humans can never be(come). To worship that which is (forever!) futile breeds frustration, confusion, resentment. That which is worshipped becomes feared, even hated. There are also some religions which teach us that the (qualities of) divinity(s) are within our reach. But if they are attained, what does this say about the divinities? Just how "divine" are Gods if mere humans can be so godly? This blurring of the sacred and the profane also produces confusion, frustration, and resentment. That which is worshipped becomes mundane, even disregarded. Of course, not all religions teach us these ways of relating, but many do.

Obviously changes are needed in how we are taught to relate with that which is divine. Many scholars of religions moan that because people do not relate well with their own concepts of the divine, they express their angst and fears against those not within their religious communities. This religious breakdown from worship to warship is readily found in history, and even today within and between religious communities. One could call this the slippery slope from faith to fundamentalism, from communitarianism to communalism.

People eager to distinguish between who is chosen and who is not, and how the chosen ought to relate to the divinity(s), play with *power* and *knowledge*. Many religions ascribe ultimate, perfect, complete power and knowledge to their divinity(s). Thus it is people themselves who generate their gods as such powerful and knowledgeable entities. For those who believe their all-powerful entities are forever beyond human grasp and expression, then (all) humans are forever condemned to living and working with less than perfect, or complete, power. This makes it illogical for any human to punish another, because power is relative to the absolute power of the divine. Since no human can comprehend that level of power, it is impossible to determine which human is "more" powerful than the next. Punishment—or oppression—is eliminated as a justified way of relating. Yet when the divine's power level *is* attained by humans, questions about the power's sacredness come into play—for why should one human be more divinely empowered than another. Again, justification for exploitation is eliminated.

For those religions which ascribe perfect, complete, absolute and infinite knowledge to their divinity(s), then, like power, humans are (forever!) condemned to relative (massive!) ignorance. Determining who is more or less knowledgeable relative to the divine's knowledge is a futile project. If, however, the extent of the divine's knowledge is attainable by humans, and if it is complete knowledge, then there would remain no mystery in the world for humans. Without mystery, without novelty, the mind (soul and body) stagnate. Why become completely all-knowledgeable if that requires absolute dying? And, why listen to anyone who claims she or he has attained complete knowledge of the divinity(s)? Distinguishing a divinely-knowledgeable prophet from a dunce becomes a meaningless project.

Gandhi counters these problematic trends in religious world views by shifting the concept of power and knowledge. By redefining God he even shifts how people relate with God. Gandhi argues that a central teaching of Hinduism in particular and of religions in general is selfless action (*anasakti*). Coupled with this is *yajna*, or acts for the welfare of others without desire of reciprocity of any kind. This self-less and other-more attitude dramatically subverts the concepts of *power* and *knowledge*. These are no longer selfish and other-competitive qualities or tools. Rather, power and knowledge are seen as mechanisms through which mutual empowerment and mutual divination can occur. Power (and knowledge) are construed as power-through. The pursuit and use of power and knowledge are no longer compared to an absolute (attainable or not), but to the present context. We are to seek and employ what power and knowledge are appropriate for the moment and act through them.

Recognizing that each moment has its own criteria of what's necessary to become more divine, Gandhi also reconceives the divine. Early in his life he called God Truth; later, he reversed this to "Truth is God." This emphasis on the contextuality of Truth expands his religious communal identity to include all peoples, regardless of their faiths (or no-faiths, in the case of atheists). Since each person holds a glimpse of what is True, then each person's contribution to a particular situation (here, a violent relationship) is necessary to understand its complexity. Only through the compilation of the various perspectives can one begin to appreciate, or worship, the Truthfulness of a particular relationship.

Worshipping *Truth* requires serving others. It is this service which is the locus and generation of the divine. In other words, it is the relationship (actually—the *quality* of the relationship), which is the source of divinity. This is why Gandhi encourages us to identify (that is, serve) with the masses (who, most likely, are oppressed and impoverished). The more people we serve, the greater our power and knowledge, and the more intense our divine-like qualities. Choosing not to serve others is to deny your embeddedness in networks of interdependence and obligation. Choosing not to serve others also denies yourself your own pursuit of divine qualities; you consciously opt to limit your knowledge and power—you choose to live a small life.

By shifting the religious concept of faith from worship to service, Gandhi also influences the religious concept of *justice*. No longer is the individual a passive recipient of God's decries on justice. Now each person is an enactor of justice. Nor is justice static, predetermined, universal, or exogenous from human society. What is just reflects the subtleties of the particular historical moment. What is moral also shifts. Gandhi's philosophy of meeting *needs* of everyone before the *wants* of a few also guides this other-oriented service. Though a child screams for yet another toy, it is just not to provide one. This is moral behaviour because it adheres to, and reinforces, a vision of justice that understands the difference between needs (physical, emotional, intellectual, spiritual) and wants. Religion, for Gandhi, becomes a binding together of human beings through other-oriented, historically and individually attuned service.

Identity

Gandhi's concept of faith as service impacts how identities are constructed. Obviously, the *self* is no longer an isolated individual seeking redemption, enlightenment, or messianic salvation from an external deity. Rather, the self is construed as a potential co-generator of divinity. Serving others enhances relationships and elevates the self from a meaningless void to a creator of (self) meaning.

Judaism also conceptualizes the individual self as a co-generator of meaning. This is done through active engagement with religious texts, precepts, and practices. In fact, the Hebrew language itself requires active participation: you must en-vowel the words (because the words are only collections consonants) and evoke meaning from texts *each time* you read. Thus, every reading of holy texts is (can or ought to be) a new interpretation of them. The individual is no longer a passive reader, but an animist—animating the letters with different breath-like sounds and meanings. Through participating with traditions and texts, each individual generates new spiritual understandings, especially of the self (Abram 1996). More broadly, each reading/interaction generates a new Jewish religion.

Just as my self is a generator of self-meaning, so is every other sentient being, particularly humans. This forces me not to interfere with other's spiritual development—for who am I to impose my self-meaning onto others, or force others to generate their self-meaning the same way I do? The concept of the *other* is a cite of contestation. On one hand, we are encouraged not to interfere with others' self development. But persistent non-interference can lead to indifference, and quickly toward intolerance and even xenophobia. On another hand, because each of us is a center of self-creation and we are to serve each other, then the other becomes a source of other-creation. That is, through serving the other, the self generates self-meaning. Or, as said earlier, not being self-interested is in my self-interest. Service becomes a reflexive process of constructing meaning (identity).

Taking this concept a step further, the broader one's range of service, the more complex, dynamic, deep, and personally-gratifying one's self-meaning. This is why Gandhi constantly encourages us to identify with (or, serve) the world, especially the oppressed—because he knows that this service enhances our individual senses of meaning. Life is based on relationships between self and other, and the more "others" one serves, the greater one's life meaning (Krishnamurti 1988).

These "others" are not only human beings. For Gandhi, and many religious traditions, the whole of the community of life is to be served. Or rather, the whole of the community of life is to be included in your conceptualization of yourself. You are a human being, a single member of a single species among millions in a vast world full of complex webs of interdependence; and you are needed! Through considering, protecting, and serving the whole community of life you expand your self-meaning. The concept of *community* thus transcends traditional anthropocentric views. In fact, from a feminist critique of traditional religious conceptualizations of community, this new perspective transcends the androcentric community. Some people urge eco-centric, or bio-centric approaches to community. How one conceives community also informs how one politicizes it through "development" programs (Sheth 1994).

Identification with the whole of life does not threaten your individuality—it reinforces your uniqueness. To be is to be known (Das 1966). To be known is to relate with others; to relate is to serve; to serve is to identify with; to identify with is to expand your soul; and expanding your soul reinforces your uniqueness—because only you expand it in this particular way. Making yourself known, and in the process making others known unto you, transcends traditional religious approaches to *diversity*. No longer is there an in-group identity *vis-a-vis* an out-group identity. Diversity is no longer a dichotomy of this religion and that religion. Rather, differences *within* religious communities are revealed, appreciated, and nourished. Religious dynamism stems less from distancing out-group otherness and more from serving in-group differentiation. Subtle differences between my religiosity and yours help us feel less (spiritually) anonymous. Everyone conforms to (religious) norms; it's how you don't that makes you (spiritually) special.

Religious identity requires active participation in an increasingly complex web of interdependent beings. There is no set, or predetermined, plan of how the community must look. In fact, though some religions speak of a messiah or messianic age, none has a blueprint of all micro-relations. The pursuit towards God(liness) is an *open-ended* process in which each individual must muddle-through (more or less) by serving an ever expanding community. Gandhi's oceanic circles are relevant here: as your soul's sense of community expands, what and who you include in your sphere of compassion also expands. Though you may be distant from some person whom you've brought into your meta-community, your service toward her/him is still felt, just as a ripple in an ocean makes its way around the world.

Techniques

Be(com)ing wholesomely human presupposes a conscious effort to maximize your sphere of compassion. Sphere, because the community of life is not two-dimensional; compassion, because there is more than just you in that community with whom you relate (thus, the "com-", or joint-feeling). Otherness persists in this spiritual sphere, but it does not threaten your self identity. Expression of your spiritual integrity manifests through service, or put differently, by balancing the alter with the ego (Das 1960). The ego is not obliterated, nor is the alter. By protecting the uniqueness of the alter (this done through service), you deepen your sense of self(ness). Through altruism you en-self yourself. Or, in different terms: your politics is your person; what is *personal is political*.

It is well known Gandhi yearns to merge politics and religion. Not politics into religion, but religion (nay, morality) into politics. Since religion, or spirituality, is highly personalized in this new conceptualization, then it follows that my personal spiritual orientation and expression is also a political statement. More importantly, following Gandhi's insistence on internal consistency, whatever my political stances, they must reflect my spiritual identification. I cannot believe in a universal God yet politically deny others the right to worship their interpretation of God (be it through a different name, language, or praxis).

On a more practical level, since divinity emanates from my relationships, then it is to my advantage to enhance the quality of my relationships (e.g., materially, psychologically). For example, Judaism and Hinduism encourage maximizing the welfare of (all) people. (Hopefully, the welfare of the more-than-human world is to be maximized, too.) This does not mean renouncing the world, or denying oneself material comforts. To renounce the world is to renounce (a part of) God. Self-denial is not taught either. Rather, self-control is encouraged: limit my consumption, minimize the suffering I cause others, and reduce my perceived needs/dependencies (wants). Hence the dictum of not stealing, among others (Smith 1991). Oppressing others is a form of stealing—their liberty, their material security, their spiritual identification processes. Elimination of oppression reduces potential (violent) expression of (spiritual and material) grievances.

This leads nicely to a brief discussion of the Golden Rule. There are many versions of this rule from around the world and across centuries, and they say essentially the same thing: what is hateful to you, do not do unto your neighbour. Gandhi himself creates several versions of this, positive and negative, from insisting we ought to refuse to have what millions cannot, to engaging in mutual toleration because no one knows the complete Truth but only fractions of it.

The universal prevalence of the Golden Rule suggests that most (every?) religions and civilizations understand the primacy of relationships. The quality of (inter/intra-personal) relationships informs (and are influenced by) the health of the society. The notion of reciprocity, then, is universal. However, we are taught how to take, and rarely how to give. A renewed recognition of the fundamental nature of reciprocity may help us reduce the animosity and competitive nature of our current relationships.

Even if that is our goal, how to get there is not so easy. Gandhi refers to the *Bhagavad Gita*'s teaching that you ought not be so concerned with the results of your actions, for the results are in the hands of God. This can be interpreted that you are not responsible for your actions, or more precisely, for the fruits of your actions. What you produce, or impact, is God's responsibility. However, this does not open the door for complete and absolute absolvement: one is and must remain a moral agent and live according to the dictates of one's moral obligations (*dharma*). You, yourself, cannot guarantee any particular result from your actions; but you can and must guarantee moral actions in the first place. Thus, even though the results are not yours to control, how you go about generating those (desired) results is your responsibility. By focusing on the quality of your moral agency you are able to give a greater assurance that particular ends obtain, but never can you guarantee those ends.

While reducing the oppressive nature of relations does not guarantee that the relationships will be enhanced, it gives space for the potentiality of enhancement. This potential improvement of relationships suggests an *open-endedness* quality of spirituality. That is, serving others leads not to a final relationship, but facilitates an ever-evolving dynamic. There is no conclusion, no finality, no absoluteness in relationships. Thus, there is no spiritual conclusion or nirvana. To seek such is to seek spiritual (and physical) death. To serve the historical moment is what Erikson terms Gandhi's "religious actualism"—whereby "his very passion and power will make him want to make actual for others what actualizes him" (Erikson 1969:399). It is the sharing of the pursuit of actualism which generates spiritual meaning.

If there is no spiritual end toward which we plod, then it seems that the *means are the ends*. *How* we relate is of utmost importance. *That* we relate we cannot deny. The quality of our relations is our responsibility and is an expression of our souls. The means—our relations—are our spiritual "ends." Making the means meaningful, though, is a delicate task each of us must attend to daily. Gandhi's notion of self-less and fearless action is a way of transforming competitive relations into pursuits of complementarity. Through complementarity you expand your notions of self, and intensify your spiritual identity by strengthening your relations with the community of life. By performing one's *yoga* (service), one deepens the divine within. The active participation (serving) with Hebraic texts also manifests (and expresses) the divine within. In fact, such texts would be dead without human interaction and interpretation. Said differently, religions die without active adherents. Religions are living entities only to the extent that their communities purposefully serve them (through relating, critiquing, en-voweling, and transmitting).

The generation, maintenance and transmission of spiritual self-meaning involves giving primacy to your relationships. No longer are you an isolated soul searching for divine providence. You do not exist in a vacuum, physically or spiritually. Enmeshed in complex webs of spiritual interdependencies, you must attend to your relationships. Not to do so is spiritual (and I'd say physical) suicide. Just as you are a creator of divinity, so, too are others (even though many of them believe in a different kind of divinity, speak a different language, or wear different clothes). Their pursuit of divinity is *just as* vital to them as yours is to you.

A change in how we think about the spiritual is needed. We can now stop thinking of spirituality as a competition against ourselves toward enlightenment/salvation. Now we can think of spirituality as a collective effort toward complementarity through altruistic behaviour. This, in essence, is the core of *consequential thinking*. The serving of others presupposes considering the impact of your actions. Not considering your influence is to contradict nature—you are denying your relatedness with the community of life. As you seek to reduce the suffering caused others, you consider the consequences of how you serve others. Thus, the spiritual pursuit becomes the life of transgressing, or rather, transcending, egoism.

5

Facing Violence

An ethnographer of warzones observes, "war's violence unmakes the world at large both for those who experience it and for those who witness it. Violence deconstructs reason. The question then arises, Does writing and reading about violence unmake the world?" (Nordstrom 1995:138). Humbly as a Gandhian scholar I ask "Does writing and reading about nonviolence make the world?" I wonder. I read the newspaper today and I doubt it could...

We surround ourselves with violence. We engage in wars all the time, even though many of us never carry or know how to use a gun. This is "The Century of Wars" (Hesse 1943:139). War, violence, oppression, exploitation, coercion—whatever you want to call it—you experience it. So do I. We are simultaneously victim and perpetrator, bystander and supporter—of violence. We teach ourselves how to be violent in every aspect of our lives and at all levels: personally, socially, nationally, globally. We pollute ourselves with gimmicks brainwashing us that violence is necessary, even good. Our massive (educational, political, social, economic, even religious) infrastructures reinforce this militarist paradigm. If you doubt this, read anything by the Worldwatch Institute, or this year's UNDP report. We invest heavily in destructive capability. And we are now paying the price.

Who is this "we"? Traditionally, the "we" includes (empowered) men. But are men the only ones who suffer violence? A clearer picture of the mess is this: no one is or can be separated from violence. Everyone, and everything, suffers. This is one of the Four Noble Truths of Buddhism; it is also an embarrassing condition today. Let's take some numbers to illustrate this point. At the beginning of this century, of those killed in wars 80 per cent were soldiers (trained combatants). By World War II, it dropped to 50 per cent. And today, only 10 per cent of the casualties of war are soldiers (Nordstrom 1994). Conventional strategic scholars might read this as a good sign: fewer soldiers are expended in violent confrontations, thus supporting arguments for bolstering military investments. On another hand, who are those maimed, tortured, brutalized and ultimately killed who are *not* soldiers (non-combatants)? Who are the 90 per cent in today's deadly wars? The vast majority of them are innocent civilians caught in warzones, most of them women and children. In fact, some of them fight and do not wear uniforms. Why do mainstream scholars in fields like strategic studies and international relations focus (only) on (male) combatant deaths? Why are non-combatants not counted as casualties of war? Why are they ignored? What's so dangerous about thinking about them? Why the silences? There are secrets being made and kept, and secrets are political and dangerous (Gokani †).

Before going into the politics of recording violence, we first need a clearer understanding of violence itself, because "definitions of violence are statements of power" (Nordstrom 1994:5). Traditional modes of thinking assume that violence is essentially, and not much more than, physical aggression over/against human beings. There are philosophical and religious attempts to justify the use of physical aggression (e.g., Just War Theory; Holy War Theory). This understanding of violence then excludes such things as male domination of women, racism, economic exploitation and environmental destruction. This narrow definition also affords mental space to justify these other modes of aggressing over/against others (and the self). Not only this, but what is considered not "violent" is employed (and condoned) during times of (physical) violence. For example, "scorched-earth policy" or destroying (everything and everyone in) a particular geographical terrain just so that the "other" cannot use/control it is a legitimated war strategy (Southern Sudan, BBC World News, May 27, 1998). Because no combatant *per se* was "harmed", such destruction of the environment is seen as a legitimate mode of relating (in warfare).

More insidiously, what is considered domestic violence is often elevated to legitimate war strategy. Rape has only relatively recently been condemned as violence against women. (I understand there are many other sex combination kinds of rape, but the majority are men raping women). But it is only rape of one's own which is bad (read, it is violence against "our"—same community's men's—women). In warfare, however, violence against the "other" is legitimate. Raping others' women (since those who fight are obviously only men) is a legitimate activity of aggressive "defense." The technique of using women's bodies to send a message to other men that they are unable (read, effeminate) to protect their women (read, chattel) becomes an endorsed tactic. The (female) body becomes the medium of a message of violence and terror to the audience: "other" men, "other" society. She is subject to (authorized) symbolic (and real) violation, mutilation and destruction. The female body is a proxy for war—not only during times of violent war, but also during times of "peace." How sexual violence is organized and managed against "other" women becomes institutionalized into the (inter)national trafficking of women (s' bodies). However, under traditional conceptualizations of violence, such domination of women(s' bodies/identities) is not considered violent and thus left (relatively) alone (by inter/national law). In short, our sex/ed/ualized identities are militarized (see Mathiak 1997; Pettman 1996; Nordstrom 1995, 1994).

What is considered violent against some and not-violent against others is obviously a double standard. A different understanding of what violence is, then, may help us eliminate this double standard. Upon reflection, there are many locations of conflict: within each individual; between individuals; between societies (intra-species); between species (inter-species) (among others). If we take Gandhi's (re)definition of violence as exploitation (oppression or coercion) then we see there are many forms of violence occurring at each of these sites. There are self-oppression, social coercion, inter-species exploitation (humans leeching on cows, as an example), among many others. These can be coupled into categories which overlap: structural violence, cultural violence, direct (physical) violence (Galtung 1996). This broader matrix of what is considered violence reduces (eliminates?) the double standard of traditional "violence."

Direct violence includes verbal and physical intended aggression against body, mind and spirit. *Structural violence* refers to "more enduring and less physically visible forms of violence—personal, domestic, community, and societal—that are provoked by unequal power relations within social structures" (Nordstrom 1994:10). This includes such "unintended" (Galtung 1996:31) violences as poverty, starvation, spread of preventable diseases, and human rights violations. *Cultural violence* is a collection of mechanisms to legitimize, protect and sustain direct and structural violence, usually through icons as national flags and anthems, and media representations supporting prejudices. Other categories are *natural violence* (that which originates within biological organisms and is unintended) and *time violence* [that which negatively impacts future (re)generation, (re)production or sustainability].

Establishment

What is now considered "violence" and where it is located and managed are indeed complex issues. The definition of violence is subverted, or rather expanded, to include a much wider array of behaviours and attitudes. No longer can we consider war, for example, as an isolated event located in a clearly defined bounded space and time with a limited (known/managed/controlled) cadre of (human) actors. There is no isolated and un-peopled "battlefield", or pure conventional "soldier", or distinct "wartime/peacetime." There are war zones with fuzzy frontiers forever shifting with the migrations of people, resources, and environmental integrity, and wars, which never end but their salience shifts and mutates into other arenas. Those involved in wars are obviously soldiers and the massive military-industrial-educational-economic complexes. There are also mercenaries, looters, humanitarian aid workers, children, spies, the infirm, inter/national financiers (like banks, corporations, private investors), politicians, inter/national monitors (like non-governmental organizations), wives and husbands, academicians or "scholars", guerrillas, arms smugglers, customs agents, news reporters, religious leaders, prostitutes, entertainers, and even microbes.

We cannot ignore the role infectious diseases play, especially in warzones where physical conditions (poverty, famine, environmental destruction and migration) are "conducive to the spread and mutation of ERID [emerging and re-emerging infectious diseases]." Movements of non/troops and supplies serve as "'vectors' (modes of transmission) for diseases to move rapidly around the globe to areas where the new host population has little natural immunity to the new pathogen[s] that [are] introduced into the local ecology" (Price-Smith 1997:21). The introduction of new pathogens is often a deadly weapon—as seen with the massive decimation of Amerindians from diseases brought over by colonizing Europeans—and is sometimes used as a deliberate war tactic. Infectious diseases influence mortality and morbidity rates of not only humans but non-humans as well.

Violence engenders refugees, weakened immune systems, impoverished environments with which to cope with deadly and debilitating microbes, and broader structures of disease transmission: prostitution, rape, prison camps, exchange of diplomats, interaction with entertainers and reporters, and economic modes of production and transportation. For example, warzone rape becomes more than just a symbolic (and real) message of conquering the other (men's women), it also becomes a way of destroying future generations by spreading HIV and other diseases. The fascination with, management and authorization of warzone sexual domination mutates into warnography—a genre of terror used in (dirty) wars (Percival 1997; Pettman 1996; Nordstrom 1995, 1994). Why would there be any question that what is allowed at home eventually becomes used at not-home? Or *vice versa*—that what "our men" do "over there" is glorified and thus is imported to/imposed upon "our homes/our bodies"? If it's so good to infect them, why not infect ourselves? Understanding violence even in its narrowest sense of physical aggression thus requires, among other things, *at least* a public health response (see Percival 1997; Price-Smith 1997; Dossey 1988).

Traditional views of violence and warfare follow patriarchal modes of bifurcating the world into disparate binarisms. On one side there is us, on the other them. One side is strong, the other weak. One is right, the other wrong. Feminist, religious, and nonviolent theories problemitize this mode of thinking. They encourage us to think about (and thus react to) violence differently than how we currently are taught. By expanding our definition(s) of violence, we can begin to recognize that our methods of relating germinate, perpetuate and exacerbate (our own) suffering. We begin to see how, for example, repressive and exploitative regimes (structural violence) are supported through mechanisms of penetration, segmentation, fragmentation and marginalization (Galtung 1996). It forces us to rethink our concept of "peace." Even though most of us are not directly engaging in direct violence, we are participants in and victims of multiple layers of violences. We do not live in peace, but rather suffer peace: peace is not what we think it is (Nordstrom 1995, 1994). The recognition of how complex, diverse and embedded our violences are demands us to think more creatively about how to face them. This is discussed below.

Identity

Our peace deconstructs our lifeworlds. We constantly dismantle semblances of constancy and sources of stability. Wars are intense periods of this. In warzones, what used to be considered reasonable becomes unreasonable, what rational irrational. For example, it used to be reasonable to trade between villages, but in warzones such trade becomes unreasonable because resources are so scarce. It used to be rational to care for your neighbours, but in war zones your neighbours sometimes become your enemies and to defend them is inviting your own destruction. What was known/stable/identifiable is destroyed. Even in our quiet lives of enjoying our occupations and (relatively) stable homes, we suffer "reason," a crisis of reasoning (Nordstrom 1995)—or as I say, identity.

Traditional views of violence dichotomize the good and the bad, the righteous and the evil. However, the good and righteous "us" engage in author(iz)ed aggression against the (unknown, bad and evil) other. Our other-oriented aggression is informed by and reifies self-oriented aggression; pain inflicted also inflicts pain. For example, make a fist and hit someone, or rather, something like a cement block. Go ahead—hit hard! What are you afraid of? Why hesitate? You're the aggressor—so hit! You cause the other pain, but now your fist throbs and you wonder why you are so dumb. Aggression is a reflexive imposition of suffering. Yet we are taught to be aggressive: academically in school, economically in business, socially in relations, internationally and more.

We are taught how to destroy ourselves. Even our own identities of *self*, based on negating and distancing ourselves from the *other*, are practices of reflexive isolation and alienation. This is identity. It is a dialectical process of increasing suppression/denial of our non-aggressiveness and magnification/approval of our (learned) aggressiveness. The self is seen as a bounded entity, forever searching accumulation and multiplication of the self (Fromm 1976; Das 1960), and assuming (in the eyes of others) one of three stances: malignant, benign or neutral. We are taught that self-defense, even with technological gadgets like guns, is respectable, even expected. The more technological (read, material, educational, political) gadgets I have, the more assistance I can mobilize for my defense (read, survival), and the more I can erect my "individuality."

What we are not taught is that reliance upon external technological assistance to mediate social problems does not bolster the individual but renders the self-dependent, weak, vulnerable and even impotent. For example, if I point a gun at you, what does this say? It says four things (among others). First, my self-confidence (to persuade you to do what I want) is so low that I must hide behind this external material object and prop my identity by its presence; my sense of "me" depends upon this thing. Second, I perceive you as strong and, more importantly, stronger than me; I am threatened by your strength and embarrassed by my weakness. Third, I continue to hold the gun to your head in fear that you will retaliate. Since you are stronger than I am then I am vulnerable to you if I remove the gun. I can't move; I can't "perform." Fourth, by interfering with your physical/emotional integrity, I have voluntarily given up the right of non-interference. You are now permitted to interfere by defending yourself. This, however, does not give you the right to destroy me, just to dismantle the interference I impose. Dismantling the threat focuses on the technology (material or mental—like racism) and is not the same as disabling (or destroying) the person rendering the technology.

We are not taught this. We are taught that having big guns is good. And we believe this. Why else do we invest over 6 per cent of global production into our militaries? Why else do we explode nuclear devices? Because we are taught, and teach ourselves, that our identities can only be meaningfully defined, protected and propagated through technological gadgets. We delude ourselves into believing our mainstream definitions of strength, power and identity. We erect massive myths, support them with intricately complex infrastructures, and declare them rational, needed, even inevitable (*Times of India*, 27 May, 1998, p.1). Such mythologies become dangerous particularly when playing with guns—nuclear guns—as are Pakistan and India today (along with other countries).

We glorify those who engage in violence against the "other" even when that other poses no, or little, threat. We also reinforce the us/them double-standard of acceptable forms of violence. For example, some people who looted and burned out an ice-cream store of a foreign company were lauded as "patriots" for "defending" domestic interests (in this case, India's "interest" to explode nuclear devices). The symbolic value of the response to the arson says much: that local opinion favours (unwarranted) destruction of property. A more insidious way of expressing discontent with foreign companies is not to cooperate with them: don't buy their products or services. But destroying their property is an act of aggression which receives, sadly, a double-standard response: if it is locally-owned property the arsonists are criminalized; if it is foreign-owned property, the arsonists are hailed as national defenders and their action echoes the vigor of pre-independence freedom fighters (*Times of India*, May 28, 1998, p.1). If this is not a confusing process of constructing mythologies of "good" behaviour, then what is it?

We re-create myths that technological wizardry will solve social ills, political oppression, and economic exploitation. Theories of development, in particular, rely heavily upon tweaking existing structures in hopes of alleviating intensifying grievances. We design our technologies to alleviate, not solve or prevent. In fact, with the explosion of virtual reality and world-wide-web technologies, we depend ever more on technology to perpetuate the myth of its panacea-like characteristics. We must recognize that technologies *cannot* solve or prevent human-created problems (Dossey 1988).

Feminist, nonviolence and religious theories encourage us to dismantle dependency upon our illusions and technologies. They suggest redefining the self differently. No longer is it a question of determining who is strong and who weak. All parties engaging in a violent conflict are strong if they choose to see themselves as strong. Some may enjoy the burden of controlling more resources (material, psychological, human), and some may enjoy the liberation of less responsibility. Nevertheless, all parties are equally viable centers of solution-generating agency. The conflict is not about becoming strong(er) but eliminating weakness. The self is not defined as a static unit allied (or not) with certain others. Rather, the self evolves through mutually constituting interactions with adversaries in a (hopefully, cooperative) search for justice, or Truth. The self, then, is a fluctuating entity expanding its sphere of interdependence.

The concept of *community*, then, also changes. Traditional violence theory perceives the community as a homogenous whole, bounded by space (and so wanting not to be bounded by time) (see *Times of India*, May 29, 1998, p.1). Political leaders speak about defending "national interests," and attempt to call them nationai "needs." But, what is a national interest? There is no one particular thing in which each and every person within a particular political border agree, and thus there can never be a completely homogeneous, definitive or eternal "national interest." To speak of them as such is to speak of myths; to defend them is to defend illusions. Sure, people want and need security; security is an "interest." Yet how you define security (or more importantly, operationalize security) may differ from how I think. To impose your way on me is to oppress me; to do so in the name of national security seems absurd.

By reconceptualizing community as a heterogeneous collection of evolving (different!) people with (different!) interests, needs, locales and visions gives (potential) voice to all members. Personal and collective identities are not imposed from above; they are generated from the in-between: our relations. Boundaries fade into ever-shifting frontiers. In-group/Out-group distinctions blur. The community expands, its need to defend itself against an (unknown/ threatening/es-strange(d)) other diminishes. The community is no longer identified with its capacity (technological gadgets) to inflict injury, but its capacity (human creativity) to include (diversity) and preserve (sustainability).

Techniques

This utopic vision of changing how we think about our (violent) selves and communities may seem ridiculous. It is, on some levels. But I think we ought to take it seriously. Conventional modes of thinking and appreciating our violence urge us to use particular methods to "solve" violent situations. These methods include coercive measures, avoidance, and intervention (mediation, arbitration, adjudication). They seek particular ends: capitulation and accommodation by the other to your desires, or (partial or total) destruction of the other. The conclusion is a win/lose situation reflecting either/or thinking. Is anyone actually winning? If so, what? Or are we all losing at these (deadly) games we play?

By changing how we think about violence, and how to cope with our violences, we may find more opportunities to pre-empt your suffering. The above reconceptualizations suggest a few ways of viewing violence differently. Because each of us, individually, is a site of contestation, we each impose and suffer violences, both consciously and unintentionally. We have the capacity to address and alter our consciouses/consiences (if we choose to). Thus, the kind and intensity of violences we participate in reflect our personal decisions. In brief, our *personal violences are political violences*.

If I deem you worthy of being violated, oppressed or exploited, then I also view myself as worthy of the same. Thus, violence begets violence. This is not a hollow philosophical statement but a concrete observation of human behaviour. Notice how children behave after watching a violent movie or television program or sport, or are surrounded by violent behaviours and attitudes—they too become violent, sometimes murderously so (see everything by Staub). So my personal violences beget your violences. The means begets the ends. Is it worth it for me to be violent? Are the ends worth the means? Are the means (imposing and suffering violences) worthy of such (selfish) ends?

Theories of non-violence, feminisms and religion suggest that violent means are *not* worthy of selfish ends, or frankly any other kind of ends[1] . Two relatively new academic fields (Peace Studies and Conflict Resolution) draw inspiration from these philosophies and put forward three general ways of coping with violent conflicts. All three reinforce the fundamental observation that *the quality of the means begets the quality of the ends*.

First, *conflict management* is a collection of strategies for reducing or eliminating violent conflict. Peacekeeping missions of the United Nations are examples of conflict management. The UN seeks to manage violent conflicts so they do not spill "out" into neighboring populations or bring "in" external parties who might exacerbate the situation. Through managing, controlling and author(iz)ing resource and population movement into and within conflict regions, peacekeeping missions sometimes obtain settlements and/or cease-fires. However, settlements or cease-fires are indications of an acceptance of the status quo; they are forms of accommodation. The fundamental nature of the relationship, along with its violence potential, remains. Second, *Conflict Resolution* techniques go beyond mere shuffling of material aspects of conflicts (e.g., persons, resources, legal rights). By focusing on the subjective relationships between parties, conflict resolution measures emphasize the fundamental role communication plays in building trust and cooperation, often called peacemaking efforts (Fetherston & Parkin 1997).

Criticisms of these methods reveal their shortcomings. These methods do not adequately consider the ways power structures operate in and around adversaries, particularly their perceptions of themselves, others and the conflict. Seeking settlements and/or improving communication, centers on elites who often have ulterior motives for engaging in violent conflicts (it's profitable for many of them). Re-distribution of political power-sharing does little to affect the structures, institutions and practices, which led to violence in the first place. Perceiving adversaries as "rational" assumes they share certain values or logic systems, and renders them culturally bound—which may not be the case. The concept of success is also construed in such a way that underlying catalysts to violence remain unchanged. Settlement seeks through containment a return to the *status quo*; resolution encourages communication and cooperation but not structural transformation (see Fetherston & Parkin 1997).

A third technique of coping with violence is *Conflict Transformation*. Here, efforts go beyond peacekeeping and peacemaking to peacebuilding. That is, the construction of positive relationships through repairing communicative networks which allow each individual to participate in the (re)production of shared cultural knowledge, social solidarities and socialized personalities (Fetherston & Parkin 1997). This is a departure from the other two mechanisms by challenging the notion of hegemony. Here, peacebuilding efforts are anti-hegemonic projects in that they seek not so much to replace existing power structures with different ones, but to supplant the need for an(y) hegemonic power structure to take root in the first place. It decentralizes notions of power and agency, and thus brings together those who were previously marginalized by hegemonic structures and empowers them through more egalitarian relations (Cooper 1995).

Gandhi recognizes the need to address violence on terms other than its own. He uses a repertoire of mechanisms quite similar to those listed above and tailors each mechanism to the exigencies of a particular situation. First, he decouples the adversaries from the violence: the people are not the violence, they are only perpetrators and victims of violence. Second, he seeks integration, or finding commonalties among adversaries—again, blurring the distinction of us/them, good/bad. Third, through communicating in *dialogue*, he offers compromises because the object is not to win the conflict but to encourage the relationship to proceed in such directions that violence (now and future) may be prevented. Fourth, Gandhi's creativity constructs alternative ways of relating which transcend/pre-empt violent tendencies of those involved. Notice, though, that Gandhi's most fundamental goal is not the (re)solution of a violent conflict *per se*, but the transformation of the relationship itself so that such violent conflicts do not obtain (Galtung 1996, 1992). The end (elimination of violence) becomes the means.

The unity of ends and means, especially when thinking about and challenging violence, presupposes *consequential thinking*. As you identify the c/overt ways you participate in and perpetuate various forms of violence it becomes apparent that you (un)consciously choose to engage in violence. In fact, by opting to live the ways we do, we choose to be violent. We reinforce oppressive power structures by cooperating with their dictates to live in particular ways. Through conforming to socially-constructed norms like separating means from ends and dichotomizing the world into binarisms, we each inflict violence upon others and ourselves—and we tell ourselves that such cycles are good, necessary and inevitable.

There is a school of thought and action that challenges this vicious cycle of conforming to violence/breeding violence. That is the school of disobedience. Laws, structures, institutions, traditions and practices exist and persist because people choose (in more or less coercive or free circumstances) to enact them. Or, put differently, these structures exist because people obey their requirements (of hierarchical, exclusionary power relations). By removing obedience these (violent) structures die (Nauriya †).

As is well known, Thoreau's decision to conscientiously refuse compliance influenced Gandhi's concept of disobedience. Disobedience is "to a law or policy that has been identified for protest but without undermining the fabric of law" (Ramaswamy 1997:181). It is a protest searching for a change without undermining (respect for) the whole legal system. It's dimensions go beyond individual conscience (as is the case for the refuser) and encourages public purposeful appeal for change. Civil disobedience focuses on "the relationship between the individual and the state and the nature and limits of political obligation" (Ramaswamy 1997:183). In contrast, criminal disobedience is (non)secret disobedience with intention to avoid punishment (Weber 1991).

But secularized civil disobedience is not enough for Gandhi. He draws on religious doctrines to emphasize that each individual is morally obligated to do what is righteous or just regardless of surrounding structures. That is, "the individual is invested with a moral law and duty (*dharma*) and is a bearer of moral authority. (S)he has a right and even the duty to judge the state and its laws, by the standards of dharma" (Ramaswamy 1997:185). Immediately religious obligations to serve others informs our reactions to violence. Remember, the state does not exist without the presence of individuals, nor does the "state" act; rather, society serves itself through the guise (structures, institutions, practices) of the state. With Gandhi, the dissociation of politics and religion fades.

But non-cooperation still leaves violent power structures relatively intact. Gandhi sees the individual conscience, responding to *dharma*, as the deciding arbiter whether non-cooperation is necessary. It is, however, "not enough merely to break laws, but, as with the general principles of satyagraha, changes of the unacceptable laws should be aimed through conversion of the majority of the populace and the law makers" (Weber 1991:85). Thus, non-cooperation must be coupled with a vision of alternative ways of relating. To establish new (different) ways of relating, old (violent) ones must be dismantled. Briefly put, rethinking how we understand and cope with violence leads us to a mode of action: *deconstructing violence through visionary non-cooperation.*

Reference

The discussion of whether *all* violences ought to be eliminated is not necessarily relevant here. Sometimes some violence is necessary to reach a common goal. For example, limiting the political and social freedom of a child to teach him/her lessons about respect may be necessary for the child's maturity and/or health and safety. In this discussion, any does not mean all.

6

Implications and Imperatives

I have traversed a broad terrain of issues. By critiquing how we traditionally perceive reality I show how we often lead ourselves into dead-ends. Much of our conventional ways of thinking encourages us to alienate ourselves, marginalize each other, decrease the value and quality of our relationships, and engage in (many kinds of) violence. Conforming to (read, obeying) traditional modes of thinking/believing is dangerous (Foucault 1984:340). As everything is dangerous, it compels us to critique, or problemitize, everything—including how we form(ulate) our identities, our relationships, our belief systems and our politics.

Theories of non-violence, feminism and religion assist us problemitizing conventional modes of believing/thinking/doing. They reveal how dangerous these modes are and can be. They offer ways of subverting and deconstructing traditional patriarchal modes, systems, institutions and practices. More importantly, they offer alternatives. They, too, are normative projects with their visions of how we ought to believe/think/do. What they propose, parts of which are in the dialogue above, are ways to understand and relate differently with the terrain of reality. By following their methods, it seems they offer more promising paths toward decreasing the prevalence of violence and promoting sustainable identities/relationships.

Like rivulets in the mountains, traditional streams lead to dam(n)s and stagnation—all for the ulterior motives of a privileged few. The different rivulets of non-violence, feminism and religion, however, do not stop at false blockades and but nourish everything/one through (re)generative cycles. As Gandhi says, we are but drops in the ocean; we are of the ocean but we are not the ocean itself. It's up to us to make our way to the ocean and participate (more) fully in the community of life. Theories of non-violence, feminism and religion can help us in this journey.

This project is an attempt to *make sense* of our relationships. It seems, in obvious and not-so-obvious ways, that traditional modes of believing/thinking/doing *de*-sensitize us and our relations. Conventional modes do *not* make sense; in fact, they dismantle, displace, and destroy our senses—all in the name of what is "good", "necessary", "inevitable." Even the notion of "common sense" is rendered meaningless in the face of our (self-imposed) violences.

Through the three critical lenses used here, we see that our traditions in fact lie to us and teach us how to lie to ourselves. For example, we tell ourselves that exploiting the environment does not undermine our human integrity or identity. However, these critiques show that such a way of believing/thinking/doing is not true. "A civilization that relentlessly destroys the living land it inhabits is not well acquainted with *truth* [of inter-species interdependence], regardless of how many supposed facts it has amassed regarding the calculable properties of its world" (Abram 1996 : 264). Said differently, a civilization that relentlessly destroys its relationships is not well acquainted with truth, or justice for that matter. It is the quality of relationships that matters—that is where truth and justice reside. It's time to make common sense what conventional thinking calls uncommon sense; and to make uncommon sense what we are taught as common sense.

Deconstructing the Establishment

The implications of this project are two pronged. First, they encourage us to deconstruct existing power structures through non-cooperation. Second, they place before us alternative ways of relating which, in essence, are obligatory for our pursuit of decreasing violence and generating justice. Thus, what is implicated becomes an imperative. *Is* leads spontaneously to *ought* (Gross 1997a).

In light of this, it seems that we need to re/de-construct our notions of what is the *Enemy*. In broad terms, the enemy is our practice of self-delusion. We delude ourselves that we are violent, that one sex[1] is more worthy than another, that we are forever doomed to profane banality. We erect structures, institutions, and practices to perpetuate and expand these delusions. We believe (in) our own creations, but not (in) our creativity.

Our lifeworlds reflect and reveal what we want them to. We exercise *power* over ourselves to disempower us. Even those men who enjoy the benefits of patriarchal hierarchical thinking and its attendant political structures suffer the consequences: they confine themselves into compartments clearly identifiable, "known" and thus control/ed/able. In their freedom, "empowered" men are slaves to their own ways of believing/thinking/doing. Men—actually all of us in conventional modes—exercise (and suffer) power as "power over." We use power over and against each other and the rest of the community of life. We exploit, oppress, marginalize, alienate, dismantle, hinder, destroy, threaten, ignore... the list goes on. (An interesting linguistic/political study would be to see how many words in our languages reinforce conventional notions of militarized power-over, and how they are used in daily life. For example, I "bombed" a test means I failed it; but my relationship is a "bomb" when I "successfully" dominate/control a woman.)

Non-violence suggests transferring the locus of traditional notions of power-over from power-over the other to power-over the self. Self-control becomes a fundamental expression of power. In Gandhian terms, power over myself (self-control) is rendering obedience to my True self. This is a seductive reconceptualization of power—it centers on me, the individual, and not on the other. By shifting the focus and onus to the individual, it seeks to liberate the self from violence. Though power-over-self diminishes violence imposed on others, it does not adequately liberate the self from other-imposed violences.

Feminisms, on another hand, suggest reshaping power as power-to. Here, power is seen as a capacity toward something. The individual is now empowered: a woman is empowered to liberate herself from exploitative relationships; a man is empowered to enlighten himself that he exploits. However, this is a slippery slope from power to liberate to power to exploit.

Gandhi's religious notion of power formulates it as power-through. That is, you draw and exercise power through your spiritual beliefs and practices. You enact power through your moral agency. But even if you act morally, there is no guarantee I will too. This conceptualization endorses individual (em)power(ment) but does little to pre-empt others using power-over the individual.

Power-over others obviously disempowers everyone; power-over-self does not protect the self; power-to does not limit the self. Power-through moral agency seems simultaneously to limit the self and render the self vulnerable. A different conceptualization of power may be useful: power-with. To be powerful, I must engage *with* others. Power is relative; strength is individual. Access to and capacity to mobilize resources (physical, emotional, mental, spiritual) together make my individual strength. I am more or less strong in comparison *with* you. (and only in particular ways). Thus, I exercise power *with* you. Notice that power-with parallels and/and thinking, not either/or.

The notion of "with" stems from the fundamental nature of existence—we relate. It is the "in-between" which concerns us here. This is where the concept "with" resides. With you, I am more or less powerful. With our relationship, I am more or less intensely embedded in the network of life. With our relationship, you are more or less exploited, oppressed, violated.

This leads to the practice of persuasion. By relating with people you can persuade them to change. Working over others is often coercive; working to and through others are sometimes oppressive and exploitative. But working with levels the playing field (even more), and brings in closer association adversaries previously subject to violence. My ability to eliminate the violence of a particular relationship stems from my ability to work (cooperate) with my adversaries, not against or through them. Similarly, my ability to eliminate violence in our relationship stems from not-cooperating with your acceptance of violence as a means of relating (Nauriya †). Power-(not)-with, or non-cooperation, reduces violence.

Notice that non-cooperation is *not* a denial or elimination of the relationship itself. Non-cooperation is a reaffirmation of the fundamentalness of relationships. A relationship is necessary for adversaries to exist; it is equally necessary for lovers to exist. Non-cooperating with a violent relationship dissociates the violence from the other; the other is not the violence, but the relationship carries it. By not consenting to participate, or obey the demands of a particular violent relationship, the non-cooperator still works with adversaries to construct different ways of relating that are not violent. Just because one way of relating is violent does not mean that *all* other ways of relating (between certain parties) are, must be, will always be, violent. The act of non-cooperation then simultaneously reduces the prevalence of violence in a particular relationship, and deconstructs the myth that relating revolves around, involves through, and devolves into violence.

This two-pronged mechanism of power-with non-cooperation seemingly dismantles traditional ways of relating. But does this leave us in a relational vacuum? No. Transgressing conventional modes of relating is itself a constructive, even creative, act. We are taught to relate violently and practice power over/against each other. By not cooperating with these teachings you subvert violent relations by challenging the presence of violence in the first place. By disobeying what you are taught (to be violent), you are then (more) free to create new and different (nonviolent/just) relationships. But remember that *a priori* you are already in relation with everyone/thing. Thus, by changing the nature of your relations (eliminating violence) you automatically reveal the more truthful quality of your relations—that they are, essentially, mutually constituting dialectics. By removing power-over/against, you reveal power-with.

The implications of non-cooperation and power-with for international relations are interesting. Traditional balance of power games nation-states play conceive power as power-over. They seek to equalize the power-overness of states by building military (and economic) capabilities ensuring mutual destruction. A country is considered strong because it can exercise power-over others. However, if (all) other countries not-cooperate with that "strong" country, then that country would be so isolated that it would need to reconsider its policies and practices. For example, if all countries decided not to cooperate with the United States because it exploits them, then the US, a highly other-dependent "soverign" state, would need to change its relationships if it thought survival with others is better than no survival. Again, international non-cooperation does not break or deny relationships, it changes the concept of power-over to power-with, and thus reduces (eliminates?) oppression and exploitation between countries. Now, if only the UN could catalyze such attitudes!

From Identity to Identity

Each of us is concerned about our relationships: with our spouses, children, pets, work, the environment, histories. Some of us run away from our relationships; we try to hide from and deny them. Some of us run into them and become overwhelmed. Others accept their fate by consenting to (perpetuate) the nature of existing relations. Still others seek to destroy relations, which is really a project of self-destruction. We ignore; we obsess. We deplore; we regress. We adore; we finesse.

What we do about our relationships reflects (and informs) our thinking. Our thinking echoes (and speaks back to) our beliefs. How we perceive (and believe we ought to perceive) ourselves, others, and our relations is crucial to our behaviour. We make ourselves known through our relations. Put differently, I am who I am because of, and through, my relations with others. The construction of my identity mutually constitutes the construction of your identity. "I" cannot exist without relating with "you." The ego requires the alter. Hence, I discover myself in, with and through you.

Removing myself from our relationship is dangerous. I can remove myself physically: moving away, attending to all my needs ("becoming independent" as it is called in some cultures, or "swadeshi"), or committing suicide, among others. I can remove myself emotionally: ignoring you, suppressing my emotions, and others. Intellectually I can remove myself by reducing the relationship to mere academic similarities/differences. Even spiritually I can remove myself by denying that we are both centers of sentience and divinity. The act of removal hurts not just you, but also me. I deny myself the chance to know myself with/in/through you, and I deny you the chance for self discovery too. Thus, "closing doors" and "burning bridges" (things we are encouraged to do when 'the going gets rough') imposes identity boundaries on yourself and on others' selves. Or, said differently, *you are necessary for the construction of my self identity, and I am necessary to you for the same reason.*

The quality of my self-meaning rests on the quality of my relations with you and others. Relating well with one person/thing/idea generates a positive self-image. No doubt. But Gandhi encourages us to expand our spheres of relating to beyond just one [e.g., person, community, idea(l)]. We are to relate with as much of the community of life as we can, and make the quality of these relations as truthful as possible. Then, and only then, can we construct for ourselves soulfully meaningful identities. Through extensive networks we reify our embeddedness and interdependencies. We also make ourselves more wholesomely human, and more human(e)ly wholesome.

So, more precisely each of us is/ought to be concerned with the expanse and quality of our relationships. Going a step further, since I seek to reduce the prevalence of violence, then I ought to be concerned about the expanse and quality of your relationships. I need to include in my sphere of compassion your relationships, and not just yours—everyone's. "If you wish to uphold basic human justice you must do so for everyone, not just selectively for the people that your side, your culture, your nation designates as okay" (Said 1994:93-4). I need to be concerned about existing relationships and those that will exist, even those seven generations from now (if we allow seven generations to emerge!). This blurs the boundary between my relations (me) and your relations (you). Where (and when) "I" begin as distinguished from where (and when) "you" begin becomes meaningless, or rather, less meaningful. Drawing boundaries on territories (physical, emotional, intellectual, spiritual) demarcating who/what is me/mine and you/yours is an arbitrary process akin to saying "History began in 1973 with my birth," and "Everything that I can see from this location in time and space I declare is mine and mine alone forever." Enprisoning the self (and also the other) in such boundaries are projects of conventional modes of believing/thinking/doing (Foucault 1984; Said 1978). Enprisoning anyone/thing is violent.

Liberating ourselves from these self-imposed identification boundaries requires listening to non-violence, feminisms and religion. These encourage recognizing the profound nature of our interdependencies and interpenetration. We are not bounded beings by self-imposed definitions. We are cross-fertilizing, overlapping, mutually constituting beings. Instead of boundaries, there are frontiers forever shifting according to the nuances of our relationships. We are beings of frontiers forever in pursuit of expanding our horizons.

In my search I encounter you. I am taught (and taught to believe) that our relationship is/ought to be one of competition [which may, and often does, be(come) violent]. Gandhi teaches us otherwise. He suggests seeking complementarities. Because power-with levels the playing field, we are able to work together rather than over/against each other. Doing so reveals to what extent we are similar and that our needs are the same (survival, well-being, identity, freedom) (Galtung 1996). In fact, because we are so similar our differences become not sites of contestation but sources of complementarity. As I learn more about you, I discover my own complexity. I become more meaningful to myself as I appreciate our differences. It is in my interest, then, to protect and promote differences. The greater the *diversity* of those with whom I relate, the more complex, dynamic, and soulfully true my self identity.

So I ask, what keeps me from expanding my horizons? What keeps me from engaging with, and not over/against, others? What barriers (real and mythological) do I erect? How can I lower the barriers to do(ing) and be(com)ing what I know is right(eous) and just(ice)? What keeps me from be(com)ing more nonviolent?

Now, ask yourself the same questions.

Technique of Relating/Serving

In today's world, the fields of non-violence, feminism and normative theology are more or less marginal. They straddle the frontier of (bare) acceptability and (outrageous) subversive. Studying Gandhi is even more subversive because he explores all these issues and more. It's sad and exciting. Exciting because these fields challenge conventional modes of thinking through critical analyses and offer different ways of believing/thinking/doing. Sad because their efforts are often shunned even when what they suggest, speaks to common sense. Maybe some day peace studies may be mainstream and strategic studies will be marginal. Ha! The best peace movement is one that does not exist: it has so successfully transformed society that its philosophy permeates all relations—and it is no longer needed. I look forward to that day when I can retire because violent conflicts (as we know them) would be only entries in history text books. Until then, though, much needs to be done.

Take you, for example. You are sitting (t)here reading this paper. Why? Precious moments of your life you filled with the meagre words I put on these pages. Why do you care? Maybe you don't. But my guess is that you do care, enough so that you are willing to engage with me, disagree with me, listen intelligently to me. Your decision to read reflects your openness to *find yourself* in these words. I've said nothing new; you knew everything I've said above. This project is merely a mirror to each of us so we can see ourselves more clearly (hopefully). After seeing how and who we are, we may understand how we became this way.

The notion of "learning" is often construed in terms of absorbing understanding *what is* and determining how to use that understanding for future manipulations. Put more powerfully, learning *what is* compels response. Exhibiting learning occurs *only* by responding (appropriately). If, in the face of what I present in this project, you do not respond in any manifestation, then I submit you learned nothing. This is ok. Again, you knew everything here and you thus already live according to what these observations demand. Or, if you knew everything and do not live according to what is compelled, then you perpetuate violences by separating what you know from what you do. It's *your* choice. Our responses are/ought to be different. But our *personal responses are also political.*

The most fundamental response this project puts forward takes inspiration from Gandhi, that of *non-cooperation*. By learning *what is*, and understanding its violence, we are compelled to non-cooperation. Or, we must unlearn, de-educate, ourselves of our violences (Nordstrom 1995, 1994). This becomes our goal. *The means are the ends, the ends are the means*. Non-cooperating with our violences is both goal and means. Through non-cooperation we deconstruct violences and reveal more just relations. By removing our consent, but not denying the fundamental (need for) relationship, we subvert conventional power hierarchies, dissolve arbitrary dichotomies, relocate spiritual meaning, and discover complementarities. Disobedience de-mythologizes our myths, envoices silences, destablizes conventional (violent) norms, and catalyzes solidarities. Non-cooperating with our violence is required. Non-cooperation with violence is just.

There is a catch, however. We can only approximate what we think is just. There is no pure justice which all peoples at all times and places will agree is so. Constructing justice, then, is a difficult task, more difficult than deconstructing what is unjust (violent relationships). A small child easily recognizes injustice when it is not fed when hungry; but it is harder to locate precisely that which *is* just (Pandeya †). Hence, it makes more sense to focus our energies on what is possible than on what is impossible. (This does not mean that there is absolutely no possible way to construct a just society which all peoples of all times and places would agree is such.) Through deconstructing and transgressing what is (known) unjust (violence), we exhibit what is just—the mutual pursuit and constitution of quality, value, purpose and meaning. These are measureless entities, but approximate them we must (Dossey 1988).

Nor can we afford to wait. How we spend our days is how we spent our life. It is up to us as individuals and collectively to approximate these values (that is, deconstruct violences through non-cooperation) *now*. As Martin Luther King Jr. reflected, justice delayed is justice denied. Hence the urgency of this project. The urgency and personal immediacy of these issues lead directly to a concern with the quality of our relations. Not only are we to relate well, *we are to relate intensely*. We intensify each and every relation by serving intensely.

Servicing a relationship requires engaging in a mutually constituting manner. This verbal and non-verbal *dialogue* promotes and feeds from *consequential thinking*. From learning how *what is* in a relationship became that way, I learn how consequences shape subsequent behaviours, attitudes, beliefs and conditions. This iterative process reinforces the notion that the individual (act/stance) implicates everything else. The letter "a" implicates the rest of the alphabet; otherwise "a" would have no context and no meaning. The word "compassion" implicates all other words; otherwise it would be meaningless. The same for you and me. I implicate you; you me. My behaviour implicates yours and *vice versa*—in our relationship. More importantly, our relationship implicates all others: in society, between societies, between humans and the more-than-human world. Consequential thinking helps us understand this mutual implication.

Attending to our relationships is challenging. We all struggle to relate and our relations are often struggles. Of this there is no doubt. We are told to service our relationships in certain ways—most of them destructive and unjust. We are taught to believe that this is how we *ought* to relate. Don't be fooled. How you relate is *your* choice. Who will decide for you—how you ought to relate? How do you want to relate?

This chapter outlines some implications of traditional modes of relating. It shows that conventional modes of relating are conventional only because people agree to make them so. People consent to en-violencing ourselves, supersaturating ourselves with violent ways of believing, thinking and doing. These observations and implications lead to imperatives, some of which are outlined here. Respond we must. I hope this makes sense. Consider this a chance to reduce the barriers that keep you violent. *How can you relate differently?* Consider this an invitation.

This really is not the conclusion of this project. Relations—life—don't end. There is no conclusion, finality or completion. This is really just the beginning.

Reference

1. Or race, class, caste, nation(ality), religion, sexual orientation, political affiliation, species, age, geographic location, food preference, or even foot size—anything which people use to divide populations into hierarchical binarisms.

Appendix A

INTERVIEW QUESTIONS & PERSONS INTERVIEWED

I talked with hundreds of people throughout the year on topics related in varying degrees to this project. These people ranged in age, class, sex, country of origin, country of residence, religion, sexual orientation, caste, education, ethnicity, occupation, primary language, and political affiliation. Each deepened my confusion about this project, and each furthered my understanding of these issues. Below are some questions I asked in informal and formal conversations. This list does not reflect any priorities; rather it hints at the complexity of this project.

1. Who defines Indian cultures? Who defines, sets the boundaries of Indian genders? What implications do these have for India's future?
2. What motivation is there to live as a "Gandhian"? What does being a "Gandhian" mean?
3. In your mind, how relevant is non-violence (as ideal and political strategy) to the (gender, environmental) movement? In what ways?
4. What justice does the (gender, environmental) movement envision and pursue?
5. What does non-violence mean to you? What is your interpretation of nonviolence through a Gandhian lens? What are the key elements, in your opinion, of Gandhi's conceptualization of non-violence?
6. Why are you involved in this movement? Why is it so important?
7. How can you motivate people to do what they know is right?
8. How can you dismantle the barrier of fear of self-change?

PERSONS INTERVIEWED

Douglas Allen	December 30, 1997 (Wardha)
Sheel K. Asopa	January 11, 1998 (Jaipur)†
Dev Asopa	January 11, 1998 (Jaipur)†

Ranjit Chaudhuri	November 10-13, 1997 (Wardha); December 27-31, 1997 (Wardha); February 1-4, 1998 (Wardha)
S.K. De	November 6-9, 1997 (New Delhi); November 10-13, 1997 (Wardha); December 27-31, 1997 (Wardha); February 1-4, 1998 (Wardha); March 4-12, 1998 (Ahmedabad)
Usha Gokani	January 29, 1998 (Mumbai); February 27, 1998 (Mumbai)†
Aaron Gross	July 7—August 6, 1997 (India & Nepal); 1997-1998 (email)
N.K. Krishnaswamy	February 1-4, 1998 (Wardha)
Sunalini Kumar	February 1-4, 1998 (Wardha); March 17-23, 1998 (New Delhi); May 17-20 (New Delhi)
Adam Loving	December 23, 1997—March 17, 1998 (India)
R.P. Misra	November 7, 1997 (New Delhi); February 1-4, 1998 (Wardha); March 20, 1998 (New Delhi); April 28, 1998 (New Delhi)
Suresh Misra	November 7, 1997 (New Delhi); March 20, 1998 (New Delhi)
Anil Nauriya	March 19, 1998 (New Delhi)†
A.N. Pandeya	July 7-10, 1997 (New Delhi); March 20 & 22, 1998 (New Delhi)†
Maulik Parekh	January 2, 1998 (Ahmedabad)
Geshe Thupten Phelgye	July 11-17, 1997 (Dharamsala); July 28—August 6, 1997 (Kathmandu, Nepal)
J. Radhakrishnan	March 23, 1998 (New Delhi)
Howard Spodek	March 9, 1998 (Ahmedabad); April 27, 1998 (Ahmedabad)

Mairetta Stepaniants	February 1-4, 1998 (Wardha)
Usha Thakkar	December 30, 1997 (Wardha); January 29, 1998 (Mumbai); February 1-4, 1998 (Wardha); March 27, 1998 (Mumbai)†
T.K.N. Unnithan	February 1-4, 1998 (Wardha)
Ravindra Varma	November 12, 1997 (Wardha)

(†—Recorded, formal interview)

SELECTED REFERENCES

Abram, David, 1996 *The Spell of the Sensuous: perception and language in a more-than-human world*. New York: Vintage Books.

Ansari, Iqbal A., 1998, "Religion and Animal Welfare: the Islamic view." *Islam and Modern Age*. 1/2 (February). Mumbai: Institute of Islamic Studies.

Babbie, Earl, 1995 *The Practice of Social Research*. 7th Edition Boston: Wadsworth.

Bhagavad Gita, 1994. W.J. Johnson (translator) New York: Oxford University Press.

Bhave, Vinoba, 1996. *Swaraj Sastra*. Varanasi: Sarva Seva Sangh Prakashan.

—— 1995. *Women's Power* Varanasi: Sarva Seva Sangh Prakashan.

Bondurant, Joan V., 1968 "Distinguishing Satyagraha From Other Forms of Action Without Overt Violence." in *Democracy and Non-violence*, pp. 112-28. Krishna Kumar, ed. New Delhi: Gandhi Peace Foundation.

Brock, Peter, 1994 "Gandhi's Non-Violence and His War Service." in Subrata Mokherjee & Sushila Ramaswamy (eds). *Facets of Mahatma Gandhi*. Volume 2: Political Ideas. New Delhi: Deep & Deep Publishers. pp. 368-84.

Bumiller, Elisabeth, 1990 *May You be the Mother of a Hundred Sons: A journey among the Women of India*. New Delhi: Penguin Books.

Burress, Lee, 1990 "A Comparison of the Ethical Principles of Selected Old Testament Prophets and Gandhi." in *Perspectives on Non-violence*, 185-192. V.K. Kool (ed). New York: Springer-Verlag.

Calman, Leslie J. 1992 *Toward Empowerment: Women and movement politics in India*. Boulder: Westview Press.

——1989 "Women and Movement Politics in India." *Asian Survey*. 29/10 (October):940-958.

Caprioli, Mary, 1997 "Democracy and Gender Parity: A prescription for peace?" Paper presented at the 38th Annual International Studies Association Conference. Toronto, Ontario, Canada. March 18-22.

Chapple, Christopher, 1990 "Ecological Non-violence and the Hindu Tradition." in *Perspectives on Non-violence*, 168-177. V.K. Kool (ed). New York: Springer-Verlag.

Chatterjee, Margaret, 1992 *Gandhi and his Jewish Friends*. London: Macmillan.

Cohn, Haim H., 1987 "Justice." in *Contemporary Jewish Religious Thought*, 515-520. Arthur A. Cohen & Paul Mendes-Flohr (eds). New York: The Free Press.

Cooper, Davina, 1995 *Power in Struggle: Feminism, sexuality and the state*. New York: New York University Press.

Crane, Jonathan, 1997a "Beyond Gandhiji's *Ahimsa*—a necessity." Paper presented at "Consultation on Religio-Cultural Approaches to Problems of Violence and Communalism." New Delhi, India. November 6-9 included in this volume as Chapter 8.

——1997b "You Have Struck the Women, You Have Struck the Rock: Voicing and creating identity by Black Women in South Africa." Paper presented at

"Interweaving Understanding: Gender Across the Disciplines." University of Notre Dame, South Bend, Indiana. February 20-21.

——1996a *An Introduction to Peace & Conflict Studies, & Research Resource Guide*. Unpublished book for the International Study of Peace/Conflict Resolution Organizations, sponsored by the Aspen Institute.

——1996b "Faltering Mystics? Martin Buber and Mohandas Gandhi." Unpublished paper. University of Notre Dame.

——1995 *Peace Movements in Israel and Northern Ireland: Case studies of political action*. Unpublished Honors Thesis. Norton, MA: Wheaton College.

Csikszentmihalyi, Mihaly, 1996 *Creativity*. New York: Harper Collins Publishers.

The Dalai Lama, 1995 *The Power of Compassion*. New Delhi: Harper Collins.

Das, Bhagavan, 1960 *Essential Unity of All Religions*. Bombay: Bharatiya Vidya Bhavan.

Dasgupta, Sugata, 1984, "Philosophical Assumptions for Training in Non-Violence." Shri Jamnalal Bajaj Institute of Studies in Ahimsa Monograph 2. Ahmedabad: Gujarat Vidyapith.

Dastur, Aloo; Usha Mehta, 1991 *Gandhi's Contribution to the Emancipation of Women*. Bombay: Popular Prakashan.

Dossey, Larry, 1988 "Non-Violence in Medical Science." Shri Jamnalal Bajaj Institute of Studies in Ahimsa Monograph 6. Ahmedabad: Gujarat Vidyapith.

Erikson, Erik, 1969 *Gandhi's Truth: On the origins of militant non-violence*. New York: W.W. Norton & Company.

Everett, Jana Matson, 1979 *Women and Social Change in India*. New York: St. Martin's Press.

Femia, J. 1981 *Gramsci's Political Thought*. Oxford: Clarendon.

Fetherston, A. B.; A.C. Parkin, 1997 "Transforming Violent Conflict: Contributions from social theory." Forthcoming in L.A. Broadhead (ed.) *Issues in Peace Research 1997-8*. London: Cassells.

Fiore, Karen K. 1995 "Was Gandhi a Feminist?" *Acorn*. Fall. pp. 23-27.

Fisher, Alan M. 1990 "Opposition to Violence: A Jewish perspective." in *Perspectives on Non-violence*, 178-184. V.K. Kool (ed). New York: Springer-Verlag.

Forcey, Linda Rennie, 1996 "The Indian Women's Movement, Ecofeminism, and the Politics of Peace." in *The Gendered New World Order*, 71-82. Jennifer Turpin & Lois Ann Lorentzen (eds). New York: Routledge.

Foucault, Michel, 1984 *The Foucault Reader*. Paul Rabinow (ed). New York: Pantheon Books.

Friedman, Maurice, 1987 "I and Thou." in *Contemporary Jewish Religious Thought*, 435-443. Arthur A. Cohen & Paul Mendes-Flohr (eds). New York: The Free Press.

Fromm, Erich, 1976 *To Have or To Be?* London: Abacus.

Galtung, Johan, 1996a *Peace by Peaceful Means*. London: SAGE.

——1996b *Conflict Transformation by Peaceful Means (the transcend method)*.

——Alfaz del Pi: United Nations Disaster Management Training Program.
——1992. *The Way is the Goal.* Ahmedabad: Navajivan Press.

Gandhi, Mohandas K. 1987. *The Essence of Hinduism*. Ahmedabad: Navajivan Press.

——1971. *Pathway to God.* Ahmedabad: Navajivan Press.

——1968. *The Selected Works of Mahatma Gandhi*. Volumes 1-6. Ahmedabad: Navajivan Press.

Vol. I: An Autobiography
Vol. II: An Autobiography (continued)
Vol. III: Satyagraha in South Africa
Vol. IV: The Basic Works:
Ethical Religion
Unto This Last
Hind Swaraj
From Yeravda Mandir
Discourses on the Gita
Constructive Program
Key to Health
Vol. V: Selected Letters
Vol. VI: The Voice of Truth

——1962. *My God.* Ahmedabad: Navajivan Press.

——1960. *Trusteeship*. Ahmedabad: Navajivan Press.

——1959. *The Message of the Gita*. Ahmedabad: Navajivan Press.

——1955. *Truth is God.* Ahmedabad: Navajivan Press.

——1949. *Ramanama*. Ahmedabad: Navajivan Press.

Ghotkoskar, Sujata; Vijay Kanhere, 1984. "The Role of Women in Social Change and People's Movements." *Social Action: A quarterly review of social trends*. 34/2 (April-June):132-144.

Ginsberg, Robert, 1990 "The Paradoxes of Violence, Moral Violence, and Nonviolence." in *Perspectives on Non-violence*, 161-167. V.K. Kool (ed). New York: Springer-Verlag.

Grimshaw, Jean, 1993 "Practices of Freedom." in *Up Against Foucault: Explorations of some tensions between Foucault and feminism*, 51-72. Caroline Ramazanoglo (ed.). London: Routledge.

Gross, Aaron, 1997a "Engaging Non-violence: reflections on the first six months of my wanderjahr." Unpublished paper for Watson Fellowship.

——1997b "Listening to Non-violence: reflections on the first nine months of my wanderjahr." Unpublished paper for Watson Fellowship.

——1996 "Searching for Non-violence: Reflections on the first three months of my wanderjahr." Unpublished paper for Watson Fellowship.

Hesse, Hermann, 1943 *The Glass Bead Game (Magister Ludi)*. New York: Henry Holt and Company.

——1930 *Narcissus and Goldmund*. New York: Bantam Books.

Hirsh, Rabbi Norman D., 1993 "The Ten Words." Unpublished Yom Kippur sermon.

——1992 "The Immortality of the Soul." Unpublished Yom Kippur sermon.

——1967 "The Weakness of Judaism." Unpublished Shabbat sermon.

Høeg, Peter, 1994 *Borderliners*. London: Harvill.

Hofstadter, Douglas; Daniel Dennett, 1981, *The Mind's I: fantasies and reflections on self and soul.* (eds.) New York: Penguin Books.

Huyer, Sophia, 1997 "Popular Movements Respond to Globalisation: Implications for social movement theory." Paper presented at the 38th Annual International Studies Association Conference. Toronto, Ontario, Canada. March 18-22.

Iyer, Raghavan N, 1973 *The Moral and Political Thought of Mahatma Gandhi.* New York: Oxford University Press.

Jaggi, O. P., 1973 *Religion, Practice and Science of Non-Violence.* New Delhi: Munshiram Mansharlal Publishers.

Jain, Devaki, 1986 "Gandhian Contributions Toward a Feminist Ethic." in *Speaking of Faith*, 255-270. Diana Eck & Devaki Jain (eds.). New Delhi: Kali for Women.

Jain, Pratibha, 1985 *Gandhian Ideas, Social Movements, and Creativity.* Jaipur: Rawat Publishers.

Johnson, Jeffrey C., 1990 *Selecting Ethnographic Informants*. London: SAGE.

Jørgensen, Bent D., 1997 "Emerging Global and Regional 'Cartographies'." Paper presented at the 38th Annual International Studies Association Conference. Toronto, Ontario, Canada. March 18-22.

Joshi, Pushpa, 1988 *Gandhi on Women: Collection of Mahatma Gandhi's writings and speeches on women.* Ahmedabad: Navajivan Press.

Kalarthi, Mukulbhai, 1962 *Ba and Bapu*. Ahmedabad: Navajivan Press.

Katz, Neil, 1990 "Evaluation Research on Nonviolent Action." in *Perspectives on Non-violence*, 109-117. V.K. Kool (ed). New York: Springer-Verlag.

Kaur, Harpinder, 1986 *Gandhi's Concept of Civil Disobedience*. Delhi: Intellectual Publishing House.

Kool, V.K. 1990 *Perspectives on Non-violence*. (ed.) New York: Springer-Verlag.

Krishnamurti, J., 1988 "The Book of Life." Pondicherry: Krishnamurti Foundation Trust.

——1980 "Freedom, Responsibility & Discipline." Pondicherry: Krishnamurti Foundation Trust.

——1977a "Inward Flowering." Pondicherry: Krishnamurti Foundation Trust.

——1977b "A Dialogue with Oneself." Pondicherry: Krishnamurti Foundation Trust.

——1973 *Beyond Violence*. Pondicherry: Krishnamurti Foundation Trust.

——1971 "Mind in Meditation." Pondicherry: Krishnamurti Foundation Trust.

——1970 "Conversations." Pondicherry: Krishnamurti Foundation Trust.

——1969 *Freedom from the Known*. Pondicherry: Krishnamurti Foundation Trust.

——1954 *The First and Last Freedom*. Pondicherry: Krishnamurti Foundation Trust.

Kumar, Radha, 1993 *The History of Doing: An illustrated account of movements for women's rights and feminism in India, 1800-1900*. London: Verso.

Kumar, Sunalini, 1998 "Feminist Theories." Unpublished Paper. LSR, New Delhi.

Kundera, Milan, 1995, *Slowness*. New Delhi: Rupa.

——1991 *Immortality*. New Delhi: Rupa.

——1984 *The Unbearable Lightness of Being*. New Delhi: Rupa.

——1978 *The Book of Laughter and Forgetting*. New Delhi: Rupa.

——1976 *The Farewell Party*. New Delhi: Rupa.

——1973 *Life is Elsewhere*. New Delhi: Rupa.

——1969 *Laughable Loves*. New Delhi: Rupa.

Kunz, George, 1990 "Psychology Ought to Honor the Paradoxical: The power of weakness." in *Perspectives on Non-violence*, 1990-96. V.K. Kool (ed). New York: Springer-Verlag.

Lavanam, 1998 "Gandhi and Atheism." Paper presented at International Seminar on Gandhi and the Twenty First Century. New Delhi & Wardha. January 30—February 4.

Mathai, M. P., 1998 "Economic Freedom, Technology and the Eco-System." Paper presented at International Seminar on Gandhi and the Twenty First Century. New Delhi & Wardha. January 30—February 4.

Mathiak, Lucy J. 1997 "Rape With the Blessing of Authority—Organized Sexual Violence in War and Conflict." Paper presented at the 38th Annual International Studies Association Conference. Toronto, Ontario, Canada. March 18-22.

McNay, Lois, 1994 *Foucault: A critical introduction.* Cambridge: Polity Press.

——1992 *Foucault and Feminism: Power, gender and the self.* New York: Polity Press.

Misra, R.P. 1990, Gandhian Model of Development and World Peace, New Delhi: Concept,

——1993, Conflict Resolution through Non-violence: Role of Universities, New Delhi: Concept.

Mitter, Sara S. 1991 *Dharma's Daughters: Contemporary Indian women and Hindu culture*. New Brunswick: Rutgers University Press.

Murti, V.V. Ramana, 1968 "Buber's Dialogue and Gandhi's Satyagraha." *Journal of the History of Ideas*. 29:605-613.

Nandy, Ashis, 1980 *At the Edge of Psychology: Essays in politics and culture*. Delhi: Oxford University Press.

Nasr, Seyyed Hossein, 1996 *Religion and the Order of Nature*. New York: Oxford University Press.

Nauriya, Anil, 1995 "Unfolding of Gandhi's Thought: The undermining of *varna*." *Janata*. October 8. pp. 5-7.

Neufeld, Beverly, 1997 "Feminism and the Concept of Community in International Relations." Paper presented at the 38th Annual International Studies Association Conference. Toronto, Ontario, Canada. March 18-22.

Nordstrom, Carolyn, 1995 "War on the Front Lines." in *Fieldwork under Fire: Contemporary studies of violence and survival*, 129-153. Carolyn Nordstrom & Antonius Robben (eds). Berkeley: University of California Press.

——1994 "Warzones: Cultures of violence, militarization and peace." Working Paper No. 145. Canberra: Australia National University.

Ochs, Peter, 1987 "Truth." in *Contemporary Jewish Religious Thought*, 1017-1023. Arthur A. Cohen & Paul Mendes-Flohr (eds). New York: The Free Press.

Omvedt, Gail, 1993 *Reinventing Revolution: New social movements and the socialist tradition in India*. Armonk: M.E. Sharpe.

Oommen, T. K., 1990, *Protest and Change: Studies in social movements*. New Delhi: SAGE.

Outhwaite, William, 1994 *Habermas: A critical introduction*. Stanford: Stanford University Press.

Pandeya, A.N. 1994a "Secular Discourse and the Republican Vision of India." *Secular Democracy*. XXIII/5 (August):13-16.

——1994b "Central Contradiction of 'Modernity'." *Secular Democracy*. XXIII/6 (September) : 29-33.

——1994c "Mahatma Gandhi: Civilizational Vision." *Secular Democracy*. XXIII/7 (October) : 17-19.

Pathak, D.N. 1998 "The United Nations and the Twenty First Century." Paper presented at International Seminar on Gandhi and the Twenty First Century. New Delhi & Wardha. January 30—February 4.

——1997 "Environmental Crisis—Emerging Context of Gandhi's Non-violence and 'Ecological Humanism'." Ahmedabad: Gujarat Vidyapith Peace Research Center.

——1985 "Intimations of Peaceful Society." Shri Jamnalal Bajaj Institute of Studies in Ahimsa Monograph 4. Ahmedabad: Peace Research Center, Gujarat Vidyapith.

Percival, Val, 1997 "Women and War: A public health approach." Paper presented at the 38th Annual International Studies Association Conference. Toronto, Ontario, Canada. March 18-22.

Peterson, V. Spike, 1997a "Whose Crisis? early and post-modern masculinism." in *Innovation and Transformation in International Studies*. Stephen Gill & James Mittelman (eds). Cambridge: Cambridge University Press. pp. 185-201.

——1997b "Are Women Human? It's not an academic question." Paper presented at the 38th Annual International Studies Association Conference. Toronto, Ontario, Canada. March 18-22.

Pettman, Jan Jindy, 1996 *Worlding Women: A feminist international politics*. London: Routledge.

Prabhu, R.K.; U.R. Rao, 1967 *The Mind of Mahatma Gandhi*. Ahmedabad: Navajivan Press.

Price-Smith, Andrew T. 1997 "Infectious Disease and State Failure: Developing a new security paradigm." Paper presented at the 38th Annual International Studies Association Conference. Toronto, Ontario, Canada. March 18-22.

Quinn, Daniel, 1997 *My Ishmael*. New York: Bantam Books.

Rabinow, Paul, 1977 *Reflections on Fieldwork in Morocco*. Berkeley: University of California Press.

Radhakrishnan, S. 1956 *Recovery of Faith*. New Delhi: Harper Collins.

——1947 *Religion and Society*. New Delhi: Harper Collins.

——1927 *The Hindu View of Life*. New Delhi: Harper Collins.

Rai, Shirin M. 1997 "Gender and Village Level Democracy in India and China: Constructing explanations for difference(s)." Paper presented at the 38th Annual International Studies Association Conference. Toronto, Ontario, Canada. March 18-22.

Ramaswamy, Sushila, 1997 "John Rawls' Theory of Civil Disobedience in the Gandhian Perspective." *Gandhi Marg*. July-September:179-197.

Ravitzky, Aviezer, 1987 "Peace." in *Contemporary Jewish Religious Thought*, 685-702. Arthur A. Cohen & Paul Mendes-Flohr (eds). New York: The Free Press.

Ray, Baren, 1995 "Gandhiji and the Dalit Question: then and now." *Mainstream*. April 22. pp. 17-22.

Richards, Jerald, 1995 "Gandhi's Qualified Acceptance of Violence." *Acorn*. Fall. pp. 5-16.

Rose, Dan, 1990 *Living the Ethnographic Life*. London: SAGE.

Routledge, Paul, 1993 *Terrains of Resistance: Non-violent social movements and the contestation of place in India*. Westport: Praeger.

Roy, Ramashray, 1984 *Self and Society: A study of Gandhian thought*. New Delhi: SAGE.

Sangharakshita, Maha Sthavira, 1995 "Heart Sutra." *Dhammamegha*. No. 61. April-June.

——1987 "The Origin and Development of the Bodhisattva Ideal." *Dhammamegha*. No. 31. January.

Said, Edward, 1994 *Representations of the Intellectual*. New York: Pantheon Books.

——1978 *Orientalism*. New York: Vintage Books.

Sargisson, Lucy, 1996 *Contemporary Feminist Utopianism*. London: Routledge.

Sarkar, Tanika, 1995 *Women and Right-Wing Movements: Indian experiences*. London: Zed Books.

Sheth, Pravin, 1994 "Theory and Praxis of Environmentalism: Green Plus Gandhi." Ahmedabad: Peace Research Center, Gujarat Vidyapith.

Singer, Eric; Janet Shope, 1997 "The Insecurity of Development: Rural women in South Africa." Paper presented at the 38th Annual International Studies Association Conference. Toronto, Ontario, Canada. March 18-22.

Smith, Huston, 1991 *The World's Religions: Our great wisdom traditions*. New Delhi: Harper Collins.

Snow, David A.; Leon Anderson, 1993 *Down on Their Luck: A study of homeless street people*. Berkeley: University of California Press.

Sonnleitner, Michael W., 1985 *Gandhian Non-violence Levels of Satyagraha*. Delhi: Abhinav Publishers.

Spodek, Howard, 1971 "On the Origins of Gandhi's Political Methodology: the heritage of Kathiwad and Gujarat." *The Journal of Asian Studies*. 30/2 (February):361-372.

Staub, Ervin, 1996a "Cultural-Societal Roots of Violence: The example of genocidal violence and of contemporary youth violence in the United States." *American Psychologist.* 51/2 (February):117-132.

——1996 "The Psychological and Cultural Roots of Group Violence and the Creation of Caring Societies and Peaceful Group Relations." in *A Natural History of Peace*, 129-158. Gregor (ed). Nashville: Vanderbilt University Press.

——1989 *The Roots of Evil: The origins of genocide and other group violence*. Cambridge: Cambridge University Press.

——1984 "Notes Toward an Interactionist-Motivational Theory of the Determinants and Development of (Pro)Social Behaviour." in *Development and Maintenance of Prosocial Behaviour*, 29-50. Staub, Bar-Tal, Karylowski, & Reykowski (eds). New York: Plenum Press.

Suresh, A., 1997 "Communal Harmony and National Integration: A challenge to interreligious dialogue." Paper presented at "Consultation on Religio-Cultural Approaches to Problems of Violence and Communalism." New Delhi, India. November 6-9.

Tagore, Rabindranath, 1988, *The Religion of Man*. New Delhi: Harper Collins.

Tähtinen, Unto, 1976 *Ahimsa: Non-violence in Indian Tradition*. Ahmedabad: Navajivan Press.

Thakkar, Usha, 1998 "Discovering New Horizons: Indian women and freedom struggle." Unpublished paper.

Udayakumar, S.P. 1997 "Local Histories and Global Futures." *Gandhi Marg.* 19/2 (July-September) : 223-228.

Unnithan, T.K.N. 1998 "Human Society in the Twenty First Century, A Gandhian Alternative." Paper presented at International Seminar on Gandhi and the Twenty First Century. New Delhi & Wardha. January 30—February 4.

——1987 "Change Without Violence: Gandhian Theory of Social Change." Shri Jamnalal Bajaj Institute of Studies in Ahimsa Monograph 5. Ahmedabad: Gujarat Vidyapith.

——Singh, Yogendra, 1973 *Traditions of Non-violence*. New Delhi: Arnold-Heinemann India.

Varma, Ravindra, 1997a "Gandhi's Philosophy of Swadeshi." Eighth Gandhi Memorial Lecture. New Delhi: Gandhi Smriti and Darshan Samiti.

——1997b "Gandhian Perception of the Ethical Foundations of Society." *Gandhi Marg*. 19/3 (October-December) : 279-286.

——1995 "Gandhi's Theory of Trusteeship: An essay in understanding." Wardha: Institute of Gandhian Studies.

Vaz, Pelgy, 1997 "Co-existence of Secularism and Fundamentalism in India." Paper presented at the 38th Annual International Studies Association Conference. Toronto, Ontario, Canada. March 18-22.

Weber, Thomas, 1991 *Conflict Resolution and Gandhian Ethics*. New Delhi: The Gandhi Peace Foundation.

Whitehead, Tony L.; Mary Ellen Conaway, 1986 *Self, Sex, and Gender in Cross-Cultural Fieldwork*. (eds). Urbana: University of Illinois Press.

7

Beyond Gandhiji's Ahimsa: A Necessity

There is no doubt that violence in this century has devolved to immeasurable depths of brutality and complexity, and it continues to plummet beyond what could even be called inhumane. And there is no doubt that searches for ways to stop violence have yet to prove themselves worthy of the name "conflict resolution"—for so few, if any, violent conflicts have actually been solved, much less, resolved. Many, if not most, of these efforts are couched in socio-economic and politico-legal-strategic paradigms, that through redistribution violence can be stemmed, maybe pre-empted. Yet violence persists, even after such efforts. Just because previous and contemporary attempts to stop violence have not "succeeded"[1] does not mean that anyone, and everyone, ought to stop looking for effective ways to stem violence. Rather, what the modern day requires is a more systematic, symptomatic, approach to addressing violent conflicts. This approach is a part of and defines a religio-cultural paradigm. One characteristic of a religio-cultural paradigm is a mechanism to curb violence by de-legitimizing its various forms. Without this mechanism societies suffer unregulated and debilitating aggressiveness.

But first, let us understand what is meant by violence. As traditionally conceived, violence means using physical force to coerce obedience. But this is a limited conceptualization of violence. Galtung describes how violence is manifest in many arenas, including nature violence, structural or indirect violence, cultural violence, time violence.[2] From this broader conceptualization it is difficult to find any piece of human society void of violence. If violence is pandemic, saturating our every moment and continuing to devolve, and we desire to pre-empt violence, we must purge ourselves of what causes this violence, not symptoms of it. This is where Gandhiji comes into the picture. He offers a way to cope with our violences. He calls his integrated path one that is religious. That it may be. But can we rely solely on Gandhiji's religious approach to problems of violence; that is, can we accept his vision unquestioningly?

Gandhi's Religious Living

As is well known and explored in an expanding discourse, Gandhiji seeks to integrate religion into politics, for he believes that his whole existence was a religious existence, all else is secondary. He creates arguments for living religiously (or righteous living) and how best to do this. Here is a general overview of his philosophical approach. He claims the central teaching of the Bhagavad Gita is *anasakti*—selfless action.[3] *Yajna*, or acts for the welfare of others without desire of reciprocity of any kind, physical or spiritual, are essentially sacrifices "which conduce the most to the welfare of the greatest number in the widest area, and which can be performed by the largest number of men and women with the least trouble."[4] Some of these acts may be seen as *tapas*, self-suffering, and may require an activist's death.[5] Gandhi's contemporary, Rabindranath Tagore, agrees with the central nature of self-less action in the Gita:

> According to the Gita, the deeds that are done solely for the sake of self fetter our soul; the disinterest action, performed for the sake of the giving up of self, is the true sacrifice. For creation itself comes of the self-sacrifice of Brahma, which has no other purpose; and therefore, in our performance of the duty which is self-sacrificing, we realize the spirit of Brahma.[6]

Gandhi stipulates that these selfless acts of sacrifice and self-suffering are to be done fearlessly, because fearlessness "heads the list of the Divine Attributes enumerated in the 16th Chapter" of the Gita.[7] Fearlessness "connotes freedom from all external fear—fear of disease, bodily injury or death, of dispossession, of losing one's nearest and dearest, of losing reputation or giving offense, and so on."[8] It is only a matter of changing attitudes about attachment for wealth, family, and health. If one fears these things, then one cannot do selfless acts. The only fear an individual is allowed is the fear of God, and only then can people cease to fear each other.[9]

But only a certain kind of motivation behind such fearless self-sacrificial action realizes the spirit of Brahma. Often people engage in selfless action because they see no other way to express their desire to love, share and connect with others, especially with their inner spirituality. As Fromm observes, "self-sacrifice is frequently the solution for individuals who ardently desire to love, but who have lost the capacity to love and see in the sacrifice of their own lives an experience of love in the highest degree."[10] This leads to a kind of heroism, where hollow, or false, love binds and blinds people to a particular way of living and perceiving the world, and where fear (of Self and Other) persists. Thus, the only motivation allowed for selfless actions of sacrifice is that of universal love. This goes beyond mutual love and to a selfless love and it does not need reciprocation.[11] "Mutual trust and mutual love are no trust and no love. The real love is to love them that hate you, to love your neighbor even though you distrust him."[12] So one can love but need not trust; or, love is a necessary but not sufficient condition for realizing Brahma through fearless self-sacrificial action, while trust is neither necessary nor sufficient for same. If this universal love requires no reciprocity and trust, it presupposes that those who are so loved are unable (or unwilling) to reciprocate or be trusted or are themselves trusting. In short, those who are loved within this universal love are nonmoral agents—Others who cannot (or will not) behave motivated by ethical considerations of others (or "love"), or be consistent and/or constant within or through historical moments (or "trusted"). This is a strange "universal" love indeed.

A picture of what Gandhi's understanding of the Gita can be sketched as follows. Universal love, such as it is, demands no reciprocity or trust but can be expressed only when one fears God alone and nothing else. Such love manifests itself in those who are humble and do not seek heroism. Humility emerges from the performance of actions for the betterment of the general welfare. The betterment of general welfare takes root in self-sacrificial actions, which are, of course, none other than nonviolent actions—*ahimsa.* (Violence, as said earlier, destroys the general welfare.) But it is the *selfless nature* of these non-violent actions that is fundamental for Gandhi. Their non-violent character is a necessary condition, but for Gandhi being nonviolent (*ahimsic*) is not sufficient to live religiously, or righteously. To live according to Gandhi's picture is to live righteously; and according to Radhakrishan, to live righteously is to live religiously.[13] Not to live righteously is to live outside religion—something Gandhi abhors; living righteously must be adhered to at all times. It is a rare person indeed who can meet all these criteria and perform such selfless sacrifices. So what Gandhi presents here is more an ideal typology or a series of ideal stages to which people ought to aspire for righteous or religious living, than it is a blueprint for mass social change or even collective righteous living. Nevertheless, this is what Gandhi espoused to the masses, and this is what he tried to live in his own lifetime.

While Gandhi presents a somewhat coherent argument to live religiously, and that *ahimsa* is a (or the only) necessary element for righteous living, this argument falls short. It does not prevent or pre-empt the violences we seek to curtail and eventually eliminate; it is not, then, characteristice of a religio-cultural paradigm. To explain this we first turn to some elements of Gandhi's religious approach: truth; trust, fearlessness and cowardice; and *ahimsa.* Following is a brief survey of Gandhi's thoughts on strategic political decisions and an introduction of his qualified acceptance of violence. In combination these pieces imply an ideology that is quite permissive of violence—quite contrary to the above sketch of righteous living. The conclusion suggests some alternative ways of integrating Gandhi and his ideas into a religio-cultural paradigm.

Truth

First, an understanding of what Gandhi means by truth is needed. Near the beginning[14] of his search for God, Gandhi thought God is Truth. But over time he saw that through the realities of *syadvaad* (maybe-ism) and *anekantvaad* (several end-ism) one person's God as Truth could negate another's God as Truth. To avoid sponsoring another war of the Titans, so to speak, Gandhi shifted his view of God to "Truth is God."

> In "God is Truth", is certainly does not mean 'equal to' nor does it merely mean, 'is truthful'. Truth is not a mere attribute of God, but He [sic] is That. He is nothing if He is not That. Truth in Sanskrit means Sat. Sat means is. Therefore Truth is implied in Is. God is, nothing else Is. Therefore the more truthful we are, the nearer we are to God. We are only to the extent that we are truthful.[15]

He argues that this notion of Truth has no *double entendre*, and that even atheists can ascribe to it and cannot deny the existence of God so defined.[16] Truth is "not something material but pure intelligence."[17]

> This Truth is not merely the truth we are expected to speak. It is That which alone is, which constitutes the stuff of which all things are made, which subsists by virtue of its own power, which is not supported by anything else but supports everything that exists. Truth alone is eternal, everything else is momentary.[18]

But, one cannot obtain Truth, for one can never experience Truth first hand, but only come near to the Truth. "No man [sic] has ever been able to describe God fully."[19] The best and individual can do is to approximate Truth or, as Gandhi would have us do, approximate God.

As each individual sees the world differently, what is Truth for one differs for another. Thus, Gandhi says, "there is nothing wrong in every man [sic] following Truth according to his lights. Indeed it is his duty to do so."[20] His acceptance of relativism is coupled with an acknowledgment of non-absolutism. "A devotee of Truth... must always hold himself [sic] open to correction, and whenever he discovers himself to be wrong he must confess it at all costs and atone for it."[21] Thus, no truth can be imposed upon others through coercive efforts.

> Truth rules out prejudice, evasion, secrecy and deception as well as exaggeration. Suppression or modification of reality. It requires that we should never be afraid of confessing our mistakes or retracing our steps. Truth also implies mutual toleration and avoidance of dogmatism and bitterness; for truth is discerned by man [sic] is always relative and fragmentary. While, therefore, it is a good guide for individual conduct, imposition of that conduct upon others will be an insufferable interference with their freedom of conscience.[22]

What is the truth ought to be compelling. That is, truth is more than just facts or information about reality; inherent in truth are relationships. If one sees an unjust relationship (for example, the truth of domination) this ought to compel one (with a free conscience) to respond accordingly (to eliminate domination from the relationship), and no coercion is necessary.

Yet, each person is only able to approximate her own vision of the Truth, or her own vision of the reality of God. What is best is not to gain this approximation, but to be it, for "to *gain* truth is to admit its separateness, but to be true is to become one with truth."[23] The way to become more truthful, or true, is through *ahimsa*, or non-violence. In fact, *ahimsa* is *the only way*: "the only means for the realization of the Truth is *Ahimsa*," and "a perfect vision of Truth can only follow a complete realization of *Ahimsa*;"[24] "Realization of Truth is impossible without non-violence."[25] Here, according to Gandhi, approximations of Truth (or God) are relatively attainable by individuals (and theoretically communities, too) through non-violent action only.

Trust, Fearlessness and Cowardice

Gandhi stipulates that any advocate of Truth must also have trust and fearlessness and be rid of cowardice. Trust, according to Radhakrishan, is fundamental in Hinduism: "He [sic] whose consciousness is anchored in God cannot deny any expression of life as utterly erroneous. He is convinced of the inexhaustibility of the nature of God and the infinite number of its possible manifestations."[26] This re-enforces notions of tolerance, especially for others' concepts of God (*sarvyadharma*). Of trust, Gandhi says "My trust is solely in God. And I trust men only because I trust God."[27] He admits that he does not trust other people directly, but only indirectly via his trust in God (or, as Gandhi believes, his trust in Truth). This is a qualified trust; it is limited by his own ability to trust God. But, again, trust for Gandhi is neither necessary nor sufficient for realizing Brahma. Hence, it could be said that trust has nothing to do with *ahimsa*. And, then again, Gandhi eliminates this conclusion. "A Satyagrahi bids good-bye to fear. He [sic] is therefore never afraid of trusting the opponent. Even if the opponent plays him false twenty times, the Satyagrahi is ready to trust him for the twenty-first time, for an implicit trust in human nature is the very essence of his creed."[28] Trust is also negatively associated with fear. The fundamental nature of trust is fearlessness. "The golden rule is to act fearlessly upon what one believes to be right."[29] But, as Galtung observes, "fearlessness cannot be built up unless there is something to fear."[30] Gandhi reflects on this:

> Perfect fearlessness can be attained only by him [sic] who has realized the Supreme, as it implies the height of freedom from delusions. But one can always progress towards this goal by determined and constant endeavour and by increasing confidence in oneself... As for internal foes, we must ever walk in their fear. We are rightly afraid of Animal Passion, Anger and the like. External fears cease of their own accord when once we have conquered the body as the center, and would, therefore, disappear as soon as one got rid of the attachment for the body. We thus find that all fear is the baseless fabric of our own vision.[31]

If fearlessness requires greater confidence, then what is to stop an individual pursuing her own truth even when that truth is a lie, and her motivations, while not centered on attachment for the body, are rooted in self-centered desires? If unfettered, approximate fearlessness (for we can never fully realize the Supreme) empowers inidividuals to pursue (and possibly impose) their Truths, which may be, in actuality, those delusions Gandhi so wants to expose and dismantle.

Fearlessness has no room for cowardice. Cowardice is a crime against one's religion and humanity. Cowards can never be moral, he declares.[32] He describes cowardice as effeminate, and one who chooses cowardice instead of action is emasculated.[33] It is interesting here to see Gandhi's link between cowardice and femininity, especially when he believes that women are in fact more powerful moral agents and *ahimsites*:

> To call a woman the weaker sex is libel; it is man's injustice to woman. If by strength is meant brute strength, then, indeed, woman is less brute than man. If by strength is meant moral power, then women is immeasurably man's superior. Has she not greater intuition, is she not more self-sacrificing, has she not greater powers of endurance, has she not greater courage? Without her, man could not be. If non-violence is the law of our being, the future is with woman. Who can make a more effective appeal to the heart than woman?[34]

If Gandhi so admired the non-violent self-sacrificing leadership and activist potentials in women, why did he associate cowardice with femininity and non-morality? This brings into question his own understanding of what it means to be an *ahimisic*. He goes on to say that inaction itself is unmanly and "rank cowardice" and it "must be shunned at all cost."[35] Thus, if inaction is abhorred, it must be avoided. Gandhi leaves no room for omission; he demands action. Supposedly he demands nonviolent action.

Ahimsa

As is commonly understood, Gandhi believes that whatever action an individual takes, that action ought to be non-violent in nature. Throughout his life and his writings he explores many dimensions of *ahimsa*. He sees that non-violence must pervade the total being, in thought, speech and action. There are different kinds of action, including passive resistance, civil disobedience, non-cooperation, and there are methods of employing them at different times during a conflict struggle (see Galtung 1992). He purports that non-violence is the law of the human species and that it is infinitely greater than and superior to brute force. But this is more than a law because laws and "policies may and do change. Non-violence is an unchangeable creed."[36] It is lawful not because it may comply with human laws, but because it adheres to and reinforces Natural Law. Or rather, it is part and parcel to the Natural Creed of the human species.

While he says that all peoples can exercise its power, only those who have a "living faith in the God of love and have therefore equal love for all mankind [sic]"[37] can actually execute non-violence's power morally. Moreover, non-violence is not for the weak-minded or weak-willed. As discussed earlier, Gandhi says no coward could be non-violent even if she would. In fact, he found it easier to communicate the power of non-violence to those who are couched in the school of violence.[38] But are those trained in violence those with an equal love for all peoples? It requires great deliberate restraint from the desire for vengeance, from aggression of any kind, and from the meek running away from conflict. "Non-violence is not a cover for cowardice, but it is the supreme virtue of the brave."[39] And again, the motivation must be pure: "[non-violence] must come from inward conviction."[40] But unlimited bravery motivated by internal conviction of one's Truth and truthfulness to morality undermines the potentiality of non-violence. "If one has... pride and egoism, there is no non-violence. Nonviolence is impossible without humility."[41] For the "owner of hard discipline" non-violence is accessible.[42] It is interesting that Gandhi thinks that one "owns" discipline and not that one "is" disciplined. This sense of ownership betrays his philosophy that a *satyagrahi* must renounce possessions including those characteristics we try to own, or have. For having discipline is not the same as being disciplined; having discipline distances an individual from the discipline itself while being disciplined integrates self with the discipline to the degree that neither is distinguishable from the other.[43] While he says that *ahimsa* requires no outside or outward training, "it simply requires the will not to kill even in retaliation and the courage to face death without revenge."[44] An individual then must have the discipline of restraint, or forbearance; an individual need not *be* restrained in her nature.

According to Gandhi, non-violence is the only method in which to engage reality, especially conflict situations. But those who are "allowed" to use such non-violent methods (in thought, speech and action) compose, despite his insistence to the contrary, a limited population. For he describes an *ahimsic* as one who is both brave yet without pride or ego, one who is humble yet not a coward, one who is trained in the ways and views of violence yet renounces them and loves all equally, one who has a living faith in (read, fearing) God yet is fearless, one who is free of external and internal limitations but owns (read, haves) the discipline of forbearance. This is a rare person indeed.

Strategic Political Decisions

Gandhi's insistence that non-violence is the only way to live and (re)solve conflicts seems to be fulfilled by and applicable to very few people indeed (those who meet his characteristic requirements). Nevertheless, what is more curious than the limitations of who can be ahimisic is Gandhi's integration of *anekantvaad* (several-end-ism) into his philosophical makings. Of renunciation (say, of violence, excessive pride or egoism) he says "it is a deliberate act, not done in ignorance."[45] Only through *intentionally* meaning to do good does an act become moral. However, "the result of our action is not within our control."[46] But since we have no control over outcomes, and since we each have our own version of reality or Truth, one must intentionally try the *best* path, or way, to attain the Truth:

> In other words, when we know a particular path to be the right one, we should set out on it without fear. We can progress only if we observe the laws of morality in this way. That is why true morality, true civilization and true progress are always to be found together.[47]

But if we find ourselves in the wrong, or morality and Truth are not obtaining from our actions, we must change our paths.[48] What we thought best at first may not be so. We must, then, find what is second best and use that. Thus, there are more ways of living and engaging than *only* non-violence. By relying on *anekantvaad* Gandhi allows himself wiggle room in his philosophy—that is, non-violence is no longer a religious doctrine to be adhered to all times: it is now a strategic political decision which can and must be changed to suit tranistory and momentary conditions. Non-violence is no longer a creed of life as he says; non-violence is a political tool to be used or not used as desired.

Acceptance of Violence

Of course Gandhi encourages reliance on non-violence as the primary way of living and engaging in conflicts. As he understands the importance of changing circumstances, and personal shortcomings to the ideals of *ahimsic* characteristics, he comes to appreciate the need for second-best strategic political decisions and actions. In his own life he decides to participate in wars (1899-1902, 1906, 1914-1918), albeit in a qualified nature (that of initiating and leading ambulance corps). He admits that he is as guilty as one who carries a weapon in war.[49] Buts Richards explains, he also had many reasons for his participation in these wars.[50] In 1918 he saw that "there is non-violence in violence.... Violence is a function of the body"[51], giving him justification to be an *ahimsic* at war. By World War II his comfort with participating in war, however qualified, diminishes to what he called providing moral support. "But even this moral support was conditional upon the justness of the Allied conduct of the war. Thus, elements of justified war morality entered into Gandhi's assessment of the war."[52]

In regards to the Indian struggle for independence from British colonial rule, Gandhi advocates the use of violence over and above cowardly submission to continued British imperialism.

> I advocate training in arms for those who believe in methods of violence. I would rather have India resort to arms in order to defend her honour than that she would, in a cowardly manner, become or remain a helpless witness to her own dishonour.[53]

> If there was a national Government, whilst I should not take any direct part in any war, I can conceive occasions when it would be my duty to vote for the military training of those who wish to take it. For I know that all its members do not believe in non-violence to the extent I do. It is not possible to make a person or a society non-violent by compulsion.[54]

> If we feel that we shall not be able to displace the British power without a violent struggle, the [Indian National] Congress must say so to the nation and prepare accordingly.[55]

He would have India as a nation be independent through violent means rather than remain under British rule.

For individuals he also allowed room for violence as an option. His arguments suggest that it is better for an individual to be violent to maintain moral integrity than to lose face, be cowardly, or act in any morally unacceptable ways. In 1920 he writes, "I do believe that, where there is only a choice between cowardice and violence, I would advise violence."[56] In 1936 he suggests that non-violence can be used to hide cowardice (or, another words, that non-violence can be ill-used) and that violence would be better: "when [non-violence] becomes a cloak for our weakness, it emasculates us. Far better than emasculation would be the bravery of those who use physical force. Far better than cowardice would be meeting one's death fighting."[57] Violence is better than non-violence hiding impotence. By 1942 he says in cases of personal self-defense:

> People must everywhere learn to defend themselves against misbehaving individuals, no matter who they are. The question of non-violence and violence does not arise. No doubt the non-violent way is always the best, but where that does not come naturally the violent way is both necessary and honourable. Inaction here is rank cowardice and unmanly. It must be shunned at all costs.[58]

In 1946 he talks of collective defense:

> If an individual or group of people are unable or unwilling to follow this great law of life [non-violence]... retaliation or resistance unto death is the second best, though a long way from the first. Cowardice is impotence worse than violence.... A coward is less than man. He does not deserve to be a member of a society of men and women.[59]

Note how he feminizes cowardice and inaction. Strange, again, that this is so especially when he reveals that he "learnt the lesson of non-violence from my wife."[60] As Erikson observes, Gandhi seeks to be both mother and father to Indians, and thus he has a tendency to mix and mingle the characteristics he abhors and desires with those associated with men and women.[61] Still, what is evident here is Gandhi's obvious acceptance of violence as an option, albeit a second-best option, but an option nonetheless, and a preferred option to acts of omission stemming from "impotence" or "cowardice".

Gandhi demands acts of commission—preferably non-violent but violence is legitimate. Again in a gendered tone he says "vengeance is any day superior to passive, effeminate and helpless submission."[62]

> Though violence is not lawful, when it is offered in self-defense or for the defense of the defenseless, it is an act of bravery far better than cowardly submission. The latter befits neither man nor woman. Under violence, there are many stages and varieties of bravery. Every man must judge this for himself. No other person can or has the right.[63]

He leaves room for each individual to defend herself violently to continue to pursue her own vision of Truth, even if that vision is no Truth.

But we must understand what legitimate violence means. The question of when it is legitimate to use physical force against other living beings raises several arguments for and against its justification. Legitimacy implies permission; it does not imply desirability. Second, legitimacy as permission is different from obligation, responsibility or duty. So understood, the question now reads "to what extent *is it permissible to use physical force* against other living beings?" Legitimacy so derived (re-)enforces the concept of permissibility.

Permission gives room for and even justifies non-action. If the goal is to decrease human killing and suffering, non-action (or act of omission) does little in this regards. A reconceptualization of legitimacy to read as restrictions of non-action could be useful here. At the same time, if the goal is to decrease human killing and suffering, demanding acts of commission, including violent acts (as does Gandhi) also does little to address the overall problem. It is possible to see the justification of using violent force against the basic needs of other (equally needy) beings (human and non-human) to secure the basic needs of humans.

However, it is not justifiable to meet non-basic wants by using force against others' basic needs, because that would be depriving others of their rights to non-interference, and to their survival (basic tenets of *ahimsa*). If it is morally unjustified to be physically violent over and against human and non-human basic needs for non-basic wants then it is equally morally unjustified to perpetuate structural violence (as an example) that imposes upon others' basic needs for non-basic wants. In short, the only violence that is morally acceptable is that which aggresses against others only in defense of basic needs; anything else is not morally acceptable and thus not justifiable even within Gandhi's schema. Simultaneously he stops just short of defining "legitimacy as obligation" (making the use of violence required) yet goes beyond "legitimacy as permissability" (violent self-defense as a viable option). He settles with "legitimacy as desirability"—that violent self-defense is desired and preferred above and before other action or non-action itself.

Implications

The above observations of Gandhi's complexity lead to a startling possibility. If Gandhi allows violence as a second-best option, it is *de facto* a viable strategic political choice. *Ahimsa*, then, is also a political choice and thus not a religious doctrine; non-violence cannot preclude other non-nonviolent actions. Though Gandhi desires, allows and even encourages the use of violent force (instead of cowardice) by people who are not complete *ahimsics*, he stipulates that their cause must be just or truthful. Yet he acknowledge that each person has her own conception of the Truth, and thus he must concede that each person has a different understanding of what is a worthy moral cause for which she may choose violence to pursue.

This, it seems, says that Gandhi supports the pursuit of arbitrary Truths and (random) acts of violence in search of closer approximations of those Truths. Hence it seems that Gandhi's acceptance of violence as a strategic political option (re)enforces and encourages what is commonly called terrorism (for example, random acts of violence done in the name of defending basic needs, like access to clean water). This is not what Gandhi wants to support ("I do not regard killing or assassination or terrorism as good in any circumstances whatsoever."[64]) but implicitly and inevitably does so by allowing the justification of violence.

Conclusion

It is obvious by now that what Gandhi espouses as *ahimsa* is not a religious creed or way of life. It is, for him, a strategic tool. Still he says *ahimsa* is a religion, "The religion of non-violence is not meant only for the *rishis* and saints. It is meant for the common people as well. Non-violence is the law of our species as violence is the law of the brute."[65] But as we can see Gandhi encourages those who cannot be 'fully' human to be at least 'brutish' and use violence, instead of being impotent or cowardly. Gandhi fudges distinctions between human morality and 'brutish' immorality. And this is done in a strategic political decision-making fashion. "For Gandhi, the best way of behaving in struggle was always the *non-violence of the brave*. But the second best was the *violence of the brave* and this would certainly cover not only the military fighting courageously for the just cause, but also the revolutionary who so does."[66]

Ahimsa presupposes fearlessness, courage, and universal love. But fearlessness untethered by rationality can lead to blind judgments and brash actions, and may do more harm than good. Courage, too, can do more harm than good when exercised in search of the title of bravery. Gandhi's kind of universal love is more a conditional love realized only through the fear of God. And trust seems like an unwanted child in his picture—neither here nor there but somehow always lurking about in the shadows. But fearlessness requires something to be feared in the first place, yet at the same time not submitting to that fear.[67] This challenges Gandhi's argument that *ahimsa* is essentially the process of respecting God's presence in others. Translated: fearless action must not submit to Other's God's Truths—thus perpetuating conflicts. So conceived, *ahimsa* is a limited way of life and worldview, and it leaks: it supports kinds of violence that we seek to diminish and prevent and it perpetuates violent conflicts, especially those of a religious nature.

What is needed is a different conceptualization of a religio-cultural approach to problems of violence. By expanding Gandhi's notion of universal (yet conditional) love to *unconditional* love, the circle of compassion is expanded and concomitantly the range of action is narrowed. That is, given the Truth that all sentient beings suffer[68], we must pursue ways to minimize suffering of *all* beings, regardless of their intentions towards our selves. This requires realizing and appreciating the fundamental principle of reality—that all things are because they are related to others, and sometimes those relations are ones of domination, repression, violence. Seeking independence is both futile and in fact perpetuates unjust relationships. The challenge is to balance all relationships so as to minimize suffering of all involved. Or, to eliminate domination, repression and other kinds of violence from all relations: with Others, nature, time and self. As Tagore observes, this is no easy task.

> Freedom in the mere sense of independence has no content, and therefore no meaning. Perfect freedom lies in a perfect harmony of relationship, which we realize in this world not through our response to it in knowing, but in being. Objects of knowledge maintain an infinite distance from us who are the knowers. For knowledge is not union. Therefore the further world of freedom awaits us there where we reach truth, not through feeling it by our senses or knowing it by our reason, but through the union of perfect sympathy.[69]

Thus, one of the most fundamental principles of a religious approach to problems of violence is compassion. This compassion is both "with-suffering" (*com-passio*, Late Latin) (sometimes associated with "pity"—or the negative aspect), and "with-feeling" (*Mit-gefühl*, German, or *soucit*, Czech) (maximal affective emotional identification—or the positive aspect). Compassion is realized through unconditional love. Such love manifests itself only through non-violent thought, speech and action. Violence as a strategic political option is eliminated. Self-defence is allowed only it it is non-violent in nature, because otherwise the religious creed of unconditional love would be broken by imposing and infringing upon others.[70] Even with the Truths of *syadvaad* and *anekantvaad* are maintained and revered by compassion *qua* unconditional love through non-violence.

Overall, *ahimsa* can no longer be regarded as a religious doctrine; it is a pragmatic political tool. Gandhi's conceptualization of *ahimsa* is a political code of postures and actions. If compassion were a central tenet of his understanding of *ahimsa* then there would be no alternative to non-violent action. There would be no "best" political strategy, nor a "second-best" option: violence. There would be no leakages and room for justifiable random acts of violence. Allowing the existence of a second-best option betrays his desire for *ahimsa* to be an all-encompassing and purely moral religious way of life. This shows that it is dangerous to believe unquestioningly all Gandhi's doctrines, advice, ethical stands and constructive programs. Thus, if we seek a religio-cultural way of (re)solving violent conflicts, Gandhi gives us a good start, but by no stretch of the imagination, is his conceptualization of *ahimsa* an end-all-be-all methodology.

References

1. This word plagues modern discourse because each person defines it differently, depending on the situation, assumptions, and ultimately desired outcomes.
2. Galtung, Johan. 1996. *Peace by Peaceful Means*. London: Sage Publications. p. 30.
3. Gandhi, M.K. 1940. *Harijan*. September 9. quoted in Gandhi's *The Message of the Gita*. 1959. Ahmedabad: Navajivan. p. 32.
4. Gandhi, M.K. 1932. "From Yeravda Mandir." in *The Selected Works of Mahatma Gandhi*, Volume IV. 1968. Ahmedabad: Navajivan. pp. 250-251.
5. "From Yeravda Mandir." op cit. p. 215.
6. Tagore, Rabindranath. 1988. *The Religion of Man*. New Delhi: Harper Collins. p. 52.
7. *Young India*. September 9, 1930.
8. *Young India*. September 9, 1930.
9. Gandhi, MK. 1933. *Speeches and Writings of Mahatma Gandhi*. Madras: G.A. Natesan & Co. p. 130.
10. Fromm, Erich. 1976. *To Have or To Be?*. London: Abacus. p. 107.
11. Gandhi, MK. 1948. *Non-violence in Peace and War*. Ahmedabad: Navajivan Press. I: p. 282.
12. Gandhi, MK. 1946. *Harijan*. March 3. p. 28.
13. Radhakrishnan. 1927. *The Hindu View of Life*. New Delhi: Harper Collins. p. 35.

14. Gandhi's life and ideas must be considered within the historical and religious moment. What is discussed here acknowledges this imperative and admist that it is not fully included in this paper.
15. Gandhi, MK. 1949. *Harijan*. March 27. p. 26. his emphasis.
16. Gandhi, MK. 1987. *The Essence of Hinduism*. Ahmedabad: Navajivan Press. p. 46.
17. Gandhi, MK. 1987. *The Essence of Hinduism*. Ahmedabad: Navajivan Press. p. 48.
18. Gandhi, MK. 1959. *Ashram Observances in Action*. Ahmedabad: Navajivan Press. Ch. 2.
19. *Harijan*. March 3, 1946.
20. From Yeravda Mandir. op cit. p. 215.
21. Gandhi, MK. 1968. *An Autobiography*. in *The Selected Works of Mahatma Gandhi*. Ahmedabad: Navajivan Press. Vol. II. p. 524.
22. *Harijan*. February 11, 1939.
23. Tagore. op cit. p. 41. His emphasis.
24. *An Autobiography*. op cit. p. 752.
25. *Young India*. November 12, 1925.
26. Radhakrishnan. op cit. p. 24.
27. *Young India*. December 4, 1924.
28. Gandhi, M.K. 1968. *Satyagraha in South Africa*. in *The Selected Works of Mahatma Gandhi*. Ahmedabad: Navajivan Press. Vol. III. p. 217.
29. *Harijan*. June 2, 1946.
30. Galtung, Johann. 1992. *The Way is the Goal*. Ahmedabad: Navajivan Press. p. 76.
31. *Young India*. September 11, 1930.
32. *Young India*. October 13, 1921.
33. As quoted in Richards, Jerald. 1995. "Gandhi's Qualified Acceptance of Violence." *Acorn*. Fall. p. 10.
34. As quoted in Fiore, Karen K. 1995. "Was Gandhi a Feminist?" *Acorn*. Fall. p. 24.
35. *Harijan*. June 28, 1946.
36. *Harijan*. April 2, 1938.
37. *Harijan*. September 5, 1939.
38. Prabhu, R. K. and U. R. Rao. 1967. *The Mind of Mahatma Gandhi*. Ahmedabad: Navajivan Press. p. 119.
39. *Young India*. October 12, 1926.
40. As quoted in Richards. op cit. p. 11.
41. *Harijan*. January 28, 1939.
42. *Harijan*. December 14, 1947.
43. Fromm. op cit.
44. *Harijan*. September 8, 1946.
45. Gandhi, MK. 1961. "The Gospel of Renunciation." Pamphlet. Ahmedabad: Navajivan Press. p. 5.

46. Gandhi, MK. 1968. "Ethical Religion." Pamphlet. Ahmedabad: Navajivan Press. p. 10.
47. Gandhi. "Ethical Religion." op cit. p. 7.
48. Iyer, Raghavan, N. 1973. *The Moral and Political Thought of Mahatma Gandhi*. New York: Oxford University Press. p. 159.
49. As quoted in Richards. op cit. pp. 5-6.
50. See Richards. op cit. pp. 8-13.
51. As quoted in Erikson, Erik. *Gandhi's Truth*. New York: Cambridge Univervisity Press. 1967. p. 374.
52. Richards. op cit. p. 7.
53. *Young India*. August 11, 1920.
54. *Young India*. September 13, 1928.
55. *Harijan*. April 9, 1938.
56. In Richards. op cit. p. 10.
57. In Richards. op cit. p. 10.
58. *Harijan*. June 28, 1942.
59. *Harijan*. September 15, 1946.
60. *Harijan*. December 24, 1938.
61. Erikson. op cit.
62. *Young India*. August 12, 1926.
63. *Harijan*. October 27, 1946.
64. In Prabhu & Rao. op cit. p. 140.
65. *Young India*. August 11, 1920.
66. Galtung. 1992. op cit. p. 24.
67. Fromm. op cit.
68. The Dalai Lama. 1995. *The Power of Compassion*. New Delhi: Harper Collins. p. 2.
69. Tagore. op cit. p. 106.
70. This argument is challenged by James Sterba. He shows how self-defence may actually be in the interests of the aggressing party, or at least, how violent self-defence is justified within a non-violent paradigm. (Citation forthcoming).

8

The Faltering Giants: Martin Buber and Mohandas Gandhi

> "We do not enter into dialogue to produce an agreement, but to produce real relationship, even friendship, which is premised upon mutual understanding, not upon agreement... [An] aim of dialogue is to understand ourselves and our faith more clearly. Dialogue is not a debate between two positions, but a truth-seeking encounter." (Eck, 197-198)

For many people around the world, the search for truth is a life-long pursuit. Some seek truth through individual meditation, others through dialogue. Martin Buber and Mohandas Gandhi are two great intellectuals of this past century who deeply influenced the way their communities sought truth. Their influence transcended their own communities and touched the lives of many others around the world. At one point, these two men attempted to engage in dialogue directly to better understand how best to stand against to the emerging evil in Europe, and the nascent Jewish state. This paper explores this attempt at dialogue. But as this story will show, evidence leading to concrete conclusions is elusive about why they said what they did, thus this is a speculative analysis and should be seen as my attempt to engage in dialogue with these two men's lives.

Gandhi (1869-1948) and Buber (1878-1965) lived during extraordinary change in the world. During the first half of the twentieth century there were huge waves of increased nationalism that pressured for independent national homelands. Two world wars wreaked havoc throughout the globe as countries sought to exercise their presumed right to sovereignty and self-determination. The number of nation-states nearly doubled within the first fifty years of this century. Among the ones that emerged after World War II were India (1947) and

This chapter has been written jointly by Jonathan K. Crane & Yoder Joan B. Kroc.

Israel (1948). But besides the political realm, Gandhi and Buber lived to see societies become dependent on electricity, the industrial revolution boom and bust and boom again, transportation and communication technologies evolve, and weapons of mass destruction be used against innocents.

Both of these men showed promise early on as intellectuals. Gandhi went to Britain to study law, where he also engaged in Christianity and other experiments. He then worked in South Africa and helped gain civil and political rights for Indians there. From 1920-1948 he masterminded India's non-violent independence movement from British rule. Buber studied languages, art, politics, education and theology in Germany and Switzerland. From 1913-1933 Buber taught and wrote in Germany, advocating the possibility that Jews can live peaceably with Germans in Germany.[1] He then emigrated to Israel, taught at Hebrew University, and supported spiritual and cultural Zionism.[2]

These men were similar in many ways. They both were highly educated and well-versed in theologies and politics. Though Gandhi was more politically active than Buber, both were prone to speaking their opinions on political matters. They also had religious backgrounds that included existential elements, they both experimented with other religions, and they both became religious leaders of varying degrees during their lives. Both spoke of engaging enemies as fellow human beings to bring about understanding and resolve conflicts. Most profound, I think, is not how they became revered and respected in their own communities, but how peoples outside their communities looked to them for spiritual, political, and social guidance.[3] One could almost expect similar statements from each on issues regarding Jews in Nazi Germany and the struggle for a national homeland for Jews.

This paper explores what these men said about those topics, and seeks explanations as to why they somehow spoke past each other. An analysis of their exchange of thoughts in 1939 precedes a brief survey of the religious, particularly mystical, influences on these men. A discussion of their religious philosophy of dialogue follows. The latter part of the paper offers speculations as to why these men disagreed, and possible indications as to why one of them, or maybe both, did not fully integrate his thoughts into his own religio-mystical or philosophical groundings.

The Exchange

In 1930, Buber is well aware of Gandhi and writes "Gandhi, Politics and Us"[4] expressing his admiration of Gandhi's struggles in South Africa and India. Though impressed by Gandhi's political activism, Buber is wary of adopting Gandhi's fervor and tactics for political struggles outside India. Buber challenges Gandhi's attempt to "introduce religion into politics" (128) by arguing that Gandhi's struggles are manifestly religious in nature and Gandhi gave them political intent (131). For Buber, "religion means goal and way, politics implies end and means" (128).

> The political end is recognizable by the fact that it may be attained—in success—and its attainment is historically recorded. The religious goal remains, even in man's[5] highest experiences of the mortal way, that which simply provides direction; it never enters into historical consummation. (128)

If political ends are attainable states of existence, then the introduction of religious ways (or pathways) "runs the danger, therefore, that the categories will mingle, that the goal will become and end, the way a means; that man, instead of treading in the path taken by that step of God through history, will run blindly over it" (131).

To maintain the integrity of politics and religion, Buber urges the recognition that "we can only work on the kingdom of God through working on all the spheres of man that are allotted to us" (137). Thus, there should be no *one* political means to serve this purpose. "There is no legitimately messianic, no legitimately messianically-intended, politics" (137). But, as all human endeavours should seek to hallow all things, Buber concludes that "we cannot prepare the messianic world, we can only prepare for it" (137). He urges that we look to Gandhi as a teacher about how to prepare for the messianic world, but that "we cannot simply follow in his steps" (137).

It was not until 1938-39 that an exchange of thoughts regarding the escalating violence in Europe and the struggles for a Jewish homeland occurred between Gandhi and Buber. In November, 1938, Gandhi wrote a column in *Harijan*, responding to letters asking his perspective on "the Arab-Jew question in Palestine and the persecution of the Jews in Germany" (39).[6] Gandhi begins by expressing his sympathies for the Jews:

> Religious sanction has been involved in both cases of the inhuman treatment meted out to them. Apart from the friendships, therefore, there is the more common universal reason for my sympathy for the Jews.... My sympathies are all with the Jews.... The parallel between their treatment by Christians and the treatment of untouchables by Hindus is very close. (39)

But he qualifies his sympathy, saying "my sympathy does not blind me to the requirements of justice" (39). Sympathy, for Gandhi, does not eliminate the need for upholding justice.

On Germany and the Holocaust, Gandhi expresses his revulsion of Hitler and suggests that still in the face of Hitler Jews ought not to feel helpless. He sees evil in how Hitler "is propounding a new religion of exclusive and militant nationalism, in the name of which any inhumanity becomes an act of humanity to be rewarded here and hereafter" (40). He then turns to the situation of the Jews and urges them not to feel helpless.

> Can the Jews resist this organized and shameless persecution? Is there a way to preserve their self-respect, and not to feel helpless, neglected and forlorn? I submit there is. No person who has faith in a living God need feel helpless or forlorn. Jehovah of the Jews is a God more personal than the God of the Christians, the Mussalmans or the Hindus, though as a matter of fact in essence, He is common to all and one without a second and beyond description. But as the Jews attribute personality to God and believe that He rules every action of theirs, they ought not to feel helpless. (41)

As Germany is "showing to the world how efficiently violence can be worked when it is not hampered by any hypocrisy," Gandhi believes that violently opposing this evil would be justified.

> If there ever could be justifiable war in the name of and for humanity, a war against Germany, to prevent the wanton persecution of a whole race, would be completely justified. But I do not believe in any war. A discussion of the pros and cons of such a war is therefore outside my horizon or province. (41)

As quickly as he suggests using violence to challenge Germany, Gandhi retreats behind his beliefs that all war is unjust, and since he seeks to uphold justice, he cannot address this topic.

Regarding the Jewish struggle for a national homeland, Gandhi decides to side with Palestinians. "The cry for the national homeland for the Jews does not make much appeal to me. Why should [Jews] not like other peoples of the earth, make that country their home where they are born and where they earn their livelihood?" (39-40). He argues that what is going on in Palestine[7] "cannot be justified by any moral code of conduct.... Surely it would be a crime against humanity to reduce the proud Arabs so that Palestine can be restored to the Jews partly or wholly as their national home" (40). He considers Jewish reliance on British military assistance an unnecessary evil, and that Jews "can settle Palestine only by the goodwill of the Arabs. They should seek to convert the Arab heart" (44). Gandhi rhetorically questions how Jews outside Palestine will take to the existence of a Jewish homeland:

> If the Jews have no home but Palestine, will they relish the idea of being forced to leave the other parts of the world in which they are settled? Or do they want a double home where they can remain at will? (40)

Gandhi then sets down his conclusion: "Palestine belongs to the Arabs in the same sense that England belongs to the English, of France to the French. It is wrong and inhuman to impose the Jews on the Arabs" (40).

On the other hand, Gandhi does not defend the "Arab excesses" (Green, 265).[8] He says of the Arabs, "I wish they had chosen the way of non-violence in resisting what they rightly regarded as an unwarranted encroachment upon their country" (*ibid.*, 265). He emphasizes his allegiance with Arabs by adding the word, "rightly," as he, too, interprets Jewish settlement in Palestine as morally reprehensible. He goes on to condone extant violent and non-violent Arab resistance, "But according to the accepted canons of right and wrong, nothing can be said against the Arab resistance in the face of overwhelming odds" (*ibid.*, 265).

Gandhi urges Jews to use non-violence to pursue their political ends. For Jews in Germany, he believes they can look to Indians in South Africa for an "exact parallel" *satyagraha* campaign.

> There the Indians occupied precisely the same place that the Jews occupy in Germany. The persecution had also a religious tinge.... There too the Indians were consigned to ghettos described as locations. The other disabilities were almost of the same type as those of the Jews in Germany. The Indians, a mere handful, resorted to satyagraha without any backing from the world outside or the Indian Government... But the Jews of Germany can offer satyagraha under definitely better auspices than the Indians of South Africa. The Jews are a compact, homogeneous community in Germany. They are far more gifted than the Indians of South Africa. And they have organized world opinion behind them. (Buber 1939, 42-43)

Gandhi expresses his belief in the strength of a non-violent *satyagraha* campaign against Hitler and the Nazi regime.

> I am convinced that if someone with courage and vision can arise among them and lead them in non-violent action, the winter of their despair can in the twinkling of an eye be turned into the summer of hope. And what today has become a degrading man-hunt can be turned into a calm and determined stand offered by unarmed men and women possessing the strength of suffering given to them by Jehovah. It will be then a truly religious resistance offered against the godless fury of dehumanized man. The German Jews will score a lasting victory over the German Gentiles in the sense that they will have converted the latter to an appreciation of human dignity. They will have rendered service to fellow Germans and proved their title to be the real Germans against those who are today dragging, however unknowingly, the German name into the mire. (43-44)

He even gives a hypothetical situation where he projects himself as a Jew in Germany facing the evil directly:

> If I were a Jew and were born in Germany and earned my livelihood here I would claim Germany as my home even as the tallest gentile German may, and challenge him to shoot me or cast me in the dungeon; I would refuse to be expelled

> or to submit to discriminating treatment. And for doing this I should not wait for the fellow Jews to join me in civil resistance, but would have confidence that in the end the rest are bound to follow my example. If one Jew or all the Jews were to accept the prescription here offered, he or they cannot be worse off than now. And suffering voluntarily undergone will bring them an inner strength and joy which no number of resolutions of sympathy passed in the world outside Germany can.... The calculated violence may even result in the general massacre of the Jews by way of [Hitler's] first answer to the declaration of such hostilities. But if the Jewish mind could be prepared for voluntary suffering, even the massacre I have imagined could be turned into a day of thanks giving and joy that Jehovah had wrought deliverance of the race even at the hands of the tyrant. For the God-fearing, death has no terror. (42)

Gandhi sees himself acting as a Jewish individual almost completely autonomous from the rest of the Jewish community. Furthermore, he imagines that his lone action would model for other Jews how to refuse such oppression. Insodoing, Gandhi calls for a Jewish non-violent campaign to bring about mass slaughter. He interprets the inevitable massacre both as deliverance (but he does not clarify deliverance to what) and as a day of thanksgiving (but he does not say who exactly would be alive to express thanksgiving).

In regards to the Palestinian campaign, Gandhi also urges the use of nonviolence, citing religious commonalties between Jews and Muslims as a motivating reason.

> The same God rules the Arab heart who rules the Jewish heart. They can offer satyagraha in front of the Arabs and offer themselves to be shot or thrown into the Dead Sea without raising a little finger against them. They will find world opinion in their favour in their religious aspirations. There are hundreds of ways of reasoning with the Arabs, if they will only discard the help of the British bayonets. (44)

As it is, Gandhi argues, the violent Jewish struggle in Palestine ascribes to Jews the evil of "despoiling a people who have done no wrong to them" (44). Overall, Gandhi challenges Jews to rise to their self-proclaimed status:

> Let the Jews who claim to be the chosen race prove their title by choosing the way of non-violence for vindicating their position on earth....[The Jew] can command the attention and respect of the world by being man, the chosen creation of God, instead of being man who is fast sinking to the brute and forsaken by God. They can add to their many contributions the surpassing contribution of nonviolent action. (Green, 265)

Buber took several months to respond to Gandhi's exposition, finally sending a letter in late February, 1939, along with one written separately by his friend J.L. Magnes (then president of Hebrew University in Jerusalem).[9] Buber opens his letter with a brief anecdote about an unhappy person listening to someone who is purported to give good counsel but is ultimately left disappointed because what is said "is yet barren of all application to his peculiar circumstances" (Buber 1939, 1). In fact, "these words are in truth not applicable to him at all" (1). Buber asks Gandhi directly, "But you, the man of good will, do you not know that you must see him whom you address, in his place and circumstance, in the throes of his destiny?" (2)

Buber begins by discussing the Jewish plight in Germany in face of the Holocaust, and challenges Gandhi's recommendation to use Indians in South Africa as an example of a resistance struggle. Buber cites book burning and destruction of temples and things sacred to Jews by Germans as experiences Indians in South Africa did not have to suffer. He asks Gandhi if he knows "what a concentration camp is like and what goes on there? Do you know of the torments in the concentration camp, of its methods of slow and quick slaughter?" (4) Buber speculates, "I cannot assume that you know of this; for then this tragi-comic utterance 'almost of the same type' could scarcely have crossed your lips". (4) Buber admits that Indians in South Africa were definitely discriminated against,

> but they were not deprived of rights, they were not outlawed, they were not hostages for the coveted attitude of foreign

> powers. And do you think perhaps that a Jew in Germany could pronounce one single sentence of a speech such as yours without being knocked down? (4)

Buber concludes that it is not convincing to "observe *satyagraha* in Germany on these similarities of circumstance". (4)

In regards to the Jewish struggle for a national homeland in Palestine, Buber expounds at length challenging Gandhi's arguments. Unlike Indians in South Africa who could look to India as a cultural and spiritual motherland, Jews do not (at this time) have a place to call home. In essence, Jews are in exile.

> Dispersion is bearable: it can be purposeful, if somewhere there is ingathering, a growing home center, a piece of earth wherein one is in the midst of an ingathering and not in the dispersion and from whence the spirit of ingathering may work its way out to all the places of the dispersion. When there is this, there is also a striving, common life, the life of a community, which dares to live to-day because it hopes to live tomorrow. But when this growing center, this increasing process of ingathering is lacking, dispersion becomes dismemberment. On this criterion the question of our Jewish destiny is indissolubly bound up with the possibility of ingathering and this in Palestine. (7)

Buber emphasizes that "every nation has a right to demand the possession of a living heart," paralleling his statement in his 1923 book *I-Thou,*

> The true community does not arise through people having feelings for one another (though indeed not without it), but through, first, their taking their stand in living mutual relation with a living Center, and second, their being in living mutual relation with one another. (Buber 1958, 45)

He accuses Gandhi of being concerned only "with the 'right of possession' on the one side: you do not consider the right to a piece of free land on the other side—for those who are hungering for it" (16).

Buber also notices a double standard in Gandhi's remarks.

> You reproach us, that, having no army of our own, we consent to the British army preventing an occasional blind murder. But in view of the accepted canons [of right and wrong] you cast a lenient eye on those who carry murder into our ranks every day without even noticing who is hit. (18-19)

Buber argues that Jews began to settle in Palestine well before the "shadow of the British gun" arrived, and that Jews did not want the British to be there in the first place (19). Jews in Palestine "do not want force" (19). According to Buber, by remaining silent on the issue of Arab violence against Jews in Palestine Gandhi tacitly endorses Arab violence on Jews, yet he explicitly condemns Jewish reliance on British protection, and occasional self-defense. Nevertheless, Buber does envision, like Gandhi, a possible solution to the problem.

> We cannot renounce the Jewish claim; something even higher than the life of our people is bound up with the Land, namely the work which is their[10] divine mission. But we have been and still are convinced that it must be possible to find some form of agreement between this claim and the other; for we love this land and we believe in its future; and, seeing that such love and such faith are surely present also on the other side, a union in the common service of the Land must be within the range of the possible. Where there is faith and love, a solution may be found even to what appears to be a tragic contradiction. (12-13)

Buber describes the Jewish wish of co-habitation with Arabs thus:

> The Jewish peasants have begun to teach their brothers, the Arab peasants, to cultivate the land more intensively; we desire to teach them further: together with them we want to cultivate the land—to 'serve' it as the Hebrew has it. The more fertile this soil becomes, the more space there will be for us and for them. We have no desire to dispossess them:

> we want to live with them. We do not want to rule, we want to serve with them. (17)

Co-service would bring about a "genuine peace" in which "both people should together develop the Land without the one imposing his will on the other" (12).

Though Gandhi discusses the use of *satyagraha* and non-violence in both Germany and Palestine, Buber responds by addressing the concept of non-violence from a more conceptual level. Buber reflects back to his time spent in Germany before his emigration in 1933:

> I observed many instances of genuine Satyagraha among the Jews, instances showing a strength of spirit wherein there was no question of bartering their rights or of being bowed down, and where neither force nor cunning was used to escape the consequences of their behaviour. Such actions, however, exerted apparently not the slightest influence on their opponents. (4)

Jewish non-violent resistance *did* exist, contrary to Gandhi's beliefs, but the few efforts were snuffed out and, as history shows, no mass campaign emerged.[11] Buber explains how Jewish non-violent resistance, no matter how hypothetical or real, would be ineffective against Germany.

> An effective stand may be taken in the form of non-violence against unfeeling human beings in the hope of gradually bringing them to their senses; but a diabolic universal steam-roller cannot thus be withstood. There is a certain situation in which from the "Satyagraha" of the strength of the spirit no "Satyagraha" of the power of truth can result. The word "Satyagraha" signifies testimony. Testimony without acknowledgment, ineffective, unobserved martyrdom, a martyrdom cast to the winds—that is the fate of innumerable Jews in Germany. God alone accepts their testimony, God "seals" it, as is said in our prayers. But no maxim for suitable behaviour can be deduced therefrom. Such martyrdom is a deed—but who would venture to demand it? (5)

Buber then puts a test case to himself, that when in the face of evil, like Germany, he will resist the evil. But he will resist by doing whatever is necessary, even if it includes the use of force.

> For I cannot help withstanding evil when I see that it is about to destroy the good. I am forced to withstand the evil in the world just as the evil within myself. I can only strive not to have to do so by force. I do not want force. But if there is no other way of preventing the evil destroying the good, I trust I shall use force and give myself up into God's hands. (21)

(As an aside, hopefully Buber would not have used force to resist evil within himself, as committing violence against the body is condemned by Jewish law).

Buber reminds Gandhi that the Gandhi declared India should, too, use force to rid itself of evil.

> But after the resolutions of Delhi, at the beginning of March 1922, you yourself, Mahatma Gandhi, wrote: "Have I not repeatedly said that I would have India become free even by violence rather than that she should remain in bondage?" This was a very important pronouncement on your part: you asserted thereby that non-violence for you a faith and not a political principle—and that the desire for the freedom of India is ever stronger in you than your faith. And for this, I love you. (19)

Buber understands that Gandhi was not advocating the use of force from the outset. Rather, the two agree on the presumption against violence, and the pursuit of peace should come through justice (though Gandhi believes such a pursuit should be done by peaceful means). Buber continues:

> We do not want force. We have not proclaimed, as did Jesus, the son of our people, and as you do, the teaching of non-violence, because we believe that a man must sometimes use force to save himself or even more his children. But from time immemorial we have proclaimed the teaching of

> justice and peace: we have taught and we have learnt that peace is the aim of all the world and that justice is the way to attain it. Thus we cannot desire to use force. No one who counts himself in the ranks of Israel can desire to use force. (19-20)

Buber frames his ultimate disposition regarding the pursuit of justice: "If I am to confess what is the truth to me, I must say: There is nothing better for a man than to deal justly—unless it be to love; we should be able even to fight for justice—but to fight lovingly" (21). Facing this conundrum of wanting justice, peace, and a homeland, Buber pleads for assistance, particularly Gandhi's. "In order to carry out a task of such extreme difficulty... we are in need of the support of well-meaning persons of all nations, and we had hope of such" (13). "We should seek, as you [Gandhi] say, to convert the heart of the Arab. Well then—help us to do so! [For this task] of conversion we need your help!" (18)

From this brief synopsis of Gandhi's and Buber's statements, it is clear they agree on some issues, but differ on others. It seems they talk past each other, where assumptions made by one are profoundly in contrast to the other's. Buber says to Gandhi, "Our one desire is that at last we may obey" God's commandment to live in Palestine (10). Gandhi does not address this commandment, but does address *how* the Jews are settling in Palestine, "I have no doubt that they are going about it the wrong way" (44). This is but one example of how these two influential intellectuals try to engage in dialogue to find truth, but in their attempt they are on different wavelengths. Buber asks Gandhi, "Of what significance is it to point to a certain something in common when such differences are overlooked?"(4) I believe that reasons behind this miscommunication stem from their religious experiences, including the influence mystical religions had on them, and their philosophies of dialogue. As mystical religions are elusive and shrouded in paradoxes, understanding how these men based their life and works on these teachings will also remain a mystery. Nevertheless, exploring their mystical religious backgrounds and philosophies of dialogue may shed light on how they viewed the world, and how people, specifically the Jews in Germany and Palestine, should engage in resolving their conflicts.

Mystical Religious Influences and The Concept of Relativism

One of the main characteristics of mystical religions is the belief that everything is imbued with holiness, all is God, and God can be experienced through relating to all as sacred elements. This theme is evident in the mystical traditions of Gandhi and Buber. In this section I briefly explore the mystical influences on Gandhi and Buber and discuss their views on relativism. Hopefully some pieces to the puzzle of why these men disagree on the above issues may come to light.

Gandhi's background is rooted in Hinduism. Within Hinduism there are many mystical strains, but of which Vaishnavism and Jainism had the greatest influence on him. Vaishnavism is a kind of monistic theology, believing that the "Supreme Soul is a loving personal god, from which matter and the individual proceed, but which remains distinct from them; through *bhakti* one returns to the bosom of God, yet the soul retains its separate identity" (Parrinder, 225). Jainism takes the Vaishnavism belief and adds a twist: perpetual change. Thus all the changes and transformations occurring in reality are sacred, including the changes within souls even though souls are eternal in scope. The Jain law of *karma* dictates pursuing passionless acts not for a better body or life, but for the betterment of the soul. This law requires five vows: non-violence (*ahimsa*), truthfulness, non-stealing, chastity (within the vows of marriage), and non-attachment (the limitations of worldly goods) (Parrinder, 241-249).

A central piece of Hindu theology is the Upanishadic teachings. Attainment of *moksha* (or ultimate release and absolute freedom) comes through one's "own existential realization of the identity of *Atman*[12] and *Brahma*"[13] (Puligandla, 142). This realization comes in the form of knowledge, and thus must be pursued in this life (here and now), and not postponed until after death—when knowledge cannot be acquired (Puligandla, 139-143). In the process of identifying with *Atman* and *Brahma* it is logical to diminish all selfishness, and the best way to do so is through *ahimsa*. Gandhi gives a translation for the four *mantras* of the Upanishads:

(1) All this that we see in this great universe is pervaded by God.

(2 & 3) Renounce it and enjoy it. There is another rendering which means the same thing, though: Enjoy what He gives you.

(4) Do not covet anybody's wealth or possession. (Gandhi 1961, 4)

Gandhi interprets these *mantras* in light of the process of renunciation:

> If you believe that God pervades everything that He has created, you must believe that you cannot enjoy anything that is not given by Him. And seeing that He is the Creator of His numberless children, it follows that you cannot covet anybody's possession. If you think that you are one of his numerous creatures, it behooves you to renounce everything and lay it at His feet. That means that the act of renunciation of everything is not a mere physical renunciation but represents a second or new birth. It is a deliberate act, not done in ignorance. It is therefore regeneration. (Gandhi 1961, 5)

But these acts of renunciation should be intentional, because only through *intentionally* meaning to do good does an act become moral (Gandhi 1968, 10). However, "the result of an action is not within our control" (ibid., 11). But since we have no control over outcomes, one must intentionally try the *best* path, or way, to attain morality.

> In other words, when we know a particular path to be the right one, we should set out on it without fear. We can progress only if we observe the laws of morality in this way. That is why true morality, true civilization and true progress are always to be found together. (ibid., 7)

In essence, because there is no way to predict outcomes, the best option is to do moral acts (like intentional renunciation and *ahimsa*) and if morality and truth are not results, changing one's path is required (Iyer, 159).

Gandhi was also influenced by Christianity, especially while he was living in Britain studying law. He views the Sermon on the Mount as the whole of Christianity (Green, 158-160). "As the miraculous birth is an eternal event, so is the Cross an eternal event in this stormy life. Therefore, we dare not think of birth without death on the Cross. Living Christ means a living Cross. Without it life is a living death" (ibid., 160). For Gandhi, it is evident that living intentionally and seeking truth through identifying with the holiness in everything is a fundamental foundation in his worldview.

Buber's mystical experiences stem from his explorations of Jewish mysticism, particularly Hasidism[14], and oriental traditions. As Jewish mysticism "seeks at its end personal union with God, achieved through spiritual exercise, meditation and contemplation...[there is] a social messianic purpose behind this aspiration for union—a belief that the mystic can influence God in his way with the world, and so hasten the time of redemption" (Parrinder, 400). It is interesting to note that in this tradition Jews can actually exert influence on God and are not just passive sacred beings in God's world. Hasidic mysticism preaches "the striving for communion with God through the cultivation and experience of joyful fervor in prayer, study, and the natural world" (ibid., 401). It's essential message is that "God can be seen in everything and reached by every pure deed" (Henry, 379).

Hasidism yearns for the manifestation of peace, particularly through reconciliation and the realization that justice and peace are necessary complements of each other. Hasidic conception of social justice can be seen in its interpretation of "an eye for an eye and a tooth for a tooth":

> (It) is not the expression of a vengeful God, but a primitive statement of basic social democracy in which no person is held of greater worth than another, because each is created in the image of God. (Friedman 1994, 41)

Love, also, is a key element in Hasidic conception of reconciliation, and it fosters dialogue:

> The 'hallowing of the everyday' means making the concrete relations of one's life essential, and real relationship includes both mutuality and passion. Mutuality means that love does not simply flow forth from the loving person to others; rather, it moves back and forth within the dialogue between them as the fullest expression of that dialogue. (ibid., 42)

> Hasidic realism recognizes that true love and true reconciliation cannot be based upon altruism and selflessness and self-denial, but only upon genuine dialogue, real mutual contact and trust between men. (ibid., 43)

But the pursuit of genuine dialogue does "not call upon man to be saintly but to be 'humanly holy' unto God—in the measure and manner of men and women, who approach God not by reaching beyond the human but by becoming human" (ibid., 43). Becoming human does not take place through "formulae or through any kind of prescribed and special action, but through the *kavana*, or intention, that one brings to one's every act" (ibid., 41). In essence, Hasidic mysticism, like Hindi mysticisms, also leads people to experiences of the holy through intentional just acts.

Buber's curiosity about other mystical religions led him to explore Hinduism, Buddhism, Taoism and Zen, of which Buddhism and Zen especially sparked his imagination. Through a comparative dialogue with these mysticisms, Buber found "Hasidism is the one mysticism in which history remains important, the one mysticism where the seemingly incompatible spheres of revelation and illumination do meet" (Friedman 1981, 162). Buber speaks of time in Zen:

> The [Hasid's] activity with things is not like the activity of a Zen monk, something that only accompanies seeing into his own nature; rather it is permeated with independent religious meaning. The realism of Zen is dialectical, it means annulment; Hasidic realism is Messianic, it means fulfilment. As in its covenant with revelation it regards the past, so in its covenant with redemption it regards the future—both in contrast to Zen, for which unconditional reality is accorded only to the moment since in it is the possibility of inner illumination. Before the moment, thus understood, the dimension of time disappears. Hasidism, so far as I see, is the only mysticism in which time is hallowed. (Buber 1988:239, as quoted in Gross, 6)

Buber also looks to oriental mysticisms for examples of how to expand one's identity to include all creation, and therefore eliminate the existence of enemies.[15] As Friedman concludes his analysis of Buber's exploratory dialogue with these mysticisms, "The way of

Taoism, like the way of Zen Buddhism and of Hasidism, is *inner* and *outer* both, and it is *between*" (Friedman 1981, 170).

What is clear from both mystical backgrounds of Gandhi and Buber is a conception that everything is sacred and *can*, through intentional moral deeds, be included in ones own identity. Yet, as an individual seeks to gain this enlightened, or existential, identity, there remains the reality of multiples—that not everything is of one identity or mind. Thus there exist different perspectives, or worldviews, and all are relative to each individual. Gandhi recommends that to pursue the unification of identity (to reach *moksha*), one must seek the truth:

> We are members one of another, and influence one another by our actions. Actions here include thoughts, so that not a single thought is without its effect. Therefore we must cultivate the habit of always thinking good thoughts. I say that truth is God not because God is without form and so is truth, but because truth is the only comprehensive attribute of God.... By looking upon truth as God we steer clear of quite a number of dangers. We lose all interest in seeing or hearing about miracles. Seeing God is difficult to understand; but seeing truth presents no such difficulty. Seeing truth is indeed a hard task, but as we approach nearer and nearer to truth we catch a glimpse of the God of truth, so that we hope to have a full view in His good time and our faith also burns brighter and brighter. (Gandhi 1987, 82-3)

While the supreme human endeavour is the pursuit of *satya*, truth, Gandhi recognizes that truth is not absolute or eternal—but relative, relative for each individual at each moment in time (Iyer, 162). As Gandhi always felt he had never found the absolute truth, he admits, "thus I must hold to the relative truth as I have conceived it" (Gandhi 1957, 6). Implicit in this statement "was his belief that all actions contained an element of error. Therefore, all positions, that of opponents as well as one's own, should be treated with equal consideration" (Chadda, 150). Gandhi summarizes his belief in relativism as follows: "Evil and good are relative terms. What is good under certain conditions can become an evil or a sin under a different set of conditions" (as quoted in Iyer, 206). While in a society there can be consensus about the desired ultimate end, Gandhi's philosophy allows multiplicity of ways to pursue the ultimate (Iyer, 69). "The crucial thing for Gandhi is not to teach people what is right, nor lead them to examine and criticize their convictions, but to get them to do what they know they ought to do" (ibid.). Thus Gandhi believe that there are many ways to pursue good and the ultimate truth, done through intentional deeds.

Buber, also, believes in the relativity of truth and multiplicity of ways to pursue peace. He states that when relative truths meet in dialogue, the *between* is where unity, and the mystery of life, exists.

> According to the logical conception of truth only one of two contraries can be true, but in the reality of life as one lives it they are inseparable. The person who makes a decision knows that his deciding is no self-delusion; the person who has acted knows that he was and is in the hand of God. The unity of the contraries is the mystery at the innermost core of the dialogue. (Buber, in Friedman 1960, 3)

His statement, "we can only prepare for the messianic world" reveals his belief that there is no *one* way to set about preparing. Thus, as each situation is different and as each person's experience is different, political decisions and even ethical stances ought to be unique and not absolute doctrines (Henry, 382).

If there are no absolutes, that is—no *one absolute* way to pursue the absolute, there is, it seems, room for these two intellectuals to agree to disagree on how Jews should best go about resolving their problems. Rather, each man speaks to the other as if he were stating an obvious absolute: Gandhi—non-violence in face of any evil; Buber—violence in face of injustice. Grob asks a painful question at this situation: "In a contest between 'absolutes' how are we to declare a winner?" (Grob 1986, 82). Edward Said refocuses the question, asking "*the* basic question for the intellectual: how does one speak the truth? What truth? For whom and where?" (Said, 88) The absolutes these men advocate are absolutes for *him*, from *his own* perspective, and thus the truths they espouse are true for him in his own circumstance. Said challenges these two men as intellectuals to step up and recognize their own relative truths:

> In the secular world, human beings construct their truths, and that, for example, the so-called objective truth of the white man's superiority built and maintained by the classical

> European colonial empires also rested on a violent subjugation of African and Asian peoples, who, it is equally true, fought that particular imposed 'truth' in order to provide an independent order of their own. And so now everyone comes forward with new and often violently opposed views of the world: one hears endless talk about Judaeo-Christian values, Afrocentric values, Muslim truths, Eastern truths, Western truths, each providing a complete program for excluding all others. (Said, 91. Emphasis added.)

Eck also challenges these men, as "what is true is always 'true for' someone, for there is always a point of view" (Eck, 193). In light of spiritual truths, she adds, "matters of truth and value are relative to our conceptual framework and worldview, even those matters of truth that we speak of as divinely ordained" (ibid.). If the world is full of relative truths, then through dialogue, or the meaningful encounter with others, can morality be created.

Religious Philosophy of Dialogue

Both Gandhi and Buber sought to engage others in dialogue to bring about morality, peace, justice, and reveal holy truths. Each developed mechanisms they employed in dialogue, nonviolence for Gandhi, and a mental construct I-Thou for Buber. These tools helped each expand his own identity so that it would be difficult for someone to be outside their realm of relation — that is, that each would have fewer 'enemies.'

Gandhi's non-violence was based on *satyagraha*, or the ceaseless pursuit of the ideal unification of all. As observed above, *ahimsa*[16], or non-violence, is the best and only way for *satyagraha*. Violence is often conceived of as turning people into objects, *ahimsa*, in opposition to violence, is the process to engage all as subjects—the essence of dialogue (Henry, 380-1). *Ahimsa* encourages both sympathy toward an enemy, and also "the denial of the very existence of an enemy" (Iyer, 180). Gandhi explains that *ahimsa* is more than just love, but is the expansion of one's identity:

> In [ahimsa's] negative form it means not injuring any living being whether by body or mind. I may not, therefore, hurt the person of any wrong-doer or bear any ill-will to him and so cause him mental suffering. This statement does not cover

> suffering caused to the wrong-doer by natural acts of mine which do not proceed from ill-will.... Ahimsa requires deliberate self-suffering, not a deliberate injuring of the supposed wrong-doer.... In its positive form, Ahimsa means the largest love, the greatest charity. If I am a follower of Ahimsa, I must love my enemy or a stranger to me as I would my wrong-doing father or son. This active Ahimsa necessarily includes truth and fearlessness. (Gandhi in Iyer, 179-80)

As people sometimes are wrong-doers and sometimes not, relations fluctuate. Gandhi says "non-violence takes account precisely of this dynamic and non-final state of all relationships among men, for non-violence seeks to change relationships that are evil into others that are good, or at least less bad" (Gandhi in Merton, 15). The surest way to transform a relationship from an evil to good one, or to engage another to become not one's enemy, Gandhi advocates the intentional expansion of one's identity:

> One can overcome evil by taking it upon oneself, whereas if one flies from it he is not certain to escape and may, even if he seems to escape, be overwhelmed. The only way to truly 'overcome' an enemy is to help him become other than an enemy. (Gandhi in Merton, 15.)

While there is no "half way between truth and non-violence on the one hand and untruth and violence on the other," Gandhi admits that "we may never be strong enough to be entirely non-violent in thought word and deed. But we must keep non-violence as our goal and make steady progress towards it" (Gandhi in Merton, 24). He argues, "no doubt the non-violent way is always the best, but where that does not come naturally the violent way is both necessary and honorable. Inaction there is rank cowardice and unmanly" (Gandhi in Iyer, 201). His statement that India should resort to arms to defend her honor "than that she should, in a cowardly manner, become or remain a helpless witness to her own dishonor" is a statement showing Gandhi's belief that *ahimsa* can be a policy choice, and not just an absolute, and that *himsa* is sometimes necessary (Chadda, 150). In Gandhi's view, "the man who starts justifying the use of force will become addicted to it, while the man who renounces it from the start may find that he has to come to terms with the practical limitations of non-violence, but he ceaselessly tries to reduce *himsa* and replace it by *ahimsa*" (Iyer, 207). Thus, for Gandhi, "the question was not one of establishing on philosophical grounds the absolute disvalue of violence and therefore the desirability of nonviolence; rather, it was a question of discovering what to do under specific circumstances" (Chadda, 150).

Like Gandhi, Buber believes the ultimate experience is relation. Of the two kinds of relations (I-It and I-Thou), the former is characterized by utility and objectification of the other. The essence of the I-Thou relation is mutuality, openness and spontaneity. Through I-Thou dialogue, one is always becoming, as each new moment and experience transforms both parties, and the relationship itself (Grob, 1983-84). The process of becoming facilitates revelation, and revelation is "neither objective knowledge nor subjective inspiration but happening, event—life lived in dialogue" (Friedman 1986, 50). Thus, according to Buber's philosophy, one should seek as many encounters with others as subjects as possible, because it is through those encounters one experiences revelation and steps closer to God:

> God, says Buber, is the eternal Thou of the human person. God is present whenever one meets one's fellow human beings or the world as Thou.... The manner in which we relate to nature, fellow human beings and God determines the quality of our lives.... Dialogue is not only awareness of the other but is something that demands responsibility to the other person. Responsibility means responding to the other person and answering the other person from the depths of one's being. (Henry, 380)

Intentional meeting with responsibility brings one closer to God, but "meeting with God does not come to man in order that he may concern himself with God, but in order that he may confirm that there is meaning in the world" (Buber 1958, 115). Such meaning comes from taking the risk to witness "with the fullness of our lives to the truth of dialogical encounter, to the 'between' as the locus of all meaning" (Grob, 83). But the ultimate responsibility for obtaining such meaning rests on each individual's shoulders, as each must "wring from each situation its maximum amount of divinity as we engage concretely in the work of what Buber calls the hallowing of the everyday" (ibid., 85). And all this can, and must, be achieved through dialogue, as Buber states:

> I believe, despite all, that the peoples in this hour can enter into dialogue, into a genuine dialogue, each of the partners, if even when he stands in opposition to the other, heeds, affirms, and confirms his opponent as an existing other. Only so can conflict certainly not be eliminated from the world, but be humanly arbitrated and led towards its overcoming. (Buber 1957, 238)

The philosophy of dialogue, pursued either through *ahimsa* and *satyagraha* or I-Thou encounters, confirms what Gandhi and Buber were taught from their mystical religious backgrounds: that *all life is sacred*. As Gandhi quips, "the essence of true religious teaching is that one should serve and befriend all. It is easy enough to be friendly to one's friends. But to befriend the one who regards himself as your enemy is the quintessence of true religion. The other is mere business" (Gandhi in Merton, 62). He continues, "For a nonviolent person, the whole world is one family. He will thus fear none, nor will others fear him" (ibid., 67). Buber echoes, "the world and I are mutually included, the one in the other. This contradiction in thought, inherent in the situation of *It*, is resolved in the situation of *Thou*, which sets me free from the world in order to bind me up in solidarity of connection with it" (Buber 1958, 1993-94). For Gandhi the "we" had to include one's opponents and enemies; for Buber, I-Thou had to include the world, and thus one's opponents and enemies as well (Eck, 209). Given this philosophy of dialogue led to an expanded sense of identity, and thus a greater ability to understand and empathize with another's plight, it is interesting to see how these two men barely use their own teachings in their exchange of letters to better understand from where the other was originating. Instead, it seems, each is content to accuse, indemnify and ignore the other's circumstance. What is most painful is not that these two great intellectuals talk past each other, but that the opportunity for a profound encounter between them is lost—an opportunity which may have revealed how close these two men really are, and how much they might have cooperated in addressing global grievances.

Expectations and Speculations

Instead we are left with Gandhi's observations and recommendations, and Buber's response. And not much else. Given that both intellectuals were similar (though, admittedly, very different in some fundamental ways) by the fact that both were well educated (by European schooling), both were at one point exiles even in their own homelands, both advocated reconciliation through non-force, both were sought advisers and teachers, both saw everything and everyone as sacred, both desired to expand his own identity to better engage and understand the world—one could expect that their approach to exchanging observations and recommendations on a particular topic would entail some efforts given by each to encompass the other's perspective, and also give similar, or at least on the same wavelength, conclusions. In reality, however, none of this happened.

While it is difficult to ascertain why another person does something, especially if that something is seemingly contrary to that person's worldview and philosophy, it is even more difficult to grasp solidly reasons why someone dead did something contrary to expectations. This is the case here. We may never know why exactly Gandhi and Buber chose to state the things they did. Nor may we even know why they chose not to enact their own philosophy of dialogue through attempting to see the world through the other's eyes, or fulfil their mystical religious teachings that all things are sacred and unified and should be revered as such. Here I can only speculate and offer some relevant explanations as to this happenstance.

While both did not live up to their own mysticisms or shared philosophy, we can apply fault to both. I believe, however, Gandhi bears a greater burden of proof for why he states the things he does. It seems Gandhi bases his statements on misinformation, or at least non-information, about the particular circumstances of Jews in Germany at this time. Despite his ignorance, he proffers recommendations that when hypothetically applied lead to defeat; but as these recommendations are based on non-information, their applicability, as Buber notes, are nil for Jews in Germany. Also, Gandhi's siding with Arabs on the question of Palestine reflects the pressures he is receiving domestically from the Hindu-Muslim tensions (Shimoni).[17] Gandhi's statements are political posturings, not recommendations based on conceptions of justice. In short, Gandhi is mixing politics into religion, just as Buber claims he is.

But there are other differences that may help explain why these intellectuals talk past each other. Both Gandhi and Buber were European-educated, and they were both influenced by where they were educated. Gandhi yearned to be similar to British gentlemen, and took on himself the behavioural patterns conducive to this (Gandhi, 1957). One aspect he integrated into his worldview is a British sense of honor and its corollary dignified means of interaction. Throughout the rest of his life, Gandhi always deferred to British authorities during wars (Anglo-Boer War, World War I, World War II) and even assisted them because it would have been wrong to challenge the British while they were already engaged otherwise — evidence of British conceptions of "fighting fair," and that it would be easier to engage in constructive dialogue with the British than with other foreign colonizers (e.g., Boers, Japan). Buber, on the other hand, was educated in central Europe and finally settled in Germany to teach. There he became identified with elite circles and associated with intellectuals revising sociological thought to reinvigorate German civil society and exercise the possibility that Jews and Germans could live peacefully together (Mendes-Flohr). Buber's pro-German Jewish efforts were thwarted by the emerging "Hitlerism," undermining Buber's sense of identity, pushing him into intellectual exile and eventual physical emigration.[18]

While Gandhi could, and did, look back on his schooling in Britain to shape his political and social attitudes and behaviours, Buber (by 1939) could, and did, not refer back to his. Also, because of Britain's sense of honor and dignity, Gandhi was given political space to voice opposition to the unjustness of British rule in both South Africa and India. Though Britain was more concerned about establishing and maintaining good relations with the Boers in South Africa than with Indian grievances about pass laws, they still treated Indian grievances with traditional British 'rationality' and 'dignity.' But the key here is that they were receptive to the grievances voiced by Gandhi and others—listening to its citizens (in varying degrees) was a strong element in British national practice. A similar attitude was afforded Gandhi in India, where at times Gandhi engaged in dialogue with British authorities under the auspices of a British sense of mutual respect. It was to Gandhi's advantage to identify with Britain, because through British-style diplomacy his ends could be attained. Buber, on the other hand, faced an unrelenting and increasingly deaf and hostile political environment. Speaking contrary to public decrees became increasingly lethal, minimizing Buber's (and all Jews') possibility for engaging in dialogue with the oppressors. Publicly identifying with Germany was no longer a political option: Germany did not want any "non-Germans" identifying with it, nor did Jews want to be identified with their oppressors. Buber faced a brick wall, Gandhi an open door.

Given these educational and political experiences, it is possible to see why Gandhi believes that Jews in Nazi Germany can and should engage in dialogue with the government: Gandhi somehow sees the German government similar to Britain's. However, while Britain has a standard of conduct that allowed the existence of oppositional parties, Germany does not. Thus Gandhi's assertion that German Jews "will score a lasting victory over the German Gentiles in the sense that they will have converted the latter to an appreciation of human dignity" is ill-placed, as German Gentiles (by decree of the government) had no intention of opening themselves up to the opportunity of conversion (Buber 1939, 1944). Buber's plea for a motherland, the right to an ingathering, reflects Buber's experience of being ignored, isolated, targeted, and exiled. His attempts to engage in dialogue with Germany proved futile and only ended in the unjust slaughter of Jews. As Jews were treated by Nazis as objects, Buber could not, by definition, transform the relation into an I-Thou relationship because one side only wanted utility, not mutuality. By like token, Buber could not see holiness in Nazi activities, challenging his mystical background that in all things the sacred exists. His belief that peace can only be pursued through justice reflects this experience.[19]

But their positions were not imposed upon them from the outside—they were not passive objects shaped solely by their circumstances. Rather, each man chose, actively decided what to say and how to respond to the other. In short, both intellectuals are at fault for talking past each other. Gandhi, while remaining true to his mystical conception that all is holy and part of a whole, does not follow his philosophy of dialogue (because of ignorance and political pressures) to understand or address the particular circumstances of his subject: Jews in Germany and in Palestine. On the other hand, Buber, inhibited by German exclusion, chooses not to utilize either his mystical belief that everyone and everything was God, or philosophy of dialogue to eliminate the existence of enemies. Though there are reasons for why they may have been influenced to do so, the ultimate factor is that they both *decided* how they addressed these issues. It is their *choice* to not fulfil their own mystical and philosophical teachings. If they *had* chosen to use their own beliefs to shape their statements, greater commonalties, and even potential agreements, may have emerged. As it is, they chose to talk past each other for reasons external to them, not because of internal inabilities.

Still, the role of the intellectual is to uphold morality and justice, and "universalize the crises, to give greater scope to what a particular race or nation suffered, to associate that experience with the sufferings of others" (Said, 44). Both Gandhi and Buber were intellectuals in exile — either physically or psychically. As such, they tend

> to see things not simply as they are, but as they have come to be that way. Look at situations as contingent, not as inevitable, look at them as the result of a series of historical choices made by men and women, as facts of society made by human beings, and not as natural or god-given, therefore unchangeable, permanent, irreversible. (ibid., 60-1)

Both Gandhi and Buber see the relativity of truths, and understand that each person and community will have different perspectives and notions of truth, and that all these are wont to change. But blind loyalty to one's own group, or perspective, is to deny one's responsibility as an intellectual in exile.

> Loyalty to the group's fight for survival cannot draw in the intellectual so far as to narcotize the critical sense, or reduce its imperatives, which are always to go beyond survival to questions of political liberation, to critiques of the leadership, to presenting alternatives that are too often marginalized or pushed aside as irrelevant to the main battle at hand. (ibid., 41)

The true intellectual in exile is a "secular being," one who "exists in a median state, neither completely at one with the new setting nor fully disencumbered of the old" (ibid., 120, 48). Said challenges Buber and Gandhi, as two intellectuals, to uphold their responsibilities and be true to their beliefs:

> However much intellectuals pretend that their representations

> are of higher things or ultimate values, morality begins with their activity in this secular world of ours—where it takes place, whose interests it serves, how it jibes with a consistent and universalistic ethic, how it discriminates between power and justice, and what it reveals of one's choices and priorities.... The intellectual has to walk around, has to have the space in which to stand and talk back to authority, since unquestioning subservience to authority in today's world is one of the greatest threats to an active, and moral, intellectual life.... The hardest aspect of being an intellectual is to represent what you profess through your work and interventions, without hardening into an institution or a kind of automaton acting at the behest of a system or method." (ibid., 120-1)

Though Buber and Gandhi both seek justice, peace, and mutuality for the whole world but prove in their letters they are wont to see the world through limited lenses, Said urges them to go beyond tribalistic perspectives.

> If you wish to uphold basic human justice you must do so for everyone, not just selectively for the people that your side, your culture, your nation designates as okay. The fundamental problem, therefore, is how to reconcile one's identity and the actualities of one's own culture, society, and history to the reality of other identities, cultures, peoples. (ibid., 93-4)

This expansion of identity to involve everyone's right to justice, peace and mutuality is what proves to be a, if not the ultimate, stumbling block for both Buber and Gandhi, more so for Gandhi.

Faltering? Speculative Answers

While it is fairly obvious that neither man fully integrated his thoughts into his own mystical beliefs or used his version of the philosophy of dialogue to understand the other, reasons why this is so remain hidden. Only speculative answers can be given, and some are sketched above. What remains are more questions, questions seeking dialogue to reveal truths that may help us better understand why these men said what they did, and how we may interpret their words for our own circumstances.

For example, to what extent has Gandhi become an intellectual no longer questioning his own authority? Because Gandhi chose to mix politics into religion and allow himself to be inhibited by popular pressures, he became institutionalized—that is, he chose to give preferential treatment to an unjust community elsewhere because it was necessary (in his view) to not upset their local counterparts. For political reasons, Gandhi objectified the issue of Jews in Palestine, thus exhibiting his own faltering of not living up to his teachings to pursue justice no matter what the price.

On the other hand, to what extent has Buber become an intellectual at home in exile, perpetually at odds with everyone? To what extend does he defer to his treatment by Germany to shape his attitude toward Jewish defense of their settlement efforts in Palestine? Because he saw the political futility of seeking meaningful dialogue with Germany, he chose to project futility on non-violent efforts in Palestine (even though he preferred them). Buber mingled religion into politics, whereby because of previous efforts to link Judaism with secular society failed, current Jewish efforts to create community could take up secular political means (violence) that would objectify the other community (Muslims). By choosing not to see the extent and meaning of the violence he was imposing upon his Arab neighbors, Buber faltered in his pursuit to engage in dialogue with the sacred subjects around him.

To what extent do these intellectuals undermine their own presumption against violence and preference for non-force, by allowing the use of force against an ultimate evil? Promoting armed resistance to the Nazi regime would be, essentially, promoting mass suicide (non-violent resistance would also be this). Suicidal violence may be noble, but if the ultimate evil persists after the resistance is eliminated, to what extent can this effort be considered just? In light of the just war tradition where the ultimate end of a just war must be a just peace, when there is no reasonable chance of success to achieve such an end engagement in warfare therefore is inherently unjust.

Finally, if all is sacred, and relative truths can bring about ultimate evils, how *should* we look to Gandhi and Buber to engage in dialogue?

Bibliography

Allport, Gordon W. 1955. *Becoming*. New Haven: Yale University Press.

Bhagavad Gita. 1962 ET. Translated by Juan Mascaró. New York: Penguin.

Buber, Martin. 1939. "Two Letters to Gandhi." Pamphlets of the Group "The Bond", Jerusalem.

Buber, Martin. 1957. *Pointing the Way*. New York: Harper.

Buber, Martin. 1958. *I and Thou*. New York: Charles Scribner's Sons.

Buber, Martin. 1991. *The Letters of Martin Buber*. Eds., Nahum N. Glatzer, and Paul Mendes-Flohr. New York: Schocken Books.

Chadda, Maya. 1987. "Satyagraha: Gandhi's approach to peacemaking." In *Education for Peace*, 148-165. Eds., Haim Gordon and Leonard Grob. Maryknoll: Orbis Books.

Eck, Diana L. 1993. *Encountering God*. Boston: Beacon Press.

Friedman, Maurice S. 1960. *Martin Buber: The life of dialogue*. New York: Harper and Brothers.

Friedman, Maurice S. 1981. "Martin Buber and Oriental Religions." in *Buddhist and Western Philosophy*. pp. 149-171. Ed., Nathan Katz. New Delhi: Sterling Publishers Private Limited.

Friedman, Maurice S. 1986. *Martin Buber and the Eternal*. New York: Human Sciences Press, Inc.

Friedman, Maurice S. 1994. "Hasidism and the Love of Enemies." In *The Challenge of Shalom*, 40-48. Eds., Murray Polner and Naomi Gordon. Philadelphia: New Society Publishers.

Gandhi, Mohandas. 1957. *An Autobiography*. Boston: Beacon Press.

Gandhi, Mohandas. 1961. "The Gospel of Renunciation." Ahmedabad: Navajivan Publishing House. Pamphlet.

Gandhi, M.K. 1962. "My God." Ahmedabad: Navajivan Publishing House. Pamphlet.

Gandhi, M.K. 1966. *To the Perplexed*. Bombay: Bharatiya Vidya Bhavan.

Gandhi, M.K. 1968. "Ethical Religion." Ahmedabad: Navajivan Publishing House. Pamphlet.

Gandhi, M.K. 1970. *Modern* vs. *Ancient Civilization*. Bombay: Bharatiya Vidya Bhavan.

Gandhi, M.K. 1980. *The Bhagvadgita*. New Delhi: Orient Paperbacks.

Gandhi, M.K. 1987. *The Essence of Hinduism*. Ahmedabad: Navajivan Publishing House.

Gordon, Haim, and Leonard Grob, eds. 1988. *Education for Peace: testimonies from world religions*. Maryknoll: Orbis Books.

Green, Martin, ed. 1987. *Gandhi in India: in his own words*. Hanover: University Press of New England.

Grob, Leonard M. 1986. "Non-violence: a Buberian perspective." *Journal of Jewish Studies*. 37/1 (Spring):76-87.

Gross, Aaron. 1996. "The Modern Jewish Encounter with Buddhism."

Unpublished Paper.

Henry, Dr. Sarojini. 1991. "Social Ethic of Mahatma Gandhi and Martin Buber." *Journal of Dharma*. 16/4:375-386.

Hodes, Aubrey. 1971. *Martin Buber: an intimate portrait*. New York: The Viking Press.

Iyer, Raghavan N. 1973. *The Moral and Political Thought of Mahatma Gandhi*. New York: Oxford University Press.

Mendes-Flohr, Paul. 1989. *From Mysticism to Dialogue: Martin Buber's transformation of German social thought*. Detroit: Wayne State University.

Merton, Thomas. 1964. *Gandhi on Non-Violence*. New York: New Directions Books.

Murphy, John W. 1983. *The Social Philosophy of Martin Buber*. Washington, D.C.: University Press of America.

Parrinder, Geoffrey, ed. 1971. *World Religions*. New York: Facts On File Publications.

Polner, Murray, and Naomi Goodman, eds. 1994. *The Challenge of Shalom*. Philadelphia: New Society Publishers.

Puligandla, Ramakrishna. 1988. "The Hindu Quest for Peace." In *Education for Peace*, 139-147. Eds., Haim Gordon and Leonard Grob. Maryknoll: Orbis Books.

Said, Edward. 1994. *Representations of the Intellectual*. New York: Pantheon Books.

Shimoni, Gideon. 1977. *Gandhi, Satyagraha and the Jews: a formative factor in India's policy towards Israel*. Jerusalem Papers on Peace Problems. 22. Jerusalem: The Hebrew University of Jerusalem.

Tillich, Paul. 1955. *Biblical Religion and the Search for Ultimate Reality*. Chicago: University of Chicago Press.

Yoder, John Howard. 1995. "*Galuth* as Calling." Lecture, Presented at Loyola Marymount University, September 23.

References

1. Thanks to Professor Yoder for pointing this out. See also Mendes-Flohr's *From Mysticism to Dialogue* for an analysis of Buber's relation with German social thought.
2. As different from political Zionism which sought to bring under Jewish (and eventually the state of Israel's) control lands included in biblical Israel/Judea. Spiritual and cultural Zionism yearned to live peaceably with Arabs in the area.
3. To see evidence of this, one need only look to the volumes of letters sent to and from these men to peoples around the world seeking advice and challenging their positions on a wide range of issues.
4. "Gandhi, Politics and Us" can be found in Buber's *Pointing the Way*, 126-138.

5. For purposes of this paper, I will leave the authors' use of "men" as such to retain source integrity. However, I expand their concept of "men" and "man's" to include *both* women and men, and in my prose I will try to express this explicitly.
6. Because of the nature of this discussion, some quotes will be lengthy, to better understand the thought processes and nuances these authors express. All quotes from Gandhi's letter and Buber's response in this section come from Buber's 1939 "Two Letters to Gandhi." Pamphlet of the Group "The Bond," Jerusalem.
7. At this time, some Jews and Arabs were co-existing peacefully in regions of Palestine, and some Jews and Arabs were engaged in more or less sporadic armed conflict. Meanwhile, the British kept a military presence in the region which sometimes intervened in these skirmishes.
8. A longer version of Gandhi's letter is found in Green, pp. 262-265.
9. For Magnes' letter, see Buber's "Two Letters to Gandhi." pp. 23-39. It is interesting to see how Magnes and Buber address many of the same issues but argue them differently. Exploration of this would be a completely different paper.
10. It is unclear from the context to whom "their" is in reference. It could be to either Arab or Jew. Still, the essence is there: that both communities have legitimate divinely motivated reasons to live in and work the land.
11. See evidence of many kinds of resistance, non-violent and violent, in Yuri Suhl's (editor) *They Fought Back: The story of the Jewish resistance in Nazi Europe*. New York: Schocken. 1967.
12. *Atman* "is the unchanging, abiding silent witness, *sakshin*. Like *Brahma*, *Atman* is unborn, uncreated, eternal, formless, nameless, and pervades all existence. *Atman* is single and unitary and is not to be identified with body, mind, ego (*jiva*). *Atman* is pure, objectless consciousness. *Atman*, like *Brahma*, cannot be captured by the senses and mind, but can be realized only in non-perceptual, non-conceptual intuition. (Puligandla, 141).
13. *Brahma* "is the unborn, uncreated, eternal, unchanging reality underlying the myriad worlds of phenomena—of the senses and mind. *Brahma* is formless and nameless and hence imperceivable and unthinkable. *Brahma* pervades all existence—smaller than the smallest and greater than the greatest. *Brahma* is neither a he nor a she but the That. *Brahma* can be realized only in non-perceptual, non-conceptual intuition." (Puligandla, 141).
14. Buber was fascinated by Hasidism and collected many of the stories into books that became insightful resources into this elusive sect of Judaism. His recent (1988) *The Origin and Meaning of Hasidism*, Atlantic Highlands, NJ: Humanities Press International. is less a collection of stories but more his interpretation of Hasidism.
15. Buber's exploration led him to the conception of dualism and non-dualism. In the introduction to his "Ecstasy and Confession" Buber takes a Vedantist position:

Not suspecting that the poor individual 'I' contains the 'World I,' most mystics have connected their experience with God, and have made of it a multiform mystery. Only in the primitive world of India is the 'I' proclaimed that is one with the 'All' and with the 'One.' The unity which the mystic experiences when he has brought all his former multiplicity into Oneness is not a relative unity, for the ecstatic man no longer has outside of himself others with whom he has community. It is the absolute, unlimited Oneness which includes all others. (Friedman 1986, 107)

16. Gandhi outlined five main principles of the creed of *ahimsa*:
    (1) Non-violence implies as complete self-purification as is humanly possible.
    (2) Man for man the strength of non-violence is in exact proportion to the ability, not the will, of the nonviolent person to inflict violence.
    (3) Non-violence is without exception superior to violence, i.e., the power at the disposal of a non-violent person is always greater than he would have if he was violent.
    (4) There is no such thing as defeat in non-violence. The end of violence is surest defeat.
    (5) The ultimate end of non-violence is surest victory—if such a term may be used of non-violence. In reality, where there is no sense of defeat, there is no sense of victory. (Iyer, 193-4)

    It is interesting to note that Gandhi continually felt he failed in his struggles—even though the creed of *ahimsa* requires no such feelings. (See "Gandhi", the film.)
17. "Since Moslem opinion in India, 'will not tolerate any non-Muslim influence direct or indirect over the holy places of Islam,' explained Gandhi, again with implicit approval, 'the most thorny part of the question' was Palestine" (Shimoni, 22). A.E. Shohet, an Indian Jew, challenged Gandhi's double standard regarding Jews and Arabs: "Particularly incisive was his comment on Gandhi's judging of the Jews by the highest spiritual standards whereas he judged the 'proud Arabs' by the 'accepted canons.' Unless this meant that Gandhi thought the Moslem Arab had inferior moral standards—and that would be an insult—Shohet pointed out it was clear evidence of a pro-Arab bias and the application of double standards of judgment." (Shimoni, 49). Others pointed out to Gandhi that Muslims were fomenting hostility towards the Jews, and Gandhi could swing Indian opinion to the Jews' side. "Gandhi's retort was that as far as Moslem opinion in India was concerned, it was artificially worked up. The Jews had nothing to fear from it, as it was not based on just grievances. He said it would not serve any useful purpose to them if he were to condemn the way in which propaganda was carried on among the Moslems of India. According to Shohet, Gandhi thus intimated,...that he considered the real object of the Muslim League's propaganda on the Palestine question to be the Indian National Congress; hence any remarks from Gandhi would only further serve that purpose and

that was why he, Gandhi, could not take such a stand publicly" (Shimoni, 50-1).

18. In a letter to Ernst Simon (February 14, 1933), Buber wrote, "Thus far Hitlerism has not harmed me directly, but I am prepared for anything, especially after what nationalistic writers such as Hans Blüher have written about my alleged attitude during the war; although it is not true, I of course left it uncorrected....As long as the present condition holds, there can be no thought of Jew-baiting or anti-Jewish laws, only of administrative oppression. Anti-Semitic legislation would be possible only if the balance of power shifts in favor of the National Socialists, but as I have said above, this is hardly to be expected. Jew-baiting is only possible during the interval between the National Socialists' leaving the government and the proclamation of a state of emergence" (Buber 1991, 394-5).
19. What is interesting is both Buber and Gandhi agree that Hitlerism is an ultimate evil, and that war against an ultimate evil is justified. And though both say it is wrong to reject violence (and non-violence) absolutely, neither one advocated mass Jewish armed resistance against this ultimate evil. Hypothetically, it would have been an ideal case of a just war. But if this case *did* happen, what would keep Jews (or anyone for that matter) from arbitrarily determining what and who is an ultimate evil and engaging in mass armed aggression? What would happen if Jews (at this time) saw Britain or Arabs as ultimate evils and began wars against them? It is difficult to see the justness in declaring war against an already established population (Arabs) who have, for the most part, done no wrong to Jews. What would happen today? Declaring war against ultimate evil a necessary (and just) good leads to this slippery-slope.

9

Towards a Culture of Peace

No doubt there is a challenge of teaching young people how to be less violent and more non-violent. The level of difficulty varies across cultures and languages. In some communities the prevalence of the concepts of non-violence makes the exploration of it fairly easy; in other communities, violence is so embedded that, to a large extent, it has become invisible, and non-violence cannot be found or recognized. For youth, especially, the challenge is to make visible to them that which they previously could not see. This paper outlines a model of teaching youth how to become aware of their violence and empower them to choose more nonviolent ways of engaging in the world.

Cultures often encourage us to be blind to our own surroundings, experiences, attitudes and habits. What Gandhi challenges people to consider is that it is possible to make visible that which we currently do not see—especially our violent tendencies. This Gandhian social critique may occur at a communal level and also at a personal level, as individuals compose (and are composed by) society. As young people experience the world primarily through their own and their peers' eyes, it is important to teach them through their own eyes and not through the eyes of one or another authority figure as that will alienate and belittle them.[1] This, then, is the integration of Gandhi's social critique with a model of teaching that empowers young people to critique themselves. All discussions require their participation, as it is their lives that we are exploring. Without their active participation in these vocalized self-critiques, the employment of non-violent teaching methods would be for naught. Experiential games, religious, Gandhian and other texts, and guest speakers are useful teaching tools for young people. Non-violent teaching requires student participation, so much so to the effect that they become their own teachers. In so doing, they reveal to themselves how much they already know—regardless of the media used to explore a particular issue. The teacher is there to help them understand that which they already know but didn't understand.

There is much discussion in this world, and especially in Western cultures, about our love lives. Rarely, though, do we explore our hate lives. Hate breeds a false sense of separation, as Gandhi was well aware of and taught publicly. From division comes evaluation (one side is better or worse than the other), and this leads down a slippery slope into defensive (and/or offensive) action to preserve or improve one's (self) evaluation. If only we did not embark on this path of separation, then we would be more inclined to be non-violent toward each other and ourselves. Making ourselves aware that we voluntarily, either consciously or subconsciously as a result of cultural training, engage in divisive and violent tendencies is the first step toward unlearning violence. Thus the first question posed to the youth was, "How is your hate life?" This leads into a dynamic exploration of the meaning of "hate": it means in our general context to desire the obliteration of the object, to annihilate it from existence. Rarely do youth actually desire the obliteration of the object of their conversations. By empowering them to explore their "hate" lives, they begin to see how often they, their peers and their cultures use this violent term—but rarely mean it. Momentary consistency, or resonance between one's beliefs, attitudes, thoughts, words and actions, is a Gandhian value. Through self-analysis, critique and change, the youths were able to become more wholesomely consistent in this Gandhian way.

From the issue of hate, related issues were explored in a similar vein. These included how we traditionally understand power and strength, the different kinds of violence we suffer and inflict, and the ways we make decisions according to adversarial mindsets. Through dynamic conversations on these and other issues the youths came to see their many roles in society: as perpetrator, bystander, victim and survivor.[2] They also understood more clearly the ways they engage their roles, especially as they attempt to influence others to do what they want them to do: through coercion, accommodation, conversion and transformation of others' opinions. This led to a deeper understanding of how we obey rules—through obedience and consent. Gandhi sought both but preferred consent as it proved that people were voluntarily complying with the rules and regulations of (his) nonviolent vision of society.

Each session is opened with a question posed at the close of the previous session. For example, after a discussion on suffering, sacrifice and compassion, questions the youth's pondered until the next discussion was "How are you compassionate? How do you engage in suffering and sacrifice?" Repeating this question the next class empowered the students to openly discuss their self-reflections. This public forum enabled them to make visible that which previously was invisible to them: their capacity to be compassionate, to take into their own deliberations the pains of other sentient beings. This is the process of transcending valuing only personal interests and becoming altruistic, again a Gandhian value. It also helps the youths recognize how responsible they actually are for their actions—even though society teaches them that life is about shirking responsibilities and seeking instant gratification. This leads to the questions: "How are you responsible? What vows do you take on?" Just as Gandhi encouraged, even commanded, people to take on vows, so, too do many religious traditions. Through discursive reflection the youths came to understand that vows empower them to become more compassionate, given their special roles in society. No longer do they see themselves as passive individuals. They see and understand themselves to be active agents, assuming responsibility, thinking consequentially, and being conscious of their acts of omission and commission.

This dynamic model of experiential and reflexive dialogue empowers youth to teach themselves things they already knew but didn't clearly see, fully understand or articulate. By challenging them to answer integrative questions (like, "How far does your compassion extend?") they push themselves to justify their current self-centered, and violent, tendencies. Failing to do so convinces them that they ought to, and can, change their worldviews, attitudes, thoughts and actions. In this way, they (re)consider their violence, teach each other how to unlearn them, and reveal to themselves their more truthful, momentarily consistent, non-violent selves.

References

1. The model is the one the author developed and used with North American Jewish teenagers in the summer of 1999 at the UAHC Kutz Camp Institute in Warwick, NY.
2. See works by Krishnamurti.

3. See works by Ervin Staub.
4. See the covers of popular magazines any day of the week to find the prevalence of this topic. Television talk shows often explore the trials and tribulations of some people's love lives. And, of course, the popularity of politicians' love lives reflects and reifies this obsession.
5. See chapters 2-6.
6. The distinction between victim and survivor, they developed, was that the former often suffered death while the latter endured injury to continue living.
7. Responsibilities, meaning that our actions intrinsically "have" consequences on and for others (and ourselves). Their insightful comments about their roles included the observation that they can never escape one of these roles; the challenge is how they will use their relative power and objective strengths in those roles for the betterment of society. Essentially, they taught themselves that no matter what role they play, they have the capacity to do justice in nonviolent ways.

PART II

APPROACHING ALTERNATIVE DISPUTE RESOLUTION (ADR) FROM GANDHIAN PERSPECTIVE

By

Jordi Agusti-Panareda

1

Introduction

> My joy was boundless. I had learnt the true practice of law. I had learnt to find out the better side of human nature and to enter men's hearts. I realized that the true function of a lawyer was to unite parties riven as under. The lesson was so indelibly burnt into me that a large part of my time during the twenty years of my practice as a lawyer was occupied in bringing about private compromises of hundreds of cases. I lost nothing thereby—not even money, certainly not my soul.
>
> —M. K. Gandhi,
> *An Autobiography* (2001)

Daughters of the same century, the theoretical and applied traditions hovering around the Gandhian approach to conflict and the Alternative Dispute Resolution (ADR) movement share, as a common thread, the search for alternative ways to think about and deal with conflict that rely on more consensual and less violent or coercive means. However, the exploration of similarities and possible interconnections and interrelations between them has been disregarded in the academic circles. Despite the great relevance of Gandhi's accomplishments and contributions to the theory and practice of conflict resolution, ADR scholars have not attempted to interrelate the two movements, let alone to embark on a Gandhian approach to Alternative Dispute Resolution. It is precisely this lacuna that this part of the volume tries to fill. It attempts to answer the following question: what are the existing and potential relations and parallels between the above-mentioned traditions: ADR and Gandhian Approach to Conflict Resolution through Non-violence. In my view, there may not be any causal link between the two traditions, we can identify important resonance between them, and that the Gandhian approach to conflict, often going beyond many of the postulates held by the Alternative Dispute Resolution movement, provides an interesting standpoint from which to examine the ADR debates. Furthermore, I have attempted to formulate certain possible reinterpretations of the ADR label and of some of its central themes from a Gandhian perspective, contending that the former can be positively enriched by the insights brought forth by the latter's approach to conflict.

In order to meet the above objectives, I have first attempted to outline the main tenets of the Gandhian approach to conflict. Secondly, I examine the existence of possible links or parallelisms between both traditions and sketch out the possibility of a Gandhian interpretation of the ADR movement. I consider the reasons and advantages offered by a Gandhian reading of conflict resolution, both in terms of its intrinsic value and its potential contribution to ADR. Finally, I have explored how certain broad ADR areas and debates might be better understood from a Gandhian perspective. More specifically, I have used the Gandhian approach to examine the distinction between dispute and conflict, to analyse the dispute processes, and to scrutinize some of the most paradigmatic criticisms against the ADR movement and reconceptualize it make it a more powerful instrument of conflict resolution.

However, two preliminary remarks are required. First, this work being based on the views, understandings and practices of Gandhi, a prolific and polifacetic thinker and activist ever experimenting, improving and changing his views and strategies, it cannot pretend to represent in its broadest perspectives the Gandhian approach to conflict and its resolution. Thus, this contribution should be understood not as an exegetic enterprise but as a personal interpretation of the insights offered by Gandhi, both in his life and writings, and by the broader Gandhian tradition. The aim is to draw subjectively the Gandhian perspective to conflict and to interrelate it creatively with an existing and varied Alternative Dispute Resolution movement.

Second, since I have tried to explore a least explored ground, the reader should treat my conclusions as preliminary and general. The strokes on the canvas are broad; the details are yet to be filled to give the painting a final touch. One of its main aims is, precisely, to defend the potential benefits of developing relationships of mutual enrichment between the Gandhian tradition and the ADR movement; that is moving further on the path I have tried to draw in following pages.

As it is often the case, the importance is not really in pointing a finger but in the direction in which it points.

Since my aim is to approach the Alternative Dispute Resolution movement from a Gandhian perspective, the first logical step would probably be to thoroughly describe and map out the two elements that I attempt to interrelate in the discussion. However I will mainly concentrate, first on the description of the Gandhian approach to conflict, devoting far less attention to the ADR movement. Furthermore, as I will argue, the Gandhian approach to conflict, especially in its interpersonal dimension, has received very little attention in general (Rath 1986:857) and has been almost totally ignored by the alternative dispute resolution literature. The task of unraveling its main tenets in relation to ADR becomes both necessary and pressing. Second, there is rich amount of writings that already tackle the issue of defining and contextualising the ADR movement and its various trends.[1] Moreover, due to its complex composition and its continuing evolution, an attempt to thoroughly describe here the ADR movement would risk both employing a disproportionate share of this paper, in an enterprise not directly related with its aims, and not offering any fresh dimension to the general ADR debate. Consequently, I will limit such preliminary task to proposing a broad definition of the ADR movement and making some general remarks on how I will use the label in this work.

ADR

The terms Alternative Dispute Resolution are often used to describe a variety of contemporary movements that 'share an interest in consensual non-violent modes of reaching agreements and an opposition to a formal, adversarial method of dealing with conflicts' (Adler 1995:67), whose nascence is usually located in the United States around the 1970's and 1980's (Menkel-Meadow 2000:2). It is with such a general definition in mind that I will use the term in this paper. Nevertheless, I am aware that, below the broad apparently shared aims of ADR one finds a myriad of tendencies and agenda that go from the alternatives of the community justice movement to the attempts by the legal system and the legal actors to incorporate new, flexible and informal processes in their mode of operating. ADR becomes, therefore, a 'fugitive label ... attached to a disparate group of evolving practices' (Palmer and Roberts 1998 : 5).

I have sometimes used generic references to the ADR movement. It might be rightly contended that, due to its internal complexity, any allusion to ADR as a whole dangerously risks inconsistency. I am well aware of that fact and, therefore, all the references to ADR in this work should be thus understood not as over generalizations referring to an entirety, but as allusions to different—either general or particular—trends and practices of an heterogeneous movement that sometimes do not share much more than a common name. I only pretend in this paper to bring forth another way of thinking about conflict into an already very varied field of both practices and thought. I do not pretend to judge ADR as a compact whole nor do I view it such a monolithic way. Therefore, whenever possible I refer directly to specific strands or authors. Other general references point to internal trends that might be by and large attributed to the movement. However, they must never be understood in a totalising sense. It is with those warnings in mind that the reader should address the dissertation that, in a more proper sense, now begins.

Reference

1. The literature is vast. On the different contemporary tendencies see Anderson (1997). An introduction to its intellectual history can be found Menkel-Meadow (1997). For general overview see Palmer an Roberts (1998).

2

Satyagraha—Gandhian Approach to Conflict Resolution

Having introduced a few remarks on the ADR label, I examine in this section the Gandhian conception and approach to conflict and its resolution. In order to so do, I will refer to the works of Gandhi himself. However, bearing in mind that Gandhi, strictly speaking, 'was not a theorist'[1] (Bondurant 1965 : 7) and that he 'never attempted to put his ideas on conflict and its resolution in a well-synthesized manner' (Rath 1986 : 856), I will also resort to the writings of those scholars that have dealt with this and related aspects of his philosophy.

At the very centre of all Gandhian reflection on conflict stands the concept of *satyagraha*. Coined during Gandhi's campaign in South Africa, *satyagraha* emerges etymologically from the combination of the two Sanskrit words *satya* (truth) and *agraha* (firmness). It was defined by Gandhi as a 'relentless search for truth and a determination to reach truth' (*Young India,*[2] 19 March, 1925). Although in its deeper and more encompassing meaning *satyagraha* should be understood as 'a complete way of life' (Fisher 1971:188) it can also be used to refer to 'the Gandhian approach to conflict resolution' (Weber 1986 : 692). It is in this latter sense that we shall examine it in the following paragraphs. More specifically, in accordance with the aims of the present work, I will attempt to summarise the basic tenets of the Gandhian *satyagraha*, focusing especially on interpersonal conflict resolution, an area which has been object little detailed exploration[3] and which constitutes a core dimension of ADR. In order to do so, I will follow three steps. First I will examine the fundamental conceptions and aims of *satyagraha*, then I will analyse the Gandhian conception of conflict and finally I will outline the basic elements of *satyagraha*'s approach to conflict resolution, referring both to its process and main precepts.

Basic Principles Underlying *Satyagraha*

Underlying *satyagraha*, we find several basic principles and conceptions which run through the whole of Gandhi's philosophy. First, the Gandhian approach to conflict is based on a particular understanding of truth. *Satyagraha* means 'truth-force' and it was, for Gandhi, both based on and directed towards truth seeking. However, Gandhi distinguished between absolute and relative truth. He argued that 'no man is capable of knowing the absolute truth' (Gandhi 1933 : 506) and that people should maintain an unceasingly open approach to those who hold different views and positions (Bondurant 1965:16).

Secondly, we find the principle of intimate unity between means and ends. According to Gandhi 'the means might be likened to a seed, the end to a tree; and there is just the same inviolable connection between the means and the end as there is between the seed and the tree' (Gandhi 1939 : 71) so that 'if one takes care of the means, the end will take care of itself' (*Harijan*, 11 February, 1939).

Thirdly, stands the concept of non-violence or *ahimsa*[4] and the rejection of coercion. *Satyagraha* excludes the use of both violence[5] and coercion[6] since, in the Gandhian scheme, 'perceptions of truth vary from person to person and no one can be absolutely certain that their perception is the correct one' (Weber 1991 : 56-57) and for Gandhi there is 'no wall of separation between means and ends' (*Young India*, 17 July, 1924). Thus, 'while truth is the goal, *ahimsa* or non-violence becomes the necessary and only means of realising it' (Weber 1991:45). According to Gandhi '*ahimsa* and truth are so intertwined that it is practically impossible to disentangle and separate them' (1945:8). *Satyagraha* can never be a method of coercion, since coercion undermines the personal development of the parties, fails to express respect for the opponent and does not clarify the truth (Weber 1991:56-58). Thus, Gandhi argued that reliance has to be placed 'upon the ability to reach the intellect and the heart' (*Harijan*, 23 July, 1938).

Fourthly, *satyagraha*, being, as I discuss below, aimed at the conversion of the adversaries, rests on the belief that all disputants are human beings and that, as such, have a capacity for reason and goodness.[7] Such principle is incompatible with a negative or dehumanised conception of the other party. Lanza del Vasto, one of the most well-known European disciples of Gandhi, saw this profound acknowledgement of the opponent as a human being as the core axiom of non-violent conflict resolution (Vasto 1971:13-50). Furthermore, *satyagraha* must be based in an acknowledgement of the relational nature of the 'self', where the 'other' becomes one of its constituents.[8] Closely related, stands the belief on the unity of life. This principle is strongly connected with the major cultural and spiritual influences in Gandhi's life—Indian thought, Hinduism and Jainism (Burrowes 1996:110). Although the belief refers to all living beings, suffice it to say here that, according to Gandhi, human beings are related, beyond social relations, through a deeper bond of a transcendental nature (Galtung 1998:52).

And finally, another essential principle of *satyagraha* is that of creative self-suffering (Weber 1991:52-54). Through its willingness to suffer for its own cause, the *satyagrahi*[9] aims at appealing to the conscience of the opponent and evoking her[10] sense of justice, while eliciting the support of third parties and the public opinion (Burrowes 1996:111). The role of self-suffering would be to 'break a deadlock' (Weber 1991:52) and 'cut through the rationalised defences which the opponent might have built in opposing the initial efforts of rational persuasion' (Bondurant 1965:228).[11]

Aims of *Satyagraha*

Satyagraha aims primarily at resolving the conflict. In the Gandhian scheme 'it is not to be tolerated that conflicts simply go on and on' since 'conflicts are to be solved' (Galtung 1985:97). The objective is a 'restructuring of the opposing elements' from which 'through the operation of non-violent action the truth as judged by the fulfilment of human needs will emerge in the form of a mutually satisfactory and agreed-upon solution' (Bondurant 1965:195). Furthermore, *satyagraha* seeks to change the attitudes rather than the mere behaviour of the opponents, it 'goes beyond redressing merely the immediate grievance that has surfaced as conflict but aims to resolve the distrust and friction that are the underlying causes of conflict' (Weber 1991: 36). A basic aim in *satyagraha* is to convert both parties so that they both see each other on the same side in a shared attempt to solve the conflict. Accordingly, the resolution cannot be imposed from the outside but has to come from an inward joint determination of the opponents. This strive for *conversion* is seen, from a Gandhian perspective, as not only the morally correct way to deal with conflict but also as the most effective method of conflict resolution (Weber 1991:34).

However, conflict resolution is not the sole aim of *satyagraha*. For Gandhi 'resolving a conflict was only one aspect of the desired outcome' (Galtung 1985:110). The Gandhian approach to conflict has much broader aspirations. First, it aims at reaching a higher degree of truth. By seeking to attain a synthesis of the relative truths held by the parties, conflict resolution provides an opportunity 'to progress towards the absolute truth' (Rath 1986 : 853). Secondly, *satyagraha* is aimed at reinforcing the unity of life, strengthening the ties of unity between human beings (Galtung 1985:110). Gandhi seemed to prefer a disharmonious relationship that no relationship at all and saw conflict as a way to bring the opponents together, i.e. as a medium through which the parties could develop a higher degree of awareness of themselves as well as of the other party (Galtung 1998:32-57). Thirdly, *satyagraha* seeks the personal transformation of the opponents. According to Galtung, 'a conflict 'resolved', but leaving the parties unchanged, was no success for Gandhi' (1985:110). Such a transformation is directed at different levels. On the one hand, *satyagraha* aims at empowering the parties and developing their autonomy to deal with conflict. The Gandhian way intends to 'relieve the individual of feelings of helplessness in conflict situations' (Weber 1991:6) and to achieve a 'higher level of self-reliance in both parties' (Galtung 1985:110). On the other hand, success in conflict resolution implied for Gandhi a higher degree of fearlessness on the parties—a necessary quality that lies at the base of his approach to conflict resolution (Weber 1991:59). In short, *satyagraha* seeks to endow the parties with the necessary capabilities and attitudes to better deal with future conflicts. Moreover, it strives to achieve 'self-realisation' and personal growth' (Weber 2001: 507). Finally, the Gandhian approach to conflict resolution also aims at social transformation. *Satyagraha*, through non-violent direct action, provides 'a way of fighting for justice' (Weber 2001:505), striving for 'the creation of a superior social structure'(Burrowes 1996:109).

The Gandhian Concept of Conflict

Satyagraha is based on a constructive reading of conflictual situations. According to Gandhi, conflict, understood in a broad sense,[12] is both 'positive and desirable' (Burrowes 1996:107). Differing from other non-violent movements,[13] *satyagraha* does not aim at avoiding conflict. For Gandhi, conflict is a 'gift, a rich opportunity, potentially to the benefit of all' (Galtung 1998:56) that 'far from separating two parties... should unite them, precisely because they have their incompatibility in common' (Galtung 1978:490). Accordingly, *satyagraha* does not seek a conflict-free society (Burrowes 1996:107). Conflict is seen as a chance to reaffirm the unity of life and to restructure the social order so as to produce a more human society (Galtung 1998:56). In short, conflict is regarded as a perfect opportunity to pursue the different aims of *satyagraha*.

In relation to its origin, Gandhi, on the one hand, understood conflict 'as built into social structures and not into people' (Burrowes 1996:107). *Satyagraha,* distinguishing between actor and structure, locates the 'evil' not in the former but in the latter (Galtung 1998:52).[14] Therefore, it involves attempts to 'change the system itself' (Rath 1986:852). According to Galtung, what is new in such a structuralist view is Gandhi's claim that such an approach is valid for all conflicts (Galtung 1985:99). Thus, the essence of *satyagraha* is to identify approaches to conflict that preserve the people while systematically demolishing the evil structure (Burrowes 1996:107). Nevertheless, according to Gandhi, the purification of the structure is not enough, 'self purification is also indispensable, and the purification both of structure and of self is an open-ended process' (Galtung 1998:53). In other words, moving beyond the strictly structuralist interpretation of some Gandhian scholars, one should be aggressive not against the opponent, but against the condition, against the antagonism but not against the antagonist (Rath 1986 : 852). In view of that, we find Ghandi's distinction between 'man and his deed'[15] and his admonition to 'hate the sin and not the sinner' (Gandhi 2001:254). On the other hand, from a more interpersonal perspective, *satyagraha* views conflict as a tension between different sets of relative truths and, therefore, it aims at synthesis, rather than at compromise as a middle ground. Moreover, in the Gandhian scheme, since nobody represents the truth, no one has also the right to force his opinion on others and therefore, conflict resolution has necessarily to be achieved through peaceful negotiations (Rath 1986 : 853-854).

The Gandhian Process of Conflict Resolution

The process of *Satyagraha* can involve several steps. Most Gandhian scholars distinguish three stages, each to be taken up only after the failure of the preceding one (Bondurant 1965; Rath 1986; Weber 1991). The first stage is aimed at reasoning with the opponent in order to achieve a just solution (Prahbu 2001:5), i.e. at persuasion through reason or negotiation. This stage seeks 'a synthesis of the two opposing claims' so that, not necessarily implying compromise and mutual concessions, and being able to result in a completely new position for both opponents, there is 'no victory in the sense of triumph of one party over the other' (Rath 1986 : 854). The second stage, taken up 'when appeal to reason through the persistent efforts of rational argument have failed to persuade the opponent' (Bondurant 1965:229), is that of persuasion by means of self-suffering. Here Gandhi points out that 'mere appeal to reason does not answer where prejudices are age-long' and that in some cases 'reason has to be strengthened by suffering' to open 'the eyes of understanding' (*Young India,* 19 March, 1925). Self-suffering aims at getting 'through the opponent's unprejudiced judgment so that he might willingly come back onto a level where he may be persuaded through rational argument' (Bondurant 1965:11). However, as Galtung points out, Gandhi has a further line of defence and, 'if appeals to reason and compassion do not lead anywhere, non-violent revolutions in the forms of non-cooperation and (defensive and offensive) civil disobedience may be the answer' (1998:52). Thus, the third stage is that of non-violent direct action, which can take these two or other forms.[16] Here Rath points out that 'while civil disobedience can be undertaken only against a governmental authority, non-cooperation can be applied in cases of personal and group conflict also' (1986:857).

This paper concentrates on the first stage of *satyagraha*, since, according to the Gandhian scheme, in dyadic conflicts the chief measures to be used should be discussion and persuasion (Weber 1991:63). *Satyagraha* will be mainly examined as a non-violent dialogical process that strives for a creative, constructive and mutually agreed solution through both determination and openness and aims to resolve the underlying conflict. However, it is also important to bear in mind the other dimensions since they are at the root of *satyagraha*'s distinctiveness and comprehensiveness and, as I will argue below, allow it to provide an interesting global reinterpretation of the ADR debates.

Precepts of *Satyagraha*

As last task in our analysis of the Gandhian approach to conflict and by way of summing up I will briefly refer to some of the main precepts of *satyagraha*. Following from all that has been said and basing myself on the works of Galtung (1998:84-96) Næss (1974:70-85) and Webber (1991:36-40; 2001:494-506), I will try to synthesize them in the following four normative points.

First, according to Gandhi, one should always act positively and non-violently to solve the conflict. Parties should seek negotiation and not continue the struggle forever. Opponents should see conflict positively as an opportunity for personal and social transformation and act in a non-violent manner, without neither humiliating or provoking the other side nor letting themselves be provoked or humiliated. The purpose should not be coercion but conversion.

Secondly, one should define the conflict well and avoid polarization. Disputants should be clear and sincere about the elements of their case and the purpose of their struggle, so that the other party could understand their position. Moreover, efforts should be made to formulate essential common interests and establish cooperation on that basis. In addition, one should be empathetic with the case of her opponent and always distinguish between antagonism and antagonist.

Thirdly, one should be willing to compromise on non-essentials but not in aspects of principle. *Satyagraha*, as it has been pointed out above, is a process of synthesis rather than compromise. Accordingly, the aim would be to seek solutions that are acceptable by both parties.

And fourthly, one should see oneself as fallible and be generous when viewing the opponent. Opponents should remember that they might be wrong and be open to admit their errors. Conversely, they should trust their adversaries without judging them harder than themselves or exploiting their position of weakness.

References

1. Although he left a copious amount of writings, Gandhi was not concerned with developing a systematic corpus of theory. Answering negatively to a friend's petition of writing a treatise on the science of non-violence he argued: 'I am not built for academic writings. Action is my domain' (*Harijan*, 3 March, 1946). 'My life' he declared 'is my message' (*The Hindustan Standard,* 7 September, 1947).

2. *Young India* and *Harijan* are the names of newspapers edited by Gandhi, where he published a great deal of his writings. Gandhi's articles can be found in his *Collected Works* (1958-1991).
3. Most scholars and activists have given attention to *satyagraha* in relation to international, social and group conflicts (i.e. Burrowes 1996; King 1958). Weber (1986; 1991; 2001) is one of the few authors that have dealt with *satyagraha* from a primarily interpersonal point of view. Nevertheless, Gandhi placed great importance to conflict resolution at the interpersonal level and warned that 'if one does not practice non-violence in one's personal relations with others and hopes to use it in bigger affairs, one is vastly mistaken' (*Harijan*, 28 January, 1939).
4. An interesting philosophical enquiry into the concept on non-violence is provided by Muller (1995).
5. Gandhi held a very wide conception of violence, which entailed not only physical aggression but referred to 'anything that would impede individual self-realisation' (Galtung 1998:61).
6. I disagree here with Bondurant when she claims that *satyagraha* contains 'a positive element of coercion' (1965 : 9). In my opinion, a coerced outcome is intrinsically incompatible with the ends of *satyagraha* described below. As Gandhi argued, 'there is not such thing as compulsion in the scheme of non-violence' (*Harijan,* 23 July, 1938); 'since satyagraha is a method of conversion and conviction, it seeks never to use the slightest coercion' (1958-1991 : XXVI : 267).
7. However Gandhi did not base *satyagraha* upon a naïf conception of human nature, stating that 'every one of us is a mixture of good and evil' (*Harijan,* 10 June, 1939).
8. See Prahbu (2001 : 6).
9. Practitioner of *satyagraha.*
10. For practical purposes, when not alluding to a particular person, I use in this paper the forms she and her as referring, respectively, both to she and he and to her and his.
11. However, several psychological studies on the effects of self-suffering have revealed that "any sweeping general statement about it 'melting the hearts' of others is a gross oversimplification" (Pelton 1974:143). In this vein, Gandhi strongly warned against the dangers of brutalizing the opponent (Burrowes 1996:112) and argued that the undertaken suffering had to be functional to the resolution of present or future conflicts (Weber 1991:52).
12. It is hard to find in the works of *satyagraha* scholars an explicit definition of the Gandhian concept of conflict. They usually refer to it, in the context of the Gandhian theory of conflict, as a state of incompatibility (Galtung 1985:95; Weber 1991:14-16).
13. In the Quaker tradition, for example, Quaker law, being directed at preventing the appearance of conflict, is primarily regarded as a mechanism of dispute avoidance (Bradney and Cownie 2000).

14. Following this structural consideration Rath states that for Gandhi '*himsa* or violence' was the primary root of conflict (1986:853). Burrowes, in an attempt to narrow it down, declares that, in the Gandhian scheme, 'conflict is the result of the structural denial of human needs' (1996:112).
15. Gandhi argues that 'whereas a good deed should call forth approbation and a wicked deed disapprobation, the doer of the deed, whether good or wicked, always deserves respect or pity as the case may be' (Gandhi 2001 : 254).
16. See, for example, Prahbu (2001 : 5).

3

Satyagraha and ADR Compared

In order to explore possible reasons for approaching ADR from a Gandhian perspective, I first investigate in this section the existence of certain parallelisms between *satyagraha* and the ADR literature and attempt to outline the advantages of adopting a Gandhian approach to conflict. Before that, however, an introductory remark on the possibility of relating and comparing both traditions is needed. Gandhi's *satyagraha* has a much broader field of application than ADR, the latter being mainly focused on the management of civil disputes, and the former encompassing a wider range of situations as, for instance, those dealt with by criminal law. Nevertheless, this does not pose any problem to our enterprise. As shown by Gandhi's concerns and remarks,[1] *satyagraha* is very much focused on the kind of disputes which are dealt by ADR.

Gandhian Resonances in the ADR Literature

Although ADR has as one of its foundational aims the development of non-violent and less coercive dispute resolution mechanisms (Jeong 1999 : 393), there is no apparent causal relation between the emergence of this contemporary movement or its search for 'alternative' mechanisms of dispute resolution and the Gandhian approach to conflict.[2] Moreover, the exploration of possible links between *satyagraha* and the ADR tradition has received nearly no attention from the academic world.[3] However, the Gandhian approach to conflict and its precepts outlined above, as any ADR scholar would notice while reading them, are often echoed by the ADR literature. Attempting to shed some light on the existence of such resonances, I briefly try to unravel certain parallelisms between *satyagraha* and several ADR trends and writings in the following paragraphs:

First, the positive view of conflict implicit in *satyagraha* clearly echoes the 'constructive' view of conflict held by many intellectual mothers and fathers of ADR. Contrary to scholars that view conflict as 'a problematic aspect of human life, requiring resolution or management', conflict situations were seen by 'founders' of ADR such as Parker Follett or by social theorists of great influence in the ADR field such as Simmel and Coser, as a positive and valuable opportunity that could contribute to the enrichment of all (Menkel-Meadow 2000 : 6-7).

Secondly, the Gandhian view of conflict as an occasion to reaffirm and reinforce human relations parallels the relationship concerns of the early developers of ADR. A leading ADR jurisprudential thinker such as Fuller, for instance, highlighted repeatedly the importance of relationships and saw as one of the main strengths of mediation the fact that 'it would bring about a more harmonious relationship between the parties' (1971:308). Fuller's focus on relationships can also be perceived in his concept of 'polycentric disputes', where the existence of a multiplicity of potentially affected parties or interests and its complex interplay might make adjudication an unsuitable dispute resolution mechanism (1978).

Thirdly, the so-called integrative approach to dispute resolution is also reminiscent of Gandhi's *satyagraha*. Although the integrative label has received different interpretations[4] and covers a broad range of literature stemming from diverse sources,[5] it usually refers to the approach that seeks to reach an integrative agreement, i.e. an agreement that, going beyond mere compromises, reconciles the parties interests' so that they are all satisfied (Pruit 1987:68). *Satyagraha*, though in the deeper meaning of a 'fusion of the two actors into one' and a 'harmonisation of their goals, i.e. their interests and values' (Galtung 1998:77, 81), also aims at this integration. Moreover, the integrative approach echoes the Gandhian approach in the strategies it suggests to achieve its objective; strategies that, without any reference to Gandhi, have filled the pages of many negotiation best-seller manuals.[6] Not being able to develop here a complete comparative study, I will just use as an example the insights of the probably most paradigmatic how-to negotiation books: Robert Fisher and William Ury's[7] *Getting to Yes* (1999). In their work, Fisher and Ury describe an integrative strategy, 'principled negotiation', whose basic precepts contain several Gandhian reverberations. The first precept, 'separate the people from the problem' (1999:17-40) clearly reminds us of the Gandhian stress on distinguishing between antagonism and antagonist (Rath 1986 : 852). The second, 'focus on interests, not on positions' (1999 : 41-57) can be associated with *satyagraha*'s instructions to define well the conflict, avoid polarization, formulate essential common interests and be willing to compromise on non-essentials (Weber 2001:494, 505-506). The third, 'invent options for mutual gain' (1999:58-83), echoes *satyagraha*'s aims to create new choices and to restructure the opposing elements of a conflict in order to achieve a synthesis that is satisfactory to all parties and superior to any one of the original positions (Bondurant 1965; Burrowes 1996:108). The fourth, 'insist on using objective criteria' (1999:84-98), parallels Gandhi's emphasis on truth as the essential base of conflict resolution (Weber 1991:43-47). Finally, even Fisher and Ury's advice on dealing with difficult situations, what they call 'negotiation Jujitsu', i.e. not reacting to an opponent's attack and deflecting it against the problem (1999:112-118), strongly recalls the basic principles of non-violent activism.[8]

Fourthly, there are important parallels between the Gandhian approach to conflict and the 'popular justice' movement—an important strand in the ideological currents underlying ADR—and, more specifically, the agendas of community based ADR programs. The latter's promise to provide a 'more consensual and non-violent process for settling disputes' (Merry and Milner 1995:3) clearly echoes some concerns of *satyagraha*. Community mediation aims 'to empower both mediators and disputants by enhancing their capacity to manage their own conflicts', hoping that 'handling local problems in community-run forums independent of the legal system' strengthens 'local self-governance and rejuvenate the self-reliant communities of the past' (Merry and Milner 1995:16,10). According to a leading inspirer of the San Francisco Community Board, Raymond Shonholtz, 'decentralized neighbourhood justice systems have the capacity to reach into a community and engage conflicts before they escalate into violence... building community cohesion and understanding' in an 'effort to empower neighbourhoods to resolve their day-to-day conflicts'(1984:16-17). Community, violence prevention, empowerment and party control over the outcome are key ideas that find important parallelisms in the Gandhian philosophy.[9] Moreover, this community justice ideals echo the importance Gandhi placed in the notions of *swaraj* (self-rule) and of *swadeshi* (self-reliance) in both the individual and the communitarian levels. On the one hand, they share *satyagraha*'s aim to reach personal and social transformation and to enhance the self-reliance and autonomy of the parties in dealing with conflict situations. On the other hand, their stress on community also relates to the Gandhian political project, centred on the creation of autonomous and self-sufficient small communities.[10]

Fifthly, although far from the mainstream ADR practice, the transformative approach to dispute resolution also bears important resemblances with *satyagraha*. Here we could mention as an example the work of Bush and Folger (1994). In their book *The Promise of Mediation* these authors suggest that 'mediation's greatest value lies in its potential not only to find solutions to people's problems but to change people themselves for the better' (1994 : xv). This transformative goal, which, according to the authors, 'remains largely unfulfilled' (1994 : xvi), can be achieved through mediation potential to foster 'empowerment'—the 'capacity to exercise autonomy, choice and self-determination' (Bush 1989 : 268)—and 'recognition'[11]—the 'evocation in individuals of acknowledgment and empathy for the situation and problems of others' (Bush and Folger 1994 : 2). Transformative mediation echoes, therefore, *satyagraha's* search for greater awareness of the other, reaffirmation of human unity, personal growth and self-realisation.[12]

In short, numerous elements of *satyagraha* reverberate in various ADR writings. However, the Gandhian view often goes deeper and well beyond these shared concerns or similarities, especially if we take as element of comparison a most of the mainstream ADR literature, very much focused in developing more efficient, court decongesting, less costly and more satisfactory dispute resolution mechanisms. *Satyagraha*, as it has already been said, based in human transcendence, aspires at conversion and strives for personal and social transformation. Moreover, with its focus towards resolving the underlying conflict and fighting its structural causes, it aims even beyond the objectives of the community justice movement or the transformative approach to dispute resolution.

Why *Satyagraha*?

The existing resemblances between ADR and the Gandhian approach to conflict already raise the issue of how both traditions might enrich each other. Furthermore, one can spot several general reasons for adopting, or at least taking into account, a Gandhian perspective when dealing with conflict. To them I turn in the following paragraphs:

As we have already seen, in spite of not being a theorist, Gandhi, through both his life and work, provided a very complete and watertight approach to conflict and its resolution. According to Galtung, Gandhi developed a full 'conflictology', very rich in both 'empirical' and 'normative' elements (1998:38). Moreover, argues Arne Næss, the concrete nature of the problems upon which one can develop the Gandhian theory of conflict do not reduce but increase its value (1958:141).

Furthermore, *satyagraha* is fully consistent with an important strand of contemporary conflict resolution theory, especially with the works of Burton and Galtung (Burrowes 1996:106; Weber 2001). The writings these two scholars, in their understanding and conceptualisation of conflict and of its resolution (e.g. in their 'positive' conceptualisation of conflict or in the importance they place on denial and satisfaction of human needs to understand conflict and its resolution) support, as I argue in this dissertation, the main tenets of *satyagraha.*[13]

In addition, beyond the reminiscences in the theoretical literature, empirical studies on negotiation strategies tend to support the adoption of *satyagraha*'s precepts. The studies by Weiss-Wink, pointing out, for instance, the positive results of concentrating on the satisfaction of the other party's intangible needs (1983:720), or Braver and Van Rohrer, stating that parties will most often cooperate if they have reason to believe that their opponent will be benevolent (1975:653), provide just a two examples. In short, as Weber, after reviewing several empirical works, concludes in a recent article, 'the empirical literature... does seem to provide a reasonably strong backing for the validity of the Gandhian approach to conflict resolution' (2001:510).

Besides, the adoption of a Gandhian approach might result in psychological advantages if used when dealing with conflict, especially at the interpersonal level.[14] As Burrowes contends, 'recent psychological studies indicate that Gandhi's conception of non-violence is likely, from the opponent's perspective, to generate the minimum degree of psychological resistance and to increase the rationality of seeking creative outcomes' (1996:115). Here Pelton's study on *The Psychology of Non-violence* (1974) becomes a necessary reference. According to Pelton, non-violent actions which, as *satyagraha,* are aimed at reducing psychological resistance, 'pave the way for trust ... successful negotiations ... and perhaps ultimately attitude change' (1974 : 205). He mentions, as aspects of non-violent action that will serve to increase trust and reduce psychological resistance, precepts of *satyagraha* like limiting oppositional attitudes to the issue itself, respecting and not humiliating the opponent, refusing to exaggerate the justness of one's position or the evils of the adversary's, standing always ready to negotiate or being willing to acknowledge de validity of the opponents arguments (Pelton 1974 : 210).

Moreover, a fundamental strength of the Gandhian approach lies in the comprehensiveness of its goals. On the one hand, aiming at solving the underlying conflict and at attaining both personal and social transformation, *satyagraha* can contribute, among other things, to a more efficient and satisfactory resolution of conflict and to the removal of structural injustices, while endowing the parties with the necessary skills to deal with future disagreements. On the other hand, *satyagraha* entails further benefits that are more difficult to measure (Weber 1991:6). An example is provided by its integration, with no contradiction, of both practical-efficiency and ethical-existential considerations. *Satyagraha* has an ultimately ethical nature. It is from an ethical perspective that we should view, for instance, its principles of unity between means and ends, ahimsa, or shared humanity of all adversaries. The Gandhian approach is, strongly based on profound moral premises and it ultimately aims at personal self-realisation. This ethical and existential stance is often lacking in the mainstream ADR literature and might make the Gandhian approach ethically superior (Weber 1991:134). Moreover, according to Gandhi, *satyagraha,* constitutes a complete lifestyle of intrinsic value, a doctrine that 'teaches us the art of living' (cited in Tendulkar 1951:VII:89). Here Iyer argues that, being *satyagraha* 'dependent on non-utilitarian assumptions', 'it would certainly be wrong to judge [it] on utilitarian grounds, on the practical results achieved' (1973:302). However Gandhi constructed his method also on the grounds of effectiveness and efficiency.[15] Hence, to sum up, conducting conflict in a Gandhian fashion may not only be instrumentally valuable but also intrinsically important in an existential sense (Weber 2001:508).

In the previous paragraphs I have pointed out several general reasons for adopting a Gandhian approach to conflict. However one might still wander if there are any more specific grounds that support a Gandhian reading of ADR or in what concrete sense the ADR debate might be enriched from its contact with the insights of *satyagraha.*[16] The fact that Gandhi was probably the twentieth century most paradigmatic living epitome of the search for alternative and non-violent means of conflict resolution should already provide a motivation to reread the ADR movement from a Gandhian perspective. Nevertheless, I believe there are also further motivations on whose basis it might be argued that *satyagraha* can provide a valuable contribution, or at least an alternative perspective, to the ADR discussions. It is towards its exploration that I direct the last and core part of this paper, which now begins.

References

1. E.g. *Harijan*, 28 January, 1939.
2. Carrie Menkel-Meadow, for instance, in a recent article on the intellectual founders of ADR (2000), does not refer, even once, to possible influences from the non-violent movement, let alone from the Gandhian *satyagraha*, in the development of ADR.
3. References to Gandhi are nearly non-existent in the ADR literature. Conversely, most works on the Gandhian approach to conflict (e.g. Galtung 1985, 1998; Rath 1986) do not draw any relationships with the ADR movement. Probably the only work that has examines the resemblances between contemporary conflict resolution theory and *satyagraha*, although mainly focused on negotiation literature, is a recent article by Weber (2001).
4. See, for instance Murray Rau and Sherman (1996:131) or Gifford (1985:54).
5. An integrative approach can be already found in the work of Parker Follett (Menkel-Meadow 2000:8) or in the work of Deutsch and his distinction between 'constructive' and 'destructive' conflict (1969;1987).
6. Having reviewed the existing negotiation literature, the Gandhian scholar Thomas Weber concludes that the precepts of *satyagraha* 'are very reminiscent of the key concepts put forward by the self-help negotiation manuals as the main components of achieving win-win solutions' (2001:507).
7. Including Bruce Patton as co-author in its second edition.
8. In this vein, see Richard B. Gregg (1935:26).
9. Some elements that hint such a resemblance can be found in a mid-eighties article on Gandhian ethics by Weber (1986:697).
10. See Parekh (1997).
11. Mediation's potential for recognition was already stressed early in the ADR debate by Fuller (1971:326).

12. Similarly, echoing *satyagraha*'s concerns for conversion, we find ADR trends which contend that mediation's true promise lies in its transformative 'power with' approach to conflict (e.g. Chornenki 1997).
13. I do not outline here the existing consistencies, since they recurrently appear in the development of the paper. However, as a mere curiosity, and although Gandhi himself would probably not have agreed with the element of comparison, I reproduce a description by Deutsch of the positive view of conflict endorsed by Burton: 'A British political scientist, John Burton (1972) has said that conflict is like sex. It is an important and pervasive aspect of life. It should be enjoyed and should occur with a reasonable degree of frequency. After conflict is over, people should feel better as a result'; Deutsch himself concludes: 'such is my orientation to conflict' (1987:38).
14. However, this statement should be taken cautiously when referring to creative self-suffering. See note 12 above.
15. See *The Amrita Bazar Patrika*, 16 of September, 1933.
16. Since the approach of this paper is from *satyagraha* to ADR, I concentrate on the benefits that the contact might have in the latter. However, although I do not tackle them here, I believe that the establishing of a relationship also benefits *satyagraha*. For instance, bearing in mind the little attention that has been given to the Gandhian approach to interpersonal conflict, the contact with ADR, being this latter dimension of conflict one of ADR's core concerns, constitutes a valuable opportunity to rediscover that often forgotten dimension of the *satyagraha* tradition.

4

Rethinking ADR from Gandhian Perspective

Looking for possible grounds to uphold the above thesis, I will tentatively explore in this section several ADR debates from the Gandhian approach to conflict. The following paragraphs, however, should not be regarded as an attempt to analyse all the effects of reading ADR from *satyagraha*, but as mere examples that hint how ADR might be reinterpreted in a Gandhian light.

From Dispute Settlement to Conflict Resolution

The terms 'dispute' and 'conflict' have been often used in a similar sense in the academic literature dealing with dispute processes and conflict resolution. A paramount example is provided by the anthropologist Philip Gulliver.[1] In his book *Disputes and Negotiations* (1979), Gulliver does not establish a distinction between the two concepts and, as pointed out by Silverman (1995:133), he sometimes employs both terms as equivalents. Likewise, looking at the existing works dealing with disputes and conflicts, expressions like 'conflict resolution', 'dispute settlement' and 'conflict management' are often used synonymously (Weber 2001: 494).[2] However, numerous scholars distinguish between the meanings of 'dispute' and 'conflict'. John Burton, in the field of international conflict resolution, refers to the term dispute as a situation regarding negotiable issues, that might just be symptoms of underlying conflicts, which he sees as deeply rooted in human needs (Burton 1990:2). In the field of ADR, to mention two examples, Crowfoot and Wondolleck refer to dispute as 'a specific conflict episode that is part of a continual and larger societal conflict'(1990:17) and Cormick (1982) distinguishes between conflict, as taking place 'when there is a disagreement over values or scarce resources' and dispute as 'an encounter involving a specific issue over which the conflict in values is joined'. In short, while the word 'conflict' usually refers to an underlying incompatibility, the term 'dispute' tends to point at a specific disagreement or manifestation of a broader conflict lying beneath.[3] Here, I use such a distinction to argue that, seen from a Gandhian perspective, the ADR movement should move beyond the predominant assumption, implicit in its acronym, that its procedures merely attempt to settle the manifest dispute, and, aiming its decision-making processes at a deeper level, aspire to resolve the underlying conflict. This move, as I will discuss below, should allow ADR to dismiss certain relevant criticisms raised against its agendas.

Many ADR scholars and practitioners implicitly or explicitly take disputes as their focal point. Marian Roberts, for example, in the field of family mediation, states that 'the primary focus of the mediator is on disputes', i.e. 'specific, identifiable issues which divide the parties and which need to be distinguished from the wider conflict' (1997:77). Disputes, in this context, are understood as 'occasions where one feels he has suffered and injury, sees another as to blame and confronts him with responsibility' (Roberts 1983:7). Furthermore, Crowfoot and Wondolleck, in the area of environmental mediation, arguing that the broader conflict cannot, in a proper sense, be resolved, state that the aim of mediation should simply be that of 'dispute settlement' (1990:17-19). Here, according to Cormick, a dispute is considered as having been settled 'when the parties find a mutually acceptable basis for disposing of the issues in which they are in disagreement, despite their continuing differences over basic values' (1982:3).

A Gandhian reading of ADR, however, makes us shift from a position of not dealing with the underlying conflict to a commitment to solve conflict in all its dimensions. From a *satyagraha* perspective decision-making processes should be aimed at resolving the underlying conflict. One of Gandhi's central precepts is that 'conflicts should be solved' and not 'brushed under the carpet' (Galtung 1998:92). Dealing with only the dispute, with the manifest claim brought forth by the parties, and not addressing the profound and often structural roots of conflict, is not the proper way to tackle the situation from a Gandhian standpoint. As Burrowes states (1996: 107), *satyagraha* attempts to solve the three corners of what Galtung (1998: 50) names the 'conflict triangle': 'the attitude, the behaviour and the goal incompatibility itself'. In addition, *satyagraha* aims at conversion, not at mere accommodation, and does not consider the conflict resolved unless an agreement satisfying the needs of both parties has been reached. Settling the immediate dispute without resolving the underlying conflict cannot be viewed as a satisfactory outcome in the light of the aims of *satyagraha*. In Gandhian terms, with such a superficial and fragile redressing of the problem we shall seldom advance in the resolution of the incompatibilities or underlying causes that prompted its emergence—thus possibly reappearing in the future. In addition, we will loose the chance that disputes, according to Gandhi, offer us to achieve, through a non-violent process, both human and social transformation. What is more, we might be misleadingly attributing the problem to the parties, while probably covering up and perpetuating perverse structures, whose demolition is one of the main aims of *satyagraha*. An illustration of such a necessary switch from dispute to conflict can be drawn, for instance, from the field of discrimination. Workplace disputes involving ethnic or cultural minority groups, for example, will sometimes arise from race discrimination or, at least, will often be heavily enmeshed in racist social and cultural understandings. Settling the manifest dispute will imply just focusing on the specific case and placing the concrete responsibility on certain parties, but it might not contribute very much to the resolution of the issues lying beneath. A Gandhian approach, viewing the dispute as an opportunity to improve the social structure, would also direct its efforts to attain a less discriminatory society, rather than focusing exclusively on the specific authors of a concrete act of discrimination. In this vein, for example, it would strive for public awareness and recognition of the existing 'injustices' stemming from racial discrimination and would seek a social commitment aimed at its removal. In its attempt it might resort to non-violent techniques, such as non-cooperation with discriminatory institutions or protest campaigns, going well beyond the mere bilateral processes of decision-making.

Yet, I do not claim that the Gandhian approach brings a totally new insight within the wide range of traditions related to ADR. Some existing approaches to mediation, for instance, try precisely to focus not only on the manifest disagreement but also on the deep causes that gave raise to it. Chinese mediation provides here and example. As shown by Alasdair Claire, change in attitude and reconciliation, focusing on the underlying issues, are often pointed out as some of its essential traits (1984:102-108). Gandhi, therefore, more than providing a totally new approach, might be viewed as reinforcing this focus on the deep roots of conflict, already present in some trends hovering around the ADR movement. However, what is distinct in *satyagraha* is that, when doing so, it is not trying to implement any specific existing values or social policies, such as it is often the case in Chinese mediation (Palmer 1988:244-252), but it strives for a joint search for justice, whose aims are defined through the dialogical interaction, conflict being, more than an occasion for enforcing existing values, an opportunity to change them (Galtung 1998: 32-96).

Although outside the *satyagraha* framework, further considerations support this move from dispute settlement to conflict resolution in a way that strongly resembles the Gandhian reasoning. I will briefly mention some of them. First, the emphasis on resolving the underlying conflict is strongly present in the contemporary conflict theories of Burton and Galtung. Both authors, while providing different understandings of conflict, stress the importance of tackling the central causes of conflict, which they see as residing on the denial of human needs (Burrowes 1996:68). Secondly, closer to the ADR field, Dugan's 'Nested Theory of Conflict' (1996), provides an additional base from which to defend a shift towards conflict resolution. Dugan's analysis illustrates the shortcomings of 'astructural' or 'neutral' approaches to conflict 'that continue to predominate in the sphere of mediation' and points to 'the need for new understandings of the practice of intervention that take us beyond the surface and help us to reach toward the structural roots of trouble' (Dyck 2000:135). Dugan develops a paradigm that distinguishes, from micro to macro, four different layers of conflict (issues-specific, relational, structural-subsystemic and structural-systemic) and argues that, being these layers 'nested' inside one another, conflicts at one level are usually related to conflicts at the other levels (Dugan 1996). Thirdly, going a step further, Dyck, both scholar and mediator, contends that 'issues-specific conflicts cannot exist entirely on their own' and that there is an 'ever present connection between issues-specific and systemic conflict' (2000:137). Finally, also echoing Gandhi's worries about ignoring the structural dimensions of conflict, certain authors have warned about how the current ADR ideology might imply a covering up of the structural and deep-rooted social conflicts (Jeong 1999:393-394). For instance, Nader (1995:435-451) argues that, under an ideology of harmony, ADR often downplays the existence of basic conflicts of interest.

However, we must refer to one objection commonly raised against those approaches that aim at resolving the underlying conflict and which would apply to our proposed Gandhian reinterpretation of ADR. Some authors contend that conflict cannot be resolved through mere decision-making processes and that, being an essential element for bringing out change in society, we should not attempt to suppress it (Crowfoot and Wondolleck 1990:17-19). It is possible to reject the objection and defend the Gandhian approach, at least on the two following grounds. On the one hand, as pointed out above, Gandhi did not seek to end up with conflict, which he valued positively, nor to build a conflict-free society. He simply claimed that we should target at the roots of conflict and aim at solving its underlying causes if any progress was to be achieved at all. It is in that sense that we should understand his appeal at conflict resolution, and not, as Crowfoot and Wondolleck state, as 'the once-and-for-all disappearance of conflict' (1990:18). On the other hand, we have to admit that conflict sometimes cannot be solved through mere negotiation, mediation or even adjudication and that its resolution might require wider implications such as structural and policy changes.[4] This should not lead us, however, as it happens in most of the ADR literature, to avoid dealing with the broader conflict and to only concentrate on the manifest dispute. A more ingenious option would be, for example, to adopt a 'problem solving' approach, in the sense proposed by Burton (1990:202-210).[5] Going further, Gandhi, aware of the difficulties of attempting to resolve the underlying conflict, included, as additional stages of his approach, creative self-suffering and non-violent direct action. From a *satyagraha* perspective, decision-making processes such as negotiation and mediation should be regarded as the starting point from where the resolution of the conflict and the possible broader changes it implies should be sought. A specially interesting element of the Gandhian approach to conflict is that it acknowledges, just as Galtung and Burton claim in their theories (Burrowes 1996:68), the possible need of wider structural reforms for its resolution, while at the same time provides mechanisms to achieve them.[6]

Even if often it might not be possible to reach a total solution[7] and albeit the possible need for additional measures, *satyagraha*, arguing both in terms of efficiency and justice, implies having conflict resolution always as an aim of decision-making processes. It can be discussed whether applying this insight to the ADR movement would bring about a revision or reinterpretation of its middle name. Further from that, it would most probably require us to rethink certain widespread assumptions.

Gandhian Assessment of Dispute Process

When attempting to interpret dispute processesing in a Gandhian light, we have to bear in mind that Gandhi did not use the distinction between dispute processing as it has been fixed today by the ADR movement and in the conflict resolution theory. In spite—or precisely because—of that fact, I believe that it can be particularly interesting to briefly examine how the debate about the use of different dispute processes and their essential characters might be seen from a Gandhian perspective. However, far from being a task of description and synthesis, this will imply a personal and subjective interpretation. Furthermore, in accordance with the limited scope of the paper, I will curb such an attempt to the drawing of some comments on three of the most paradigmatic dispute process mechanisms analysed by the ADR literature, i.e. negotiation, mediation and adjudication.[8]

Negotiation, the Primordial Means in *Satyagraha*

The nature of non-violence is dialogical. The Gandhian approach to conflict is based on creating the conditions for the establishment a fruitful dialogue between the parties. In this sense, as I have already discussed, the immediate goal of *satyagraha* in a bilateral conflict is to reach a synthesis of the two opposing claims.[9]

In such an enterprise, negotiations are seen by the Gandhian view as more than mere 'processes of communication, involving the exchange of information, potentially leading to common understanding and joint decision-making' (Palmer and Roberts 1998:18). Negotiations, in addition, are regarded as dialogical non-violent processes containing the opportunity to realise, and aimed actualising, the objectives of *satyagraha*. Therefore, in a Gandhian light, the negotiation process cannot be conceptualised without making reference to its fundamental aims of conflict resolution, search for truth, conversion, reaffirmation of the unity of human beings, empowerment, self-realisation of the parties and social transformation.

Moreover, Gandhian negotiation, becomes in *satyagraha* the primordial means of conflict resolution. The unity of means and ends is a cornerstone of Gandhian philosophy. Since it is through this bilateral or multilateral dialogue that the aims of *satyagraha* are, or at least can be, best met and most suitable accomplished, negotiation becomes the basic process of conflict resolution in the Gandhian scheme. The dialogical structure of negotiation, where parties themselves retain the decision-making power, and in which *satyagraha*'s principles and precepts are applied,[10] offers the most suitable means, in Gandhian terms, to reach the ends of *satyagraha*. I will attempt to develop and defend this thesis in the following lines. Some of the arguments do not apply negotiation in an exclusive manner. Others do stress its unique appropriateness.[11]

A first line of reasoning in defending the primordial character of negotiation comes from the fact that, in the Gandhian approach, conflict cannot be considered totally resolved until both parties reach an agreement. As I have argued above, in seeking conflict resolution, *satyagraha* aims at achieving a mutually satisfactory and agreed-upon solution (Bondurant 1965:195). If the resolution of conflict depends on the satisfaction of the needs of the parties, all the opponents have to be meaningfully involved in determining the outcome (Burrowes 1996: 114).

Moreover, the striving for truth, a central aim of *satyagraha*, can only be accomplished through an open and unconstrained dialogue involving the parties. As it has been explained, Gandhi did not held an absolutist view of truth. As a result, he directed *satyagraha* at reaching a higher truth through the synthesis of the relative truths of all the involved parties. Such an objective, from a Gandhian perspective, is best reached in a dialogical process where the parties can interact directly in order to reach a synthesis by themselves. As Galtung explains, the task of the parties in *satyagraha* is 'to explore each other's views as perspectives together in order to transcend the conflict and create a new system' (1998: 57).

In addition, the referred negotiation process provides an opportunity to develop *satyagraha*'s aim to empower the parties, both in the sense of improving their skills to better deal with conflict in the future and in the sense of enhancing their personal *swaraj* (self-rule). In Weber's words, the Gandhian approach 'gives the individual mastery over their own life, provides them with a mode of conflict resolution that does not rely on expert and institutional methods over which their control is lost' (1991:133).

Moreover, conversion or, at least, the reaffirmation of human unity, constitutes another of *satyagraha*'s fundamental aims that cannot be fully achieved outside the dialogical process of negotiation. *Satyagraha*, which pretends 'to restore oneness, or to create oneness' (Galtung 1998:56) with the opponent, 'is not used against anybody but done with somebody' (Weber 1986: 692). As Galtung points out, seeing conflict 'as a medium through which the parties can develop a higher degree of awareness of themselves as well as the other party', Gandhi goes as far as to 'reject third party intervention' (1998:57).

Lastly, negotiations should also be the preferred mode of decision-making if we bear in mind that a fundamental objective in *satyagraha* is personal self-realisation. From a Gandhian point of view, assuming personal responsibility in negotiations rather than leaving the process on the hands of arbitrators or adjudicators, offers an increased opportunity for personal growth by exposing parties to the views of the other, while it provides an opportunity for self-reflection (Weber 2001:507).

Having said that, Gandhi distinguished his model of ideal negotiations from the more common form of negotiations undertaken by lawyers in representation of the conflicting parties. In the view of *satyagraha*, even when a civil case is in the hands of lawyers a settlement may be reach short of actual judicial adjudication, but rarely will one party see the other's point of view and have undergone a process of 'conversion' thereby removing the source of future such disagreements and the possible need for ensuing litigation (Weber 1986:695-96). It is through the direct participation of the two parties in a process of negotiation that the different aims of the Gandhian approach to conflict are best met.

Avoiding Judicial Adjudication

The criticisms of judicial adjudication have played a fundamental role in the development of the ADR movement. A great deal of ink has been spilled in pointing out the inadequacies and drawbacks of adjudication as a mechanism of dispute resolution.[12] Here I do not intend to reproduce all the debate about the advantages or disadvantages of adjudication. In accordance with the general aim of this paper, I just intend to expose a Gandhian view of this decision-making process, referring it basically to the judicial context.[13]

Although Gandhi worked as a lawyer for a long time, or perhaps precisely because of that fact, he was very critical about the functioning and the desirability of court adjudication as a means of settling disputes, let alone of resolving underlying conflicts. Having practiced for over twenty years, before leaving the profession to devote himself to public service, he had observed: 'I have not a shadow of doubt that society would be much cleaner and healthier if there was less resort to law courts than there is' (*Young India,* 3 December, 1919). In *satyagraha* the appearance of a case in court is seen as a 'failure' that generally precludes the Gandhian dialectic from ever coming into play between the parties (Weber 1986: 695).

Most of the Gandhian criticisms to judicial adjudication can be inferred from what it has been said in the last section about the suitability of negotiation. However, although some of the arguments will be similar from those just stated above, it is worth to explicitly formulate in a few words a Gandhian assessment of such a decision-making process.

First, adjudication, from a Gandhian perspective, is flawed in its root, since it is based on violence and coercion, in both its dehumanising structure, which takes the decision-making power away from the parties and precludes their self realisation, and in its means, being ultimately rooted in the threat of state coercion. From violent or coercive means, in the Gandhian logic, can never flourish desirable ends.

Secondly, the intrinsic structure of adjudication, its adversarial and antagonistic configuration[14] is incompatible with *satyagraha*. Conversion, i.e. both parties ending up seeing themselves in the same side striving to solve the antagonism, becomes nearly impossible, since litigation is based on dialectical confrontation. In fact, adjudication is often nothing but a dialectical battle,[15] out of which the parties can hardly ever emerge as friends, as it is intended by the Gandhian approach to conflict.

Thirdly, the binary and distributive, often winner/looser, character of adjudication[16] also obstructs the logic of *satyagraha*. An agreed upon solution, a fundamental goal for *satyagraha* cannot come from the defeat of one party. What is more, the binary nature of litigation will usually polarise and drive the parties still further apart (Murray, Rau and Sherman 1996 : 19).

Fourthly, truth, in its Gandhian understanding, cannot emerge out of adjudication. The nature of its process, relying on confrontation and on the imposition of an external resolution, cannot lead to a synthesis of relative truths reached and agreed by the parties. Although the idea of a pursuit of truth might be strongly criticised in a postmodern context, such an assertion is echoed in the contemporary work of well-renowned scholars. Menkel-Meadow, for example, when criticising adjudication, contends that 'binary oppositional presentations of facts in dispute are not the best way for us to learn the truth' since it is distorted by 'polarized debate' (1996 : 6).

In short, adjudication might settle the dispute, but seldom will it contribute to resolve its underlying causes,[17] nor to achieve the aims of conflict resolution envisaged by Gandhi. Adjudication inhibits the logic of *satyagraha* from taking place while it imposes an external solution that, with salomonic determination, breaks the Gordian knot of conflict instead of undoing it. Therefore, from a Gandhian perspective, adjudication should be avoided as much as possible in our dealing with conflicts.

The Gandhian Mediator[18]

Although negotiation has been presented as the primordial means of dispute resolution, sometimes such a process might not desired by, or suitable for, the parties. The Gandhian approach that I build in this paper does not assume that all conflicts can or should be negotiated. In some cases, where negotiation is not a suitable option, mediation provides a form of third party intervention aimed at facilitating the resolution of the conflict, which is far more consistent with the aims and principles of *satyagraha* than adjudication. In this sense, as proved by the introductory quotation of this paper, Gandhi himself, when working as a lawyer, conceived the exercise of the legal profession as mainly directed to mediate between disputing opponents and to 'unite parties riven asunder' (Gandhi 2001:133).[19] While the outcome sought in it is an accommodation between the parties, mediation can lead to the conversion aimed at by *satyagraha* and so come close to the Gandhian ideal.

The Gandhian mediator would act as a *satyagraha* catalyser, helping the parties to jointly reach an agreed-upon and mutually satisfactory solution, aiming to resolve the underlying conflict, to reach a higher degree of truth, and to achieve transformation in both the opponents and their larger social environment. In this latter sense, the Gandhian model of mediation would be directed to the development of those skills and attitudes in the parties that contribute to the building of a non-violent society, of a culture of peace. As stated by Boubault, referring in general to non-violent mediation, 'every choice towards mediation constitutes a progress from the perspective of a non-violent society' (1993:11).

In its relation to the different existing models of mediation in the ADR literature, Gandhian mediation would highly resemble in certain aspects the transformative model of mediation proposed by Bush and Folger (1994) mentioned above. The Gandhian mediator would aspire at both fostering empowerment of the disputing parties and recognition between opponents. However, the Gandhian model aims even deeper. *Satyagraha*, as we have seen, implies more than empowerment and recognition. The Gandhian mediator, attempting to implement the principles, precepts and objectives of *satyagraha* is also a non-violent activist. I will try to say something about this combined role in the following lines.

Mediation and non-violent advocacy are usually understood as two different roles that mutually exclude each other. While the mediator is often seen as a neutral third party that helps opponents to achieve a joint decision, the non-violent activist is frequently understood as a partisan that intervenes non-violently in conflict in order to support certain interests. However, as it is implied by several scholars and mediators these two roles overlap, complement, and are mutually supportive and dependent of each other (Lederach 1995:14). Dyck, in a recent article, observing that the interaction between mediation and non-violent activism 'remains unfortunately scarce', claims that 'the roles of mediation and non-violent advocacy/activism are best carried out when it is understood that they are each part of a larger framework of conflict resolution or peacebuilding that makes room for them both' and that 'the energies and skills of both mediation and non-violent activism should come into play in the practice of both roles' (2000:130). I believe that is in this sense that we should understand Gandhian mediation, which, being engaged and directed at pursuing the aims of *satyagraha*, integrates the activity of both the mediator and the non-violent activist. The Gandhian model, while attempting to bring the parties together and to facilitate them reaching a joint decision, also aims at resolving the underlying conflict, attaining a higher degree of truth and achieving personal and social transformation.

However this activist engagement poses serious questions to certain implicit and widespread assumptions that lie beneath the mainstream western practice of mediation. We have already referred to the prevalent focus of numerous mediation practitioners in dispute settling (Crowfoot and Wondolleck 1990 : 17-19; Roberts 1997 : 77) and to the shift towards conflict resolution that *satyagraha*, and consequently Gandhian mediation, would imply. Here, to illustrate how *satyagraha* might contribute to the existing debate on the understanding of mediation, I will briefly refer to the issue of the mediator's neutrality and attempt to assess it from a Gandhian perspective.[20] Neutrality or impartiality is often seen as an important aspect in the conduct of the mediator. In this vein, the Standards of Conduct for Mediators approved in 1994 by the American Bar Association Section on Dispute Resolution, state that: 'the concept of mediator impartiality is central to the mediation process' and that 'a mediator shall mediate only those matters in which she or he remains impartial and even-handed'. A Gandhian approach to mediation, which, amongst other aims, intends to get at the roots of conflict and to change the underlying structures from which this emerges, can prove incompatible with such a neutral or impartial form of intervention.[21] As Dick questions: 'if a mediator were to truly seek to work from a full awareness of a given interpersonal conflict's possible connections to inequitable relational patterns or structures, could he or she still claim a place for the stance of strict neutrality without running a very high risk of simply perpetuating those inequities that give rise to the conflict in the first place?' (2000: 138). Thus, in a Gandhian light, the ideal of a neutral mediator would be both misleading and, in the sense of reinforcing the existing homeostasis, potentially dangerous. Close to this *satyagraha* reading we find, in the contemporary mediation literature, Kraybill's argument that 'neutrality is an illusion' since 'we are advocates of something all the time whether we are conscious of it or not' (2000: 291, 292). Similarly, as a mediator, Dyck argues that 'when we remain unconscious of that which we are advocating—that is neutrality—it is highly likely that we will act (read: mediate/advocate) in such a way as to reinforce whatever relationships and structures are currently in place' (2000:141). Thus, *satyagraha* does not only acknowledge an inevitable partiality but supports a commitment towards it, for example, in the Gandhian mediator's attempts to empower the weak parties, to improve existing relationships or to dismantle unjust structures. Moreover, if necessary, the process of *satyagraha* might have to move from the negotiation and mediation phase to the further stages of non-violent direct action, with a possible direct involvement of the mediator in them. An example of this latter possibility is provided by Gandhi's intervention in a dispute between textile labourers and mill owners over salary increase that took place in Ahmedabad around February 1918 (Bondurant 1965 : 65-73). In that conflict the labourers demanded a fifty per cent increase in their salaries due to a sharp raise in general prices and the mill owners called Gandhi to intervene as a conciliator. Gandhi moved to Ahmedabad and investigated the situation on his own. After a failed attempt to bring the conflict to a panel of arbitrators, Gandhi concluded that a thirty-five per cent increase was a just demand and advised the workers to ask no more and no less than that amount. When the mill owners rejected the proposal, not seeing any prospects for a fair outcome, Gandhi became the leader of the labourers, launching a *satyagraha* campaign. In short, the implicit engagement that underlies Gandhian mediation is incompatible with the notion of mediation neutrality and leads to an active role of the mediator directed at securing the aims of *satyagraha*.[22]

Overcoming Criticisms

Having briefly described some of the insights that a Gandhian perspective might bring into our understanding of dispute processes I will finally turn to the broader picture in order to briefly sketch how a *satyagraha* reading of ADR can help us both to overcome certain paramount criticisms that have been often directed against such a movement.

Satyagraha, with its integral and distinct approach to conflict resolution, can provide some clues to the overcoming of several criticisms that have been often directed to the ADR literature. Jeong, summarizing those critical appraisals, states that ADR 'given its emphasis on how to settle disputes without regard to power disparities...can be seen as another mechanism of social control', that 'the supposed neutrality of a third party favours compromise and conceals the biased impact of power imbalance on the outcome' and that 'since ADR is embedded in individualism, it is not looking to structural inequalities in the society as a reason for conflict' thus leading to 'the privatisation of dispute settlement' (1999:394). Reinterpreting ADR in a Gandhian light these criticisms can be thoroughly questioned, if not even dismissed. In the following lines, bearing in mind that its arguments should be elaborated much further, I will outline how these critical accounts might be recast from the point of view of *satyagraha*.

First, critics often argue that ADR processes such as mediation, due to its informality, lack of procedural safeguards and emphasis on consensuality are not suitable to deal with disputes where considerable power imbalances exist between the parties and that in those cases adjudication becomes the most suitable process (Abel 1982; Fiss 1984; Levine 1984). The Gandhian approach to conflict puts such a criticism into question since, combining in the process of *satyagraha* both negotiation and non-violent direct action, it provides an alternative to adjudication that is precisely designed to empower the weak, without resorting to the use of state coercion. It is in this sense that it should be also understood *satyagraha*'s deep empowerment claim. As Galtung points out, 'Gandhi's approach to power ... was through power-over-oneself rather than through building up new types of power-over others', so that, as an 'alternative balancing power-over-others with a mere counter-power of the same kind' *satyagraha* would aim at 'the development of that power-over-oneself which consists in controlling fear, dependence and submissiveness, and thus destroying the bases upon which conventional forms of power rest' (1985:100, 101).

Secondly, an important strand of criticism to ADR, and specially to community justice agendas, points out that, through an emphasis on settlement and harmony, the ideology of ADR can lead to covering the structural causes of conflict (Nader 1995: 435-451). Here, *satyagraha*, requiring a shift from dispute settlement to conflict resolution, also provides some clues into the dissolution of this critical claim. Reading ADR from a Gandhian view would imply targeting decision-making processes to the solving of the deep roots of conflict and the transformation, or even demolition, of the 'unjust' social structures (e.g. gender or ethnical discrimination) from which the dispute has emerged. Thus, not only a Gandhian interpretation does overcome the mentioned criticisms but contains their expressed concerns as central aims.

Thirdly, some critics have argued that ADR, in favouring settlement and moving away from adjudication, implies loosing an occasion for the assertion by courts of legal and political values, in the sense that 'when parties settle, society gets less than what appears, and for a price it does not know it is paying' (Fiss 1984:1085). In this vein, for example, Luban argues that settlement contributes to the 'erosion of the public realm' (1995: 2619). Here, a Gandhian reading can also help overcome the criticism. On the one hand, *satyagraha* does not aim at settlement, understood as compromise, but at conflict resolution in its deeper sense. Just as Fiss (1984), Gandhi also approached disputes as unique occasions for social transformation and, therefore, for the assertion of public values. The difference is that Gandhi saw the process of *satyagraha*, which, aspiring at a mutually agreed solution, is heavily based on negotiation and mediation and avoids adjudication, as the most suitable forum in which to implement this aim. On the other hand, from a Gandhian approach, leaving the affirmation of public values to courts, i.e. to external thirds inserted in the structure of the state, would be regarded as depriving ourselves of personal *swaraj*, as surrendering both our capacity for self-rule and an opportunity for self realisation in our social interaction. Conversely, in the Gandhian scheme, it is precisely the process of *satyagraha,* through personal and social transformation, that leads to an enrichment of the public sphere.

In short, the important stress placed by Gandhi on the deep and internal indissociability between means and ends, although not unique as an insight,[23] dissolves a false dilemma that is usually taken as the fundamental dichotomy underlying ADR debates. It is often claimed by ADR critics that consensuality, harmony and reconciliation, on the one hand, and justice, on the other, are two alternative and even incompatible ends of dispute processes, and that ADR favours the former while judicial adjudication aims at the latter. Fiss, in his paramount criticism to settlement oriented ADR processes, argues that 'parties might settle while leaving justice undone' (Fiss 1984: 1085). However, when read in a Gandhian light such a dilemma disappears. Gandhi's approach to conflict, echoing both ADR concerns and processes, on the one hand, entails a search for justice, i.e. in Gandhian terms, a search for truth, structural personal and social transformation and the resolution of the underlying conflict; on the other hand, while it does not aim to reach a compromise over the dispute, but a synthesis of the parties needs and relative truths, it aims at empowerment and takes the uncoerced consent of the parties as a basic premise. In *satyagraha* this two aspects are not seen as alternatives. The process of *satyagraha*, both adopting many of the processes of ADR but also going further and incorporating non-violent direct action, combines these two insights, not as different reconciled aims, but as inseparable aspects of a unique struggle, as interrelated, indecipherable, means and ends. Going further, a *satyagraha* standpoint is incompatible with an idea of justice that it is ultimately based, as in judicial adjudication, on the threat of coercion. This view is perhaps incompatible with a widespread iconic image and symbolic understanding of such ideal, involving sword, scales, and blindness. However, form a Gandhian perspective, this external and imposed justice, *blind* to the underlying and structural elements of conflict, that adjudicates through a *scale* calculus of rights and wrongs and which finally relies on the *sword* of coercion, might not be that just after all.

References

1. Sometimes referred as 'one of the most significant contributors to the study of disputes' (Caplan 1995:1).
2. Weber himself seems to use sometimes the terms 'conflict' and 'dispute' indistinctively (i.e.1991:16).
3. Using other terminology, the distinction is echoed by different authors (e.g. Deutsch 1969:10; Galtung 1985:95).
4. Burton, in this vein, distinguishes between 'conflict settlement', usually achieved through negotiation, mediation, arbitration or judicial adjudication, and 'conflict resolution', which only takes place when the outcome totally meets the needs of all the parties (Burton 1984:143).
5. Burton's technique is described as a facilitated analysis of the underlying sources of a conflict by the opponents themselves, i.e. a process in which both policies and institutional frameworks are adjusted in order to meet the needs of all the parties (Burrowes 1996:76).
6. Here certain criticisms to ADR directed, for instance, from feminist theory (e.g. Grillo 1991), could be reinterpreted as favouring this shift towards conflict resolution and social transformation, at which the Gandhian approach aims. Thought in *satyagraha*'s lines, if conflict was to be properly resolved, the gender dimension, as a structural feature, should not be ignored when dealing with any particular dispute. Moreover, the systemic or structural analysis and strive for change, a basic aim of feminist theory (Conaghan 2000:375), constitutes a primary target and concern in *satyagraha.*
7. Burton, for instance, argues that there are some areas of conflict in which there might not be possible resolution. To deal with those areas he proposes an approach he terms provention. The purpose of provention, paralleling the aims of *satyagraha*, is to take steps to remove the sources of the conflict, including its structural causes, and to promote the conditions for collaborative and valued relationships in order to control behaviours (Burton 1990:18).

8. I am aware that such forms of decision-making are often intermeshed and that, treating them as ideal types or models might lead to 'an analytical clarity typically absent in real-life processes' (Palmer and Roberts 1998:18). It is bearing in mind the limitations of such an abstract approach that I undertake the analysis in the following paragraphs.
9. Bondurant develops that point saying that the *satyagrahi* does 'all he can do to persuade the opponent of the correctness of his own position, but, while he carries on his own persuasive activity, he allows the opponent every opportunity and, indeed, invites him to demonstrate the correctness of his (the opponent's) position and to dissuade him of his own position ... His effort is to allow for the emergence of the best restructuring of the situation ... He seeks a victory not over the opponent, but over the situation in the best (in the sense of the total human needs of the situation) synthesis possible... this differs acutely from the notion of compromise' (1965:196).
10. Due to the limited scope of the present work I will not engage in a deep examination of the Gandhian way to conduct negotiations. For an outline of both the process and precepts of *satyagraha*, i.e. the basic guidelines of Gandhian negotiation, see section three above.
11. I am aware, however, that sometimes direct negotiation might not be a desired or even a recommendable mode of proceeding for certain parties. I will tackle this issue when dealing with Gandhian mediation.
12. Here we could mention from early classical works (e.g. Fuller 1978) to more contemporary criticisms (e.g. Menkel-Meadow 1996).
13. I will not analyse other roles, processes or interventions that the courts might deploy in the settling of disputes and will base my discussion in examining an ideal type, adjudication, which often comes entangled with other forms of intervention. I admit that employing the ideal type of judicial adjudication—as an adversarial and dichotomous process in which an independent judge reaches a decision that is heteronymously imposed to the parties, backed by state coercion, and based on legal rights and wrongs—might be totally misleading if we want to properly understand the activity of the courts. In this sense, Trubeck, Sarat, Felstiner, Kritzer and Grossman state that 'most of the literature advocating alternatives to litigation naively assumes that what occurs in courts is adjudication' (1983 : 122). Similarly, Shapiro argues that 'judges tend to share the same means of conflict resolution with other triadic figures, and most of those we would label judges engage in a great deal of mediation' (1981 : 15). However I do not concentrate here in examining the complex range of activities that courts perform, which would entail a complex sociological and ethnographical enterprise. I will limit my comments to the above-defined ideal type of judicial adjudication, which might not be present in total purity in the working of courts. Such a prototype, however, is in the minds of certain judges and lawyers and, although being just an aspect of judicial decision making, still plays an important role, which, in my opinion, justifies its examination and assessment from a normative perspective.

14. Auerbach observes: 'Conflict is channelled into adversary proceedings with two combatants in every legal ring; but beyond the implicit assumption that every fight and any winner is good for society, the social good is ignored ... as rights are asserted, combat is encouraged; as the rule of law binds society, legal contentiousness increases social fragmentation' (1983:10).
15. Thus, for example, it is no surprise to find a recent article on lawyer ethics by Yarn (2000) defending a vision of the attorney as a 'duellist's friend'.
16. As Aubert points out 'the verdict of the court has an either/or character' (1969 : 268).
17. It is often claimed that adjudication focuses on symptoms rather than on underlying causes (Murray, Rau and Sherman 1996:70).
18. A more general overview of the non-violent understanding of mediation is provided in the dossier 'La médiation' (1993), published by Non-violence Actualité.
19. Weber argues that 'Gandhi saw lawyers as mediators rather than the conductors of ordinary legal negotiations' (1986 : 696).
20. Gandhian mediation also diverges from other common understandings of mediation. *Satyagraha*'s aim to reach a higher truth provides a good example of such contrast, an illustration of which we find, in the ADR literature, through Shaw's words, when arguing that 'mediation is not a search for the truth' and that 'while the truth of falsity of the facts the parties bring may be relevant to a court proceeding, they are not what the issues are all about in mediation.' (cited in Murray, Rau and Sherman 1996:303).
21. However this questioning of impartiality and the social transformative role of Gandhian mediation, does not entail, as in some other forms of partial intervention, an 'expectation that the mediator place communal interests before the parties needs' (Palmer and Roberts 1998:110). Gandhi saw no tension in *satyagraha's* strive for both personal and social transformation.
22. This understanding of mediation is already present in the first case Gandhi dealt with as a lawyer. For an interesting description by Gandhi himself see his autobiography (2001:133).
23. Numerous other relevant figures of the XXth century, such as Aldous Huxley (1938) and Hannah Arendt (1970) also provided an important contribution to reinforcing the idea of a necessary accordance between means and ends.

5

Concluding Remarks

The first letter of the ADR acronym is usually employed as referring to the word 'alternative'. Nevertheless, some authors prefer to interpret it as alluding to the term 'adequate' (Menkel-Meadow 2000:2). A Gandhian reading allows us to redefine ADR as both a complete and adequate alternative. The 'adequate' dimension should be here understood as correspondence between means and ends. This constitutive interrelation is one of the most distinctive aspects of *satyagraha*. Its implications have been shown throughout this dissertation. In a Gandhian light, the search for adequate non-violent means or processes has a direct effect on the quality of the outcome and should thus be our primary concern when reflecting upon dispute resolution mechanisms.

The 'alternative' in *satyagraha* goes beyond the common ADR understandings. Jeong, analysing the trajectory of ADR, contends that 'compared with the original goal of empowerment, its function has turned out to be supplementary to and supportive of the existing legal system' (1999 : 394). Moreover, even in the views of the community justice movement, ADR was often seen as a complement, rather than a total alternative.[1] *Satyagraha* however, strives to develop a complete alternative in conflict resolution. This statement, nevertheless, begs a question: alternative to what? The answer in Gandhian terms is simple: alternative to violence and coercion. '*Satyagraha*', Gandhi claimed, 'was conceived as a complete substitute for violence' (*Harijan*, 15 April, 1933). As an approach to conflict, *satyagraha* excludes using any form of violence or coercion. Thus, if understood—like they generally are—as primarily based on the institutionalised coercive power of the state, this exclusion refers both to law and, as a primary means through which legal norms are applied, to judicial adjudication.[2] The Gandhian project is aimed at providing a complete alternative model of social and political organisation, which rejects any reliance on violent or coercive means, even if they are state-sponsored or bound to the rule of law.[3] It is worth noting here that Gandhi mistrusted both the use of law as a means and its capacity for bringing about social change. He argued that 'a change of heart can never be brought about by law, it can only be effected through inner conversion' and that 'when such is accomplished then there is no longer any need of compulsive laws' (cited in Bose 1974 : 144).

Beyond apparently anarchist implications, the preceding reflections hint at additional ways in which the Gandhian approach to conflict might have a say in the ADR debate. They could contribute, for instance, to the contemporary discussion over the cooption of the ADR movement by the legal system and its actors. *Satyagraha*, in the same line as some contemporary ADR scholars (e.g. Menkel-Meadow 1991), with its refusal to employ coercive means, the personal and social function it attributes to conflict resolution and its mistrust and uneasiness towards the modern state,[4] gives us additional arguments to oppose current trends towards legal institutionalisation of ADR. Similarly, concerned with personal empowerment, it would also reject existing professionalisation tendencies in informal dispute processing.

Going a bit further, the Gandhian model reveals us that a set of techniques and processes or a merely institutional change can have a limited effect in the way we deal with conflict. Aiming at providing a complete substitute for violence, Gandhi did not only rely in techniques or procedural devices. We can attempt to create adequate structures and mechanisms but, as Weber points out, the resolution of conflicts along Gandhian lines 'depends to a large degree on how far the principles of *satyagraha* have been internalised' (1991 : 63). Gandhi, conceiving *satyagraha* as an entire way of life, relied more on personal and social rather than institutional transformation. When aiming to achieve a more suitable way to deal with conflict, in a Gandhian light, broader social and personal factors or conditions might be equally or even more important than legal institutionalisation or the provision of alternative dispute resolution mechanisms. The introduction of new processes might not be enough. Perhaps a wider change would be needed if ADR were to deliver its most ambitious promises.

Although perhaps self-evident, it might be useful to bear in mind these Gandhian insights when reflecting about alternative ways to deal with conflict. If, as Jeong states, 'ADR has lost sight of its original purpose' (1999 : 394), a Gandhian approach might offer it a chance to recover some of the original goals of empowerment, and interpret them in a broader perspective. *Satyagraha* provides an alternative to both the way we deal with conflict and the way we understand ADR. From a Gandhian perspective, the ADR movement could be redrawn as an attempt to provide an approach to conflict resolution that, going beyond the provision of certain dispute processes and separated from the violence and coercion of the legal system, could attempt to construct not a mere complement but a complete and substitute alternative to deal comprehensively and creatively with conflict and its different manifestations.

Summing up this paper's arguments, the Gandhian approach to conflict offers a distinct framework from which to interpret and deal with conflict that, while sharing important resonances with numerous ADR postulates, often goes well beyond many of them. *Satyagraha*, consistent with theoretical, empirical and psychological findings of contemporary conflict literature, offers a uniquely comprehensive and integrative perspective to conflict and its resolution from which to reconsider several aspects of the contemporary ADR debate, both reaffirming certain existing strands and providing new alternatives. In this vein, a Gandhian reading of ADR first, suggests a shift of our attention from dispute settlement to conflict resolution; secondly, provides new understandings of the existing processes of decision-making, which, having negotiation as the primordial means of conflict resolution, avoid resorting to adjudication and redefine the figure of the mediator, in a new light, as a *satyagraha* activist; thirdly, endowing it with a framework from which to respond to its major criticisms, redraws ADR as both, in its own terms, an adequate and complete alternative.

This Gandhian approach can generate various reactions. It might be criticized, strongly questioned and even dismissed. Then, as a different voice, it is always worth considering. Conversely, it also might be said that, while interesting, it does not provide an entirely new contribution. I do not contend that the Gandhian insights offer a totally innovative perspective. Gandhi himself often said that there was nothing new in his project.[5] It might be that we knew its merit already. Then, however, it is always worth remembering. Even if only for this purpose, Gandhi's message, as his influence has proved, can be of an extremely valuable assistance.

References

1. Shonholtz, stating the aims of community mediation, declares that 'the effort to empower neighbourhoods to resolve their day-to-day conflicts is complementary to ... the traditional justice system' (1984).
2. The present work is of a far too limited scope to enter into debates on the nature of law or on its conceptualisation as a form of violence. Here I just pretend to point that *satyagraha* offers a total alternative to violence, and thus to law if we follow the widespread understanding of the latter eminently as institutionalised state coercion. For an interesting account on the violence of the legal system see Robert Cover (1986).
3. For a comprehensive exposition of the Gandhian political thought see Iyer (1973).
4. We should bear in mind that 'for Gandhi the vital task today was to explore alternatives not just to contemporary forms of government but to the very institution of the state' (Parekh 1997 : 81).
5. Gandhi often declared: 'I have nothing new to teach the world. Truth and Non-violence are as old as the hills' (*Harijan*, 28 March, 1936).

Bibliography

Abel, R.L. (1982) 'The Contradictions of Informal Justice', R.L. Abel (ed.), *The Politics of Informal Justice, Volume 1, The American Experience*, New York: Academic Press.

Adler, P. (1995) 'The Future of Alternative Dispute Resolution: Reflections on ADR as a Social Movement', S.E. Merry and N.A. Milner (ed.), *The Possibility of Popular Justice: A Case Study of Community Mediation in the United States*, Ann Arbor: University of Michigan Press.

Anderson, P. (1997) 'Trends in ADR since 1990', *The Practical Litigator*, Vol. 8, pp. 7-144.

Arendt, H. (1970) *On Violence*, London: Allen Lane.

Aubert, V. (1969) 'Law as a Way of Resolving Conflicts: The Case of a Small Industrialized Society', L. Nader (ed.), *Law in culture and society*, Chicago: Aldine.

Auerbach, J.S. (1983) *Justice Without Law? Resolving Disputes without Lawyers*, New York: Oxford University Press.

Bailly, Y., F. Bazier, G. Boubault and I. Filliozat (eds.) (1993) *La Médiation*, Montargis: Non-violence Actualité.

Bondurant, J.V. (1965) *Conquest of Violence. The Gandhian Philosophy of Conflict*, Berkeley: University of California Press.

Bose, N.K. (1974) *My days with Gandhi*, New Delhi: Orient Longman.

Boubault, G. (1993) 'Conflict: Danger ou Chance à Saisir?' Y. Bailly, F. Bazier, G. Boubault and I. Filliozat (eds.), *La Médiation*, Montargis: Non-violence Actualité.

Bradney, A. and F. Cownie (2000) *Living without Law: An Ethnography of Quaker Decision-making, Dispute Avoidance and Dispute Resolution*, Aldershot: Ashgate.

Braver, S.L. and V. Rohrer (1975) 'When Martyrdom Pays: The Effects of Information Concerning the Opponent's Past Game Behaviour', *Journal of Conflict Resolution*, Vol. 19, No. 4, pp. 652-62.

Burrowes, R.J. (1996) *The Strategy of Non-violent Defense: A Gandhian Approach*, Albany: State University of New York.

Burton, J.W. (1984) *Global Conflict: The Domestic Sources of International Crisis*, Brighton: Wheatsheaf.

Burton, J.W. (1990) *Conflict: Resolution and Provention*, Basingstoke: Macmillan.

Bush, B.R.A. (1989) 'Efficiency and Protection, or Empowerment and Recognition? The Mediator's Role and Ethical Standards in Mediation", *Florida Law Review*, Vol. 41, pp. 253-86.

Bush, B.R.A. and J.P. Folger (1994) *The Promise of Mediation: Responding to Conflict Through Empowerment and Recognition*, San Francisco : Jossey-Bass.

Caplan, P. (1995) 'Introduction: Anthropology and the Study of Disputes', P. Caplan (ed.), *Understanding Disputes. The Politics of Argument*, Oxford: Berg.

Chornenki, G.A. (1997) 'Mediating Commercial Disputes: Exchanging 'power over' for 'power with", J. Macfarlane (ed.), *Rethinking Disputes: The Mediation Alternative*, London: Cavendish Publishing.

Clayre, A. (1984) *The Heart of the Dragon*, London: Collins/Harvill.

Conaghan, J. (2000) 'Truth, Justice and the Pursuit(s) of Feminism', *Journal of Law and Society*, Vol. 27, pp. 351-58.

Cormick, G. (1982) 'Intervention and Self-Determination in Environmental Disputes: A Mediator's Perspective', *Resolve*, Winter 1982, pp. 1-7.

Cover, R. (1986) 'Violence and the Word', *Yale Law Journal*, Vol. 95, pp. 1601-29.

Crowfoot, J.E. and J.M. Wondolleck (1990) *Environmental Disputes: Community Involvement in Conflict Resolution*, Washington: Island Press.

Deutsch, M. (1969) 'Conflicts: Productive and Destructive', *Journal of Social Issues*, Vol. 25, No. 1, pp. 4-41.

Deutsch, M. (1987) 'A Theoretical Perspective on Conflict and Conflict Resolution', D.J.D. Sandole and I. Sandole-Staroste (eds.), *Conflict Management and Problem Solving: Interpersonal to International Applications*, London: Francis Pinter.

Dugan, M. (1996) 'A Nested Theory of Conflict', *A Leadership Journal: Women in Leadership—Sharing the Vision,* Vol. 1, No. 1, pp. 9-20.

Dyck, D. (2000) 'The Mediator as Non-violent Advocate: Revisiting the Question of Mediator Neutrality', *Mediation Quarterly,* Vol. 18, No. 2, pp. 129-49.

Fisher, M.W. (1971) 'Contrasting Approaches to Conflict', J.V. Bondurant (ed.), *Conflict: Violence and Non-violence* Chicago: Aldine Atherton.

Fisher, R., W. Ury and B. Patton (1999) *Getting to Yes: Negotiating Agreement Without Giving In*, London: Random House.

Fiss, O. (1984) 'Against Settlement', *Yale Law Journal*, Vol. 93, pp. 1073-90.

Fuller, L. (1971) 'Mediation—Its Forms and Functions', *Southern California Law Review*, Vol. 44, pp. 305-39.

Fuller, L. (1978) 'The Forms and Limits of Adjudication', *Harvard Law Review*, Vol. 92, pp. 353-409.

Galtung, J. (1978) *Essays in Peace Research. Peace and Social Structure*, Copenhagen: Ejlers.

Galtung, J. (1985) 'A Gandhian Theory of Conflict', Selbourne (ed.), *In Theory and In Practice: Essays on the Politics of Jayaprakash Narayan*, Delhi: Oxford University Press.

Galtung, J. (1998) *The Way is the Goal: Gandhi Today*, Ahmedabad: Gujarat Vidyapith Peace Research Centre.

Gandhi, M.K. (1933) *Speeches and Writings of Mahatma Gandhi*, Madras: Natesan.

Gandhi, M.K. (1939) *Hind Swaraj*, Ahmedabad: Navajivan.

Gandhi, M.K. (1945) *From Yeravda Mandir: Ashram Observances*, Ahmedabad: Navajivan.

Gandhi, M.K. (1958-1991) *The Collected Works of Mahatma Gandhi*, New Delhi: Publications Division, Ministry of Information and Broadcasting, Government of India.

Gandhi, M.K. (2001) *An Autobiography or The Story of My Experiments with Truth*, London: Penguin Books.

Gifford, D. (1985) 'A Context-Based Theory of Selection Strategy in Legal Negotiations', *Ohio State Law Journal*, Vol. 46, pp. 41-94.

Gregg, R.B. (1935) *The Power of Non-violence*, London: Routledge.

Grillo, T. (1991) 'The Mediation Alternative: Process Dangers for Women', *Yale Law Journal*, Vol. 100, pp. 1545-1610.

Gulliver, P.H. (1979) *Disputes and Negotiations: A Cross-Cultural Perspective*, New York: Academic Press.

Huxley, A.L. (1938) *Ends and Means: An Enquiry into the Nature of Ideals and into the Methods Employed for their Realization*, London: Chatto and Windus.

Iyer, R.N. (1973) *The Moral and Political Thought of Mahatma Gandhi*, New York: Oxford University Press.

Jeong, H. (1999) 'Conflict Management and Resolution', L.R. Kurtz and J.E. Turpin (eds.), *Encyclopaedia of Violence, Peace and Conflict*, London: Academic Press.

King, M.L. (1958) *Stride Toward Freedom: The Montgomery Story*, New York: Harper & Row.

Kraybill, R. (2000) 'The Illusion of Neutrality', Schrock-Chenk (ed.), *Mediation and Facilitation Training Manual: Foundations and Skills for Constructive Conflict Transformation*, Akron: Mennonite Conciliation Service.

Lederach, J.P. (1995) *Preparing for Peace: Conflict Transformation Across Cultures*, Syracuse: Syracuse University Press.

Levine, M.I. (1984) 'Power Imbalances in Dispute Resolution', in *A Study of Barriers to the Use of Alternative Methods of Dispute* Resolution, Vermont Law School.

Luban, D. (1995) 'Settlements and the Erosion of the Public Realm', *Georgetown Law Journal*, Vol. 83, pp. 2610-62.

Menkel-Meadow, C. (1991) 'Pursuing Settlement in an Adversary Culture: A Tale of Innovation Co-Opted or 'The Law of ADR'', *Florida State University Law Review*, Vol. 19, No. 1, pp. 1-46.

Menkel-Meadow, C. (1996) 'The Trouble with the Adversary System in a Postmodern, Multicultural World', *William and Mary Law Review*, Vol. 38, pp. 5-44.

Menkel-Meadow, C. (1997) 'Symposium on Alternative Dispute Resolution: Introduction: What Will We Do When Adjudication Ends? A Brief Intellectual History of ADR', *UCLA Law Review*, Vol. 44, pp. 1613-1630.

Menkel-Meadow, C. (2000) 'Mothers and Fathers of the Invention: The Intellectual Founders of ADR', *Ohio State Journal on Dispute Resolution*, Vol. 16, No. 1, pp. 1-37.

Merry, S.E. and N.A. Milner (1995) 'Introduction', S.E. Merry and N.A. Milner (eds.), *The Possibility of Popular Justice: A Case Study of Community Mediation in the United States*, Ann Arbor: University of Michigan Press.

Muller, J.M. (1995) *Le Principe de Non-violence. Parcours Philosophique*, Paris: Desclee de Brouwer.

Murray, J.S., A.S. Rau and E.F. Sherman (1996) *Processes of Dispute Resolution: The Role of Lawyers*, Westbury: Foundation Press.

Nader, L. (1995) 'When is Popular Justice Popular?' S.E. Merry and N.A. Milner (eds.), *The Possibility of Popular Justice: A Case Study of Community Mediation in the United States,* Ann Arbor: University of Michigan Press.

Næss, A. (1958) 'A Systematization of Gandhian Ethics of Conflict Resolution', *Journal of Conflict Resolution*, Vol. 2, No. 2, pp. 140-55.

Næss, A. (1974) *Gandhi and Group Conflict: And Exploration of Satyagraha*, Oslo: Universitets-Forlaget.

Palmer, M. (1988) 'The Revival of Mediation in the People's Republic of China: Extra-Judicial Mediation', W.E. Butler (ed.), *Yearbook on Socialist Legal Systems 1987*, New York: Transnational Books.

Palmer, M. and S. Roberts (1998) *Dispute Processes: ADR and the Primary Forms of Decision-making*, London: Butterworths.

Parekh, B. (1997) *Gandhi*, Oxford: Oxford University Press.

Pelton, L.H. (1974) *The Psychology of Non-violence*, New York: Pergamon Press.

Prahbu, J. (2001) 'Gandhi: Visionary for a Globalized World', *Revision*, Vol. 24, No. 1, pp. 2-8.

Pruit, D. (1987) 'Creative Approaches to Negotiation', D.J.D. Sandole and I. Sandole-Staroste (eds.), *Conflict Management and Problem Solving: Interpersonal to International Applications*, London: Francis Pinter.

Rath, B.S. (1986) 'Gandhi and Conflict Resolution', *Gandhi Marg*, Vol. 7, No. 12, pp. 850-57.

Roberts, M. (1997) *Mediation in Family Disputes*, Aldershot: Arena.

Roberts, S. (1983) 'The Study of Dispute: Anthropological Perspectives', J. Bossy (ed.), *Disputes and Settlements. Law and Human Relations in the West*, Cambridge: Cambridge University Press.

Shapiro, M.M. (1981) *Courts, A Comparative and Political Analysis*, Chicago; London: University of Chicago Press.

Shonholtz, R. (1984) 'Neighborhood Justice Systems: Work, Structure, and Guiding Principles', *Mediation Quarterly*, Vol. 5, pp. 3-30.

Silverman, M. (1995) 'The 'Inhabitants' vs. the 'Sovereign': A Historical Ethnography of the Making of the 'Middle Class' in an Irish Corporate Borough, 1840-1', P. Caplan (ed.), *Understanding Disputes. The Politics of Argument*, Oxford: Berg.

Tendulkar, D.G. (1951) *Mahatma: Life of Mohandas Karamchand Gandhi*, Bombay: Jhaveri and Tendulkar.

Trubeck, D., A. Sarat, W. Felstiner, H. Kritzer and J. Grossman (1983) 'The Costs of Ordinary Litigation', *UCLA Law Review*, Vol. 31, pp. 72-127.

Vasto, L.D. (1971) *Technique de la Non-violence*, Paris: Denoël.

Weber, T. (1986) 'Legal Ethics/Gandhian Ethics', *Gandhi Marg*, Vol. 7, No. 10, pp. 692-706.

Weber, T. (1991) *Conflict Resolution and Gandhian Ethics*, New Delhi: Gandhian Peace Foundation.

Weber, T. (2001) 'Gandhian Philosophy, Conflict Resolution Theory and Practical Approaches to Negotiation', *Journal of Peace Research*, Vol. 38, No. 4, pp. 493-513.

Weiss-Wik, S. (1983) 'Enhancing Negotiatior's Successfulness: Self-Help Books and Related Empirical Research', *Journal of Conflict Resolution*, Vol. 27, No. 4, pp. 706-39.

Yarn, D.H. (2000) 'The Attorney as a Duelist's Friend: Lessons from the Code Duello', *Case Western Reserve Law Review*, Vol. 51, pp. 69-113.

Index